CONFIDENTIAL

The Life of Secret Agent
Turned Hollywood Tycoon
Arnon Milchan

Meir | Joseph
Doron | Gelman

Gefen Books

Cover Design: Darko Bovan
Typesetting: David Yehoshua

Images courtesy of New Regency Productions, unless specified otherwise.

Back cover quotes:
Peres quote: Authors interview, Feb. 8th, 2010, Presidents Residence, Jerusalem.
Chernin quote: September 18, 2008 at gala honoring Arnon Milchan, Paramount
Studio, Los Angeles.
Murdoch quote: January 27, 2011, News Corporation press release.
Netanyahu quote: September 18, 2008 at gala honoring Arnon Milchan, Paramount
Studio, Los Angeles (via video message).
Redstone quote: Authors interview.
Robert De Niro quote: "The Last Tycoon," *Los Angeles Magazine*, April 2000, in
article by Ann Louise Bardach.

First Edition 2011

1 3 5 7 9 8 6 4 2

Gefen Books
600 Broadway
Lynbrook, NY 11563, USA
1-800-477-5257
orders@gefenpublishing.com

Distributed in Israel by:
Gefen Publishing House Ltd.
6 Hatzvi Street
Jerusalem 94386, Israel
972-2-538-0247

www.gefenpublishing.com
Comments to the authors at confidentialbook@gmail.com

Printed in Israel   *Send for our free catalogue*

Library of Congress Cataloging-in-Publication Data

Doron, Meir, 1954-; Gelman, Joseph, 1960-
The life of secret agent turned Hollywood tycoon Arnon Milchan / Meir Doron, Joseph Gelman.
p. cm.
Includes a filmography and index.

ISBN 978-0-615-43381-3 (alk. paper)

1. Milchan, Arnon. 2. Motion picture producers and directors–United States–Biography.
3. Spies–Israel–Biography. 4. Businessmen–Israel–Biography. I. Gelman, Joseph. II. Title.

PN1998.3.M513D67 2011   •   791.4302'32092–dc22 [B]   •   2011016156

To our loving wives and children,
who tolerated our late-night writing sessions
and general obsession to get this story told

⫴ Contents

Acknowledgments

We would like to thank all those who helped in the writing of this book, especially those who agreed to talk on the record, such as Israeli president Shimon Peres, Viacom chairman Sumner Redstone, former chairman of Warner Brothers Terry Semel, Meir Teper, and Dr. Michael Ledeen at the Foundation for Defense of Democracies, among others. We are also very thankful for the many sources who talked "off the record." You know who you are.

We would like to thank Hadas Klein, Ety Kanner, Dvora Ben Yitzhak, Yair Lapid, Roger Schneider, and Aya Markovitch in Israel. A big thank you to Jane Bulmer at New Regency Films and Gal Shor of *Israel Weekly* in Los Angeles. Thanks to Gary Ginsberg who at the time was at News Corporation in New York, but has since moved to Time Warner. We also thank David Kuhn of Kuhn Projects in New York for his early guidance.

We are thankful to all of those talented journalists and researchers whose diverse body of work over the years undoubtedly helped us piece together this story: people like Yossi Melman, Ronen Bergman, Dan Raviv, Ben Caspit, Dr. Avner Cohen, Seymour Hersh, Wolf Blitzer, Ann Louise Bardach, John M. Goshko, Jack Mathews, Bob Woodward, Thomas Reed, Danny Stillman, and many more.

We would like to thank Ilan Greenfield for immediately grasping the importance of the material spelled out in this book, and of course, a big thanks to our editors, Kezia Raffel Pride and Katie Roman. Thank you to all of the staff at Gefen Publishing House who have worked so hard on this project.

And last but most important, we are thankful to Mr. Arnon Milchan himself, for leading such an incredible life, and for agreeing to respond to the many assertions made in this book, even though, as would be the case with any human, not all are flattering. It takes a man of special confidence and honor to do so, and for that we are grateful.

Joseph Gelman and Meir Doron

Prologue

I would rather nobody write a book about me.

Arnon Milchan

The evening of September 18, 2008, the Paramount studio lot could have easily been mistaken for a high-profile movie premiere. Powerful searchlights reached up into the sky as A-list stars walked the red carpet accompanied by blinding camera flashes. But this event was different; the more than seven hundred attendees were powerful studio executives and community leaders who had come to honor not a movie, but a man.

Arnon Milchan arrived with his wife Amanda, seemingly uncomfortable both in his tuxedo and with all of the lavish attention heaped upon him. He quickly sought refuge in the anonymity of the crowd. But there would be no escaping the numerous speeches praising him, and the elaborate film documenting his cinematic achievements.

Although his name is connected to Hollywood blockbusters such as *Pretty Woman, The War of the Roses, L.A. Confidential, Fight Club, Mr. and Mrs. Smith*, and the Oliver Stone–directed conspiracy epic *JFK*, few in the audience had any awareness of the secret life of the man they were about to publicly honor with a Lifetime Achievement Award. To paraphrase Winston Churchill, Milchan is a riddle wrapped in a mystery inside an enigma. This book lifts that shroud of mystery.

This is the controversial story of a secret agent, of nuclear proliferation, billion-dollar high-tech defense transactions, ideology, patriotism, and the awe-inspiring Hollywood career of a mysterious mogul.

Arnon Milchan, born in Israel in 1944, has led the kind of life that Ian Fleming and John le Carré loved to write about, that Steven Spielberg or perhaps even Oliver Stone like to make movies about. Milchan is a real risk taker, charming yet tough, secretive yet famous – but only among famous people. He's a superagent in the real-world sense, and the closest thing to a real-life James Bond that one could imagine. He understands fine wines and high-stakes gambling, deception, exotic cars, exotic weapons, and exotic women, and maintains a private $600-million art collection spread among his grand dwellings around the world – from Monaco to South Africa, from Paris to Malibu to Israel.

We began this endeavor as unauthorized biographers and quickly evolved into detectives, peeling away layer after hidden layer, revealing the narrative of a unique man and his deep involvement in Israel's clandestine struggles for survival.

For many months, without Milchan's knowledge or approval, we immersed ourselves in court records and obscure articles from both the Hebrew and English presses, as well as in novels and private memoirs. We leaned heavily on our direct knowledge of the culture and language from which our main subject emerged, talked privately with the key figures mentioned in this book, and visited most of the locations described.

We have made every effort to chronicle the events as honestly and as completely as possible – fairly, accurately, and by placing matters in their full historic context. Many quotes attributed to Milchan and others are extracted or translated from rare interviews given over the decades to the international press. Other sources include a self-published autobiography of Milchan's grandfather, as well as a series of obscure manuscripts (fiction and nonfiction), written under an assumed name, by a person directly involved in Milchan's secret life. We discovered this author through the investigative process, confronted him in person, and confirmed his real identity.

Many revelations are unique to this book.

Following the completion of the manuscript, we surprised Milchan with its existence, and extended him an opportunity to respond. Initially, he was highly reluctant and perhaps even a little concerned. Eventually, he agreed to meet after we gave him every assurance of our good faith and honorable intentions. Through a few amicable meetings, we were able to confirm the accuracy of most of our assertions in this book, and corrected a number of factual errors. For his part, Milchan refused to confirm or deny the numerous sensitive defense-related assertions.

However, through the highest authorities in Israel, we have more than confirmed the overall security-related and highly sensitive contentions spelled out in this book. There were many sources, but the ultimate confirmation came from the mouth of Israeli president Shimon Peres himself, in a private interview that we conducted with him at the president's residence in Jerusalem on February 8, 2010:

> Arnon is a special man. It was I who recruited him. Working secretly, from outside the official system, he brought extraordinary ideas and a level of creativity that greatly contributed to our country. When I was at the Ministry of Defense, Arnon was involved in numerous defense-related procurement activities and intelligence operations. His strength is in making connections at the highest levels in countries around the world, including important countries with which Israel does not officially maintain relationships. His activities gave us a huge advantage, strategically, diplomatically and technologically…

And he continues to do so to this day, though only on the strategic level.

Few people in Hollywood, or anywhere else, are aware of Milchan's exploits, and many of his closest friends will be surprised as they read what follows. As Sumner Redstone, the legendary owner of the media giant Viacom, told us: "Beyond the whispers and the movies, few people know of Arnon's role in supplying Israel with its defense needs, and in creating its ultimate deterrence capabilities. I and most people don't know the details, but I suspect just enough to consider him a great man. For me, he is 'Mr. Israel.' He has introduced me to every Israeli prime minister since the 1980s."

Global media tycoon and News Corporation chairman Rupert Murdoch states, "Arnon Milchan is a multifaceted, passionate enthusiast for all he touches. He is an Israeli businessman, an Israeli political enthusiast, a Hollywood producer and a remarkable art collector. He is a loyal and generous friend who also happens to be a great long-term and trustworthy partner."[1]

Or as Peter Chernin, chairman and CEO of Fox Entertainment, once joked in reference to Milchan, "Never, never tell jokes about a man with easy access to weapons of mass destruction."[2]

Indeed, they may be unaware of the details of his secret life, yet almost every person on the planet would recognize any number of his contributions to our popular culture. (We've named the chapters of this book after his films – for a full filmography see the back of the book.)

As with any man in the arena, he's made a few profound mistakes, and has been involved in some controversial endeavors. He's rubbed a few people the wrong way and seems to spark a higher level of vitriol, and even jealousy, from some of his "victims," many of whom would be more than happy to work with him again, despite everything.

This complex man, who for so long has lived a multifaceted existence by compartmentalizing his life, now seeks alternative and more public avenues to leave his mark on the world, well beyond intelligence gathering, high-tech defense procurements, and Hollywood blockbusters. Milchan is heavily involved in politics, or as he puts it "politically active well behind the scenes." Years ago he was uncomfortable with the very mention of the word *politics*, just as he was uncomfortable with the word *rich*, especially when in reference to himself. But time and experience have cured him of this discomfort.

1. Fox press release, January 14, 2011.
2. Gala honoring Milchan, September 18, 2008.

At age sixty-five, Arnon Milchan has yet to write his last chapter. He sees his next opportunity, his next dream, his next movie, as bringing peace to the Middle East.

And as in any Hollywood blockbuster, the thriller that has been his life thus far will surely have a sequel in one form or another.

1 ‖ Man on Fire

I was away, not involved in the business at all at that time.

Arnon Milchan, *60 Minutes*, March 5, 2000

Arnon Milchan was nervous – very nervous. He had just received a phone call at his Paris apartment from a *Newsweek* reporter seeking his reaction to the stunning indictment of Dr. Richard Kelly Smyth, president of Milco Ltd., an Israeli intelligence front company, for shipping krytrons to one of Milchan's Tel Aviv companies.

Publicity is something that any secret agent tries to avoid, and Milchan was particularly averse to it.

In the coming days, newspapers around the world reported that krytrons were used as sophisticated triggers for the detonation of nuclear bombs. Indeed, krytrons have been around since the late 1930s, but the fact that they were, among other things, a primary mechanism for triggering nuclear weapons, was until that very day in May 1985 unknown to the general public.

Media analysts predicted "severe implications" for US-Israeli relations.[1] According to Smyth, Milchan's company had pushed him hard for the krytrons, and like the long list of other highly sensitive materials that

---

1. Doug Frantz and James O'Shea, "Israel Arms Deals Strain US Ties," *Chicago Tribune*, November 16, 1986.

Milchan had gathered over the years for his country, he knew perfectly well what they were for.[2]

In all, Milchan's company Heli Trading Ltd. had ordered 810 krytrons, which Smyth shipped without the proper State Department munitions export license. Now, US Customs and the FBI had moved in and all hell had broken loose. The entire Milco operation was in jeopardy. Milchan feared that a politically ambitious and publicity-hungry US prosecutor would come hunting for him.

After a short conversation with the *Newsweek* reporter, which consisted mostly of pleading ignorance, Milchan booked the first available flight to Tel Aviv, where, within hours, television crews and photographers were camped out in front of the building where he maintained a penthouse, and the phone was ringing off the hook. He ignored it all.

But there was one call that he could not avoid – the one from his mother, Shoshanna, who, after finally reaching him on the phone, burst into tears and said, "Everyone is calling my son an arms dealer. It's embarrassing." Arnon was devastated. He had never seen himself as an "arms dealer," and now his own mother was laying the charge at his feet.

"Mother, nobody calls Boeing or Rockwell an arms dealer, and nobody calls Raytheon an arms dealer. These are the kinds of companies that I am working with. It's not like I'm instigating wars in third-world countries and shipping them guns. I'm doing this to help our country survive."[3] It was little consolation for a mother who knew nothing of these sorts of things. She only knew that she had to face gossiping neighbors, and on that front the damage had been done.

Milchan did not even bother bringing up the matter with his handlers at LAKAM, a top-secret agency within Israel's sophisticated intelligence network that was unknown to the United States at the time. He quickly dressed in a sweat suit and exited the building, hoping that none of the reporters would recognize him. After all, he was not a well-known public figure, and few if any images of him had yet circulated in public.

---

2. Jon Schiller, *Irrational Indictment and Imprisonment: For Exporting Krytrons to Israel* (Charleston, SC: Booksurge, 2008), 2.

3. Personal interview with Arnon Milchan, November 2009.

His gamble worked. As he exited the building, he was swarmed by reporters who clearly didn't recognize him, so he told them that "Mr. Milchan" had gone to his office in Jaffa on the other side of town.

The reporters scrambled on a wild goose chase as Milchan calmly got in his car and drove directly to Jerusalem for a private meeting with his close friend and mentor, the Israeli prime minister at the time, Shimon Peres.

"Shimon, they are accusing me of doing it for personal gain. You know that I didn't do it for me; I did it for the country. Now I'm asking for your help."

Peres listened quietly. "What do you expect them to do, Arnon? What do you want me to do?"

Arnon firmly but respectfully raised his voice in despair. "I don't know, Shimon! Call Reagan or whoever and have them fix this. Why should I be the scapegoat?"

There was a long pause.

"Arnon, what do you want me to do? Go public and explain how the president of the United States and I got together to use you to get things for Israel that can't be obtained through regular channels?"

Arnon continued to plead. "All I am asking is that something be done to make this go away."

Peres was sympathetic and felt almost like a father to him, but he made no promises: "Let me carefully consider how to handle the matter; in the meantime, I want you to go home and try to relax."[4]

Peres knew that there was no such thing as "relaxing" for Arnon Milchan. He knew that he was one of the most productive and creative operatives that Israeli intelligence had ever fielded. Over the years LAKAM chief Benjamin Blumberg, and later Rafi Eitan, presented him with long lists of highly sensitive items needed for Israel's secret defense programs and other unobtainable defense-related materials, and through a sophisticated web of front companies around the world he delivered like no one else.

---

4. Based on the authors' personal interview with Milchan and Marvin Shanken's "An Interview with Arnon Milchan," *Cigar Aficionado* (Sept./Oct. 2008).

Milchan's mission was to secure these items by any means necessary – everything was fair game. In exchange, he would be treated by his government as a prince among his people. "He was working on missions for us, so if he found himself in trouble, I felt it our duty to help," said Shimon Peres.

Rules that applied to others did not apply to Milchan; perhaps it was not a "license to kill," but very close to it. He fronted secret bank accounts for the State of Israel – accounts that would be used to finance his country's most covert and sometimes deadly intelligence operations around the globe. He then parlayed his growing personal wealth through Hollywood and into some of the highest-profile and most profitable motion pictures ever produced, making him an icon of popular culture and one of the richest men on the planet in the process.

As he arrived back at the penthouse from his meeting with Peres, he saw that the mob of reporters was also back from the wild goose chase, and they were not very happy. Against the advice of everyone around him, according to his longtime personal assistant, Ety Kanner, Milchan agreed to invite them into his house for a short press conference in hopes of disarming them. He proceeded to explain that he had no personal connection to the krytrons matter and was unaware of the details of the event.

Whether Peres made that call to President Reagan has never been definitively confirmed, but something was clearly done. What unfolded changed lives forever.

2 ‖ The New Age

When I told Arafat I was an eleventh-generation Israeli, he said: "You're more Palestinian than me."

Arnon Milchan

A child was brought forth on the sixth of December, 1944, at the infirmary on Binyamin Street in the small but influential Jewish town of Rehovot in what was then the British Mandate of Palestine. These were grim and uncertain days in human history, as Europe was in flames and many members of the newborn's extended family would never be heard from again. It was the darkest hour. Yet, as Israeli president Shimon Peres told us, "Arnon was born as the sun began to rise, and has since lived on the sunny side of life."[1]

His ancestors on one side can be traced back to the great medieval biblical commentator Rashi, and on the other side almost to King David.

His father Dov stood nervously outside as the nurse popped her head through the door and announced, "It's a boy." He was quickly swarmed by family and friends hugging and kissing him: "Mazal tov!"

"The residents of Rehovot lived as a single family. The private and the public were as one. There was a feeling that all were sitting in the same boat, rowing toward an unknown shore," wrote his grandfather, Chaim

---

1. Personal interview with Shimon Peres, February 8, 2010.

Eliezer, who himself had arrived on the shores of the desolate land, from Poland, in the late 1890s.[2]

His parents, Dov and Shoshanna, chose for their only son the name Arnon, which is the biblical name of a river that cuts through the Moab Mountains in what is today Jordan, and flows westward to the eastern shore of the Dead Sea. In ancient times, the area was home to the kingdom of the Moabites, a people often in conflict with their Israelite neighbors to the west.

Ironically, the family name, Milchan, is derived from the Polish word *milczec*, which means "to be silent," or "to carry a secret," a virtue that would come in handy in later years.

In 1944, Rehovot was a bustling regional hub of a few thousand people and one of the most economically successful settlements in all of British-controlled Palestine. Situated among rolling hills, covered in lush orange trees and vineyards, sowed by the sweat and toil of Arnon's grandfather, it was the kind of place where no one locked their doors, children played freely, and everybody knew just about everyone else in town.

Arnon grew up among a large extended family, running through the vineyards and citrus groves and playing endlessly with friends in open fields between the houses until dark. With the "minor" exception of the ongoing Arab-Israeli conflict, for Arnon it was an idyllic and carefree life in many ways.

That perception contrasted greatly with the grown-up world around him. Unbeknownst to the young boy, one of the main Jewish underground weapons factories was hidden practically under his very feet, under the town's citrus packing house, and his family was involved in the manufacture of explosives under the cover of their fertilizer business, all in the wider struggle for Jewish independence.

On the evening of November 29, 1947, the entire population of the town, including three-year-old Arnon in his mother Shoshanna's arms, congregated around the main café and listened intently to the radio as the votes on United Nations Resolution 181 were announced.

---

2. Chaim Eliezer Milchan, *Yemei dor* [Days of a generation] (self-published, 1959).

The creation of a Jewish national homeland in the British Mandate of Palestine had been authorized by the international community. A spontaneous outburst of joy and relief swept through the crowd, which cried, danced, and sang throughout the night.

Six months later, Israel declared its independence. A small country mostly made up of farmers, merchants, and Holocaust survivors now faced the daunting task of enduring the promised military onslaught.

There was no time for celebrations after that first night. True to their word, all the surrounding Arab countries attacked in an all-out effort to destroy the fledgling, poorly equipped, and outnumbered nation before it was able to get off the ground.

Rehovot was bombed nine times from the air by the Egyptian air force; tens of people in the small town were killed and wounded. Numerous houses were hit and the original town hall structure, a short walking distance from the Milchan home, was totally destroyed in an enormous explosion. Like everyone else in town, Arnon, now four, scrambled for cover in a makeshift trench that had been dug in the backyard of their house.

The Holocaust and the entrenched Arab-Israeli conflict that exploded all around him during his early childhood would, by the nature of things, come to define most of Arnon's life and his attitudes. Metaphorically speaking, he would never really leave little Rehovot.

Over the years, the town and its immediate surroundings evolved from the quaint Mediterranean agricultural community that Arnon's grandfather helped found at the turn of the century into a massive technological and scientific center, critical to Israel's very existence. The entire area is one giant hornets' nest, buzzing with top-secret security-related activity; a world-renowned research facility, nuclear-tipped, intermediate-range missile silos, cutting-edge chemical and biological weapons programs, a nuclear squadron at the nearby Tel Nof air force base, a heavy water production plant, and much, much more. Arnon would play a role in making all of that happen.

A year after the war ended, in 1950, a dispute broke out between Arnon's father and his three uncles over the question of who would control various parts of the family business, Milchan and Sons. An agreement was reached in which Arnon's father, Dov, would get the fertilizer business and the other brothers would manage the rest, including the fuel distribution company that was quickly becoming the most lucrative part of their businesses. Within three years after the breakup, Dov felt compelled to pack up and leave Rehovot with his wife and children, and make his way separately in the new state.

Arnon, his younger sister, Dalia, and his parents, Dov and Shoshanna, departed Rehovot in 1953 for the growing suburbs of North Tel Aviv. Now that the fertilizer business was no longer part of Milchan and Sons, Dov needed a new name for the company. Out of respect for Arnon's grandfather and the family patriarch, Chaim Eliezer, Dov named the new company Milchan Brothers, even though his brothers had no stake in the company at all.

The new offices were located in the Tel Aviv agricultural wholesale market, in close proximity to the Ministry of Defense and the Mossad. The business next door, Dagon, was a grain trading company owned by the Gillerman family. Their son Danny became a close friend to Arnon and years later became Israel's ambassador to the United Nations.

Arnon's childhood coincided with the critical early years of Israel's development. He grew up among the establishment of the old Ashkenazi aristocratic elite, among the country's wealthiest and most educated, who had emigrated mostly from Europe in the late 1800s and early 1900s. This was a society that believed the keys to the kingdom – the world of business, politics, and privilege – rightly belonged to them.

It was during this period that Arnon's parents began to observe certain behaviors in their son that were outside the norm. Although bright in the extreme, he seemed hyperactive and incapable of sitting even for short periods.

Of course, hyperactivity also involves distractibility factors, impatience, impulsiveness, and in some cases, such as with Arnon, an affinity for danger: "There is something in me that wants to or needs to do scary things. I need a dose of danger to breathe."[3]

---

3. Arnon Milchan, *60 Minutes*, March 5, 2000.

It is generally recognized that people affected by hyperactivity should seek out careers that involve rapidly changing circumstances and environments that require constant stimulation, and to avoid careers that involve repetition or excessive focus on a single task, mental or physical. Arnon Milchan would choose the right career.

The most obvious trait to anyone observing the young Arnon was his boundless energy, and there was one place for him to expend that energy during childhood: on the field playing sports, a place where he almost made a career. His natural physical talents, his incredible energy, and his extreme competitive spirit paved the way for his acceptance into the elite fraternity of Maccabi Tel Aviv's youth team, the dominant soccer team in the country. Arnon was elated.

But there was a slight problem. A few years earlier, his vision had been tested and judged to be exceptionally poor. "The kid can't see a thing," the ophthalmologist told his parents as he handed them the prescription for a thick pair of glasses, which Arnon requires to this day. Although advances in optometry have since made the matter much more manageable, in those days glasses were actually made out of glass – and children wearing glasses were discouraged from participating in aggressive contact sports, like soccer, to avoid eye injuries.

Arnon did not disclose his vision problem, and it took time for his coach to realize that he even had an issue. By the time he did, Arnon had already solidified his place as a starting forward and the leading scorer on the team three seasons in a row.

He continued to play soccer for years. He had a burning ambition to play for the adult team and was completely confident that he would lead Maccabi Tel Aviv to national championships as its star. He believed he would even lead the national team to international success, and would ultimately coach the team in a lifetime career in the sport. To the astonishment of the young players, to this day Arnon Milchan continues to practice with the Israeli national squad whenever possible. He remains a big fan of soccer in general and Israeli soccer in particular.

Aside from soccer, there was another passion that Arnon developed during this period: the cinema. As a restless young man with a limitless imagination, he was mesmerized by the international films that slowly and belatedly made their way to the first movie theaters of Tel Aviv, and he imagined himself creating his own stories for the world to see. If there was one place that Arnon could sit still, it was in his own personal *Cinema Paradiso*. These encounters were his first real contact with the wider outside world and stimulated not only his imagination, but the beginning of his ambition to go out into that world and immerse himself in it, tasting every possible part of it.

With test results showing him to be a highly gifted child, Arnon was sent to a boarding school in Hertfordshire, in southern England. This kind of arrangement was the way Israel's wealthiest elite guaranteed a cosmopolitan upbringing for their children. It also meant that their children would acquire an important additional language as well as exposure to what they considered to be "high culture."

In Arnon's case, his parents also hoped that the environment of a strict English preparatory school would help him gain the kind of discipline and self-control that he was unable to achieve in the notoriously casual environment of Israel.

This journey was Arnon's first exposure to a big world outside of little Israel, and his first lengthy separation from the safety and security of the only home he had ever known. He was reluctant to separate from his family, friends, and especially from his team. But he was eager for the new adventure.

The all-boys English boarding school was not particularly successful in taming the highly energetic young man, or in keeping him seated and focused on his studies. But academia wasn't everything. Shortly after arriving, the boarding school's soccer coach discovered that he had a new star for his team, and the good news for Arnon was that talented soccer players always received preferential treatment.

It was in Hertfordshire that Arnon first encountered small instances of anti-Semitism. When his close friend and the only other Jewish student at the school, Yosef Malikson, won the school's highly prized tennis championship, the principal loudly declared that this was the first time that any Jewish student had won the tennis championship. Whether he said it in good spirit or not, it suddenly dawned on the young Milchan that others tended to look upon him differently because of his heritage.

Arnon and Yosef struck up a close friendship that has lasted to this day. One evening the two boys snuck past guard dogs and through a formidable fence to escape the school grounds in order to frequent the pub in a nearby town in hopes of meeting girls. Upon returning, the boys were caught red-handed, and their punishment was not subject to an appeal – public expulsion. The entire student body was lined up to witness the offenders, serving as examples to others, being driven off the premises in humiliation.

Dov Milchan would have none of it and arranged for his son to be picked up in unique fashion. When Arnon's escort arrived as scheduled, everyone was stunned to see the fancy white Rolls Royce, driven by a classically dressed English chauffeur. As the car came to a dramatic stop at the bottom of the stairs of the courtyard, the chauffeur quickly exited the vehicle, removed his hat, and rushed to open the door for the expelled student, to the amazement of the entire student body and the staff. Before entering the Rolls Royce, Arnon turned with a wide grin on his face, waved to his fellow students, and gave a thumbs-up to the staff.

Following his expulsion from boarding school, a special academic schedule was established for the rowdy young man. When most kids his age were preparing for their matriculation examinations, Arnon was tested and accepted to London City College while taking separate classes at the London School of Economics.

Within a year and a half, at the age of eighteen, he received his military draft orders and returned to Israel. Arnon was drafted into a unit that few are even aware exists: Foreign Transfer Unit 1030. This boutique detachment was composed mostly of multilingual individuals with foreign travel experience. His job was to generate required documents and accompany senior military officers when they traveled abroad, as well as to act as a confidant, interpreter, and facilitator.

He has never publicly discussed his military service, which, in fact, was his first real encounter with Israeli intelligence. During this period, he developed knowledge, friendships, and contacts that would last a lifetime.

Two attractive women – Dvora Ben Yitzhak, who served as the unit's financial controller, and Ety Kanner – would became trusted figures in his personal and professional life.

He served in the unit on reserve duty during the Six-Day War of 1967, and the Yom Kippur War of 1973. However, his most meaningful national service occurred well beyond the military, beyond the Israel Defense Forces, and beyond the borders of his country.

3 ⦀ The Mirror Has Two Faces

I had the choice of becoming a professional soccer player or going to university. I made a mistake and went to school.

Arnon Milchan, *LA Jewish Journal*, September 24, 2008

Following his military service, Arnon headed to Geneva, Switzerland, to continue his studies, this time focusing on chemistry in order to prepare for the family fertilizer business.

In Switzerland, he was again free of worries, playing soccer and beginning to make a name for himself as something of a playboy. He was a fine-looking young man, well connected, with unlimited possibilities.

With increased maturity, his hyperactive symptoms became less apparent. He slowly learned to adapt his behavior and to control overt physical manifestations such as extreme restlessness that had once plagued him. While studying abroad, Arnon developed a passion for tennis that would stay with him for a lifetime. Geneva was also where he discovered European cinema.

One day, in a frantic message from home, Arnon received the unexpected shock that permanently changed his life: his father's health had taken a disastrous turn and Dov was now incapacitated. In that single moment in 1965, Arnon's worry-free European paradise was cut short. In an instant, the pristine, well-manicured, orderly, cosmopolitan environment to which he had become accustomed was put on indefinite hold.

Upon hearing the news, a fear that he had never known before gripped him. He packed his bags and booked the first flight back to a rough-and-tumble world, not much more than a tiny Middle East backwater at the time.

As the flight departed Geneva International Airport, he gazed out the small window at the picturesque Swiss farms below and couldn't help but think of his grandfather, Chaim Eliezer Milchan, whom he had been very close to his entire life until the previous year when Chaim had passed away. It had been his first exposure to the reality of death and the loss of a loved one. He remembered that he had sobbed uncontrollably, and he began to brace himself for what he imagined could be an even greater blow.

From the airport, Arnon rushed to Ichilov Hospital in Tel Aviv. He sprinted up six flights of stairs to where his fifty-four-year-old father lay at death's door. As he arrived at Dov's bedside, Shoshanna explained that what started off as an infection in the pancreas had escalated into septic shock, damaging Dov's heart, lungs, and kidneys.

In the coming days, Arnon refused to leave his father's bedside, following his every movement and every breath, determined to see him through this crisis.

Within a number of weeks, to the surprise of his doctors Dov experienced a miraculous improvement and was sent to a rehabilitation facility at Kibbutz Givat Brenner. The family breathed a sigh of relief. Arnon began to plot his return to Geneva. And then things took a sudden turn for the worse.

Dov experienced intense abdominal pain that was diagnosed as a gallstone attack. In his already weakened condition, he was rushed into surgery, which he would not survive. To this day, Arnon believes that his father's death was the needless consequence of medical negligence.

The extended family arrived at the cemetery in Rehovot and longstanding differences were swept aside as a wave of emotion overcame everyone present. As Dov was laid to rest near his parents, Chaim and Esther, it suddenly dawned on Arnon, the only son, that he had lost the only emotional and financial support system that he had ever known. He struggled to show steadfastness but tears forced their way out. All of his fears were realized. A great weight was suddenly thrust upon him. He understood that his family would now look to him for leadership, strength, and their livelihood. He feared that he was unprepared for such responsibility; he was only twenty-one years old.

Through his tears, Arnon noticed many people at the funeral whom he did not recognize as they filed past the grave placing stones as a final expression of respect. A tall, lean man with a serious demeanor was keeping his distance behind the other mourners. Only after the crowd thinned following the services did he approach Arnon to offer his personal condolences: "Your father was an important man who did many important things for Israel. I know that you will follow in his footsteps," he whispered quietly in Arnon's ear.

Shortly after the funeral, Arnon made his way to his father's small office at the Agricultural Wholesale Market in Tel Aviv. It was a squalid scene and in vast contrast to the carefully tended streets of Geneva. As he made his way through the squawking chickens and agricultural waste, he suddenly gained a new appreciation for the sacrifices that his father had made for him. He entered the modest offices at the front of a small warehouse, where he was quickly surrounded by the company's few employees as they expressed their sympathy.

Arnon began to assume responsibility for the family business, Milchan Bros. Ltd. He rushed into this new world with a great deal of youthful enthusiasm, determined to uphold the family legacy, even though he would quickly learn that he had no idea what the family legacy actually was.

Dov had shielded his wife, his daughter, and his son from anything relating to the family business or finances, and they were all largely ignorant of the intricacies of Milchan Bros.

Arnon's expectations of himself and of the company that he took control over were sky-high, but he was brought back down to reality when he learned that Milchan Bros. was in a horrible financial state.

Import regulations had been loosened and the company's monopolistic advantage in the fertilizer business had been greatly diluted. Farmers began to import directly from manufacturers abroad, bypassing Israeli dealers altogether. Arnon was stunned to learn that the company had only the equivalent of $61,000[1] in reserve in Israeli liras. "The situation seemed grim. Milchan Bros. was on the edge of bankruptcy and I didn't even fully understand that," Arnon said. "In the days to come, the sharks began circling."[2]

Various competitors, vendors, and even employees began to challenge the new owner's business savvy and stomach for the job. Arnon was forced to fend off numerous schemes to maneuver him out.

As he sat frustrated in his father's office, contemplating disaster, he noticed a number of cabinets in the corner that he had yet to inspect. After looking at them curiously for a moment, he walked over and opened the drawers. He grabbed as many files as he could and brought them back to the desk to investigate.

Within moments, photographs of space-age missiles and fancy brochures lay sprawled across the desk, and it suddenly dawned on Arnon that his father had been involved in business far beyond fertilizers.

Arnon's father was the kind of man who played his cards close to the vest, especially in matters involving national security. Everything was on a need-to-know basis, and really, no one needed to know.

Dov had intended to gradually introduce his son to this side of Milchan Bros., but his sudden death prevented an orderly transition over what he had assumed would be a period of years. For Arnon, it was a stunning turn of events. He now began to understand the words whispered in his ear at his father's funeral, and why that mysterious person had been there to begin with.

He made phone calls and questioned the small secretarial staff, who themselves were uninformed. As it turned out, Milchan Bros. was also in the defense import and export business for the state; according to Arnon, his father handled some of Israel's lucrative military contracts.[3]

---

1. Elaine Dutka and Alan Citron, "A Mogul's Bankroll – and Past," *Los Angeles Times*, February 28, 1992.

2. Ben Caspit, "The Flying Producer," *Ma'ariv* (Israel), October 12, 2005.

3. Ann Louise Bardach, "The Last Tycoon," *Los Angeles Magazine* (April 2000): 77.

It is not surprising, perhaps even understandable, that some may have concluded that Arnon was a vulnerable pushover. They turned out to be wrong in an embarrassingly big way. The many sharks that repeatedly tried to displace him had no idea who they were dealing with, and grossly underestimated him.

Milchan quickly moved to consolidate his hold on the company. With youthful energy, he approached all of his suppliers, explained the situation, and charmed them into increasing their lines of credit.

He then proceeded to bring in his own team. One of his first moves was to take advantage of the maternity leave of the office manager. He called up the former controller of his military unit, Dvora Ben Yitzhak, and asked that she fill in for three months. Three months turned into a thirty-year rollercoaster ride.

Arnon may have been naïve and inexperienced, but in some ways it worked to his advantage. He had the confidence that only a young person, completely unaware of what couldn't be done, would have.

In very short order, he turned the small company that was mostly involved in brokering imported agricultural fertilizers and chemicals to local farmers into a wheeler-dealer on the international stage, involving tens of millions of dollars, and later much more than that. He reached out to every major chemical and fertilizer company in Europe and in the United States, seeking to become their exclusive representative in Israel.

However, it was one invention, one patent, one purchase, and one gamble that secured the company finances and propelled him to the next level: it involved an Israeli product that to this day is considered one of the most enterprising inventions from a tiny country that over time has become a world powerhouse of innovation.

It all happened by chance. As Arnon's desperate maneuvers to save the company began to show results after signing the Swiss companies Sandoz and Ciba-Geigy,[4] he set an appointment for a meeting at the world's second largest chemical manufacturer, DuPont, in Wilmington, Delaware. On the long flight over, he contemplated the ineffectiveness of the current fertilizer distributed by Milchan Bros.

---

4. Sandoz and Ciba-Geigy merged in the nineties to create Novartis.

Coincidentally, the stranger sitting next to him on the flight was a logging company executive from Canada. During their casual conversation, Milchan was fascinated to learn that tree bark was not used for any product and was simply disposed of after wood was processed.

He became curious about the chemical content of tree bark and wondered if there were any possible fertilizer benefits to this byproduct, which at the time was considered waste.

Upon arrival, he shared his thoughts with DuPont executives, who were at a loss about what to do with the enthusiastic young businessman from Israel and his strange ideas about bark. He was referred to the only Jewish executive in the company at the time, a man by the name of Irving Saul Shapiro, DuPont's lawyer.

Shapiro was impressed by Milchan and invited him to spend the weekend at his house. He also invited a group from the local Jewish community to meet the young man from Israel and hear his stories from the embattled country. By Monday, Milchan had secured a close friendship with Shapiro, a contract for exclusive representation of DuPont in Israel, and a commitment to finance experiments with bark in Israel.

A key Milchan contact, Shapiro would later become the chairman and CEO of DuPont from 1973 to 1981. It was the beginning of a long and close relationship with the company, which had been an integral part of the Manhattan Project (the research group that developed the nuclear bomb during World War II), and has long been a supplier of nuclear and defense-related material.

After this successful trip and upon his return to Israel, Milchan hired four agronomists from the Hebrew University Faculty of Agriculture in Rehovot, who developed a tree bark formula for experimentation. But no farm in Israel was willing to allow the formula to be tested on their orchards. After searching long and hard, Milchan finally came to an arrangement with Kibbutz Kfar Hanasi in the northern Galilee, which agreed to allow the experimentation on a portion of their orchards in exchange for Milchan financing a dental clinic in the kibbutz. Milchan agreed, under the condition that the clinic be named after his late father. The kibbutz obliged.

The experiments were a failure, but Milchan refused to give up. Eventually, he and his team realized that the fertilizer would be many times more effective if developed in a spray form, and delivered directly to the leaves and branches of the trees themselves. The formula was perfected over time and proved to be an important, revolutionary product for citrus growers around the world.

In addition to its agricultural effectiveness, the nutrient originally known as NU Green proved extremely profitable both for DuPont and for Milchan, and remains so to this day.

"This is a man who made his fortune by screwing with nature," a colleague criticized later.[5] It has been said that since Milchan got involved in the fertilizer business, oranges have never tasted the same.

The orders started rolling in, first from Israel and eventually from around the world. The legend of the young Milchan who made a quick fortune was born, and rapidly circulated around the small country.

Over time, he reached out to many more chemical and biotech companies, including some of the largest in the world, such as Germany's Bayer, Switzerland's Syngenta, Chemtura, and Seedco. In partnership with these companies, Milchan went on to play a key role in additional field experimentations that led to significant increases in agricultural production in Israel throughout the 1960s and 1970s, technology that would then be exported by Milchan Bros. and others, benefiting developing nations around the world.

As interesting as his agricultural endeavors were, it is also clear that over time these pursuits became something of a convenient cover for where the overwhelming portion of his success came from: defense-related contracts. And as in the agriculture sector, he would sell Israel as a prime testing ground for the latest weapons systems from some of the world's largest aerospace companies.

Milchan subscribed to every imaginable defense-related magazine, particularly publications having to do with aviation. He quickly learned the names of every major defense manufacturer and studied the latest developments in aviation and military electronics systems. He sent countless letters

5. Screenwriter Shawn Slovo in Bardach, "The Last Tycoon," 77.

of introduction to defense manufactures around the world offering to represent them in Israel. To his surprise, a number of companies expressed interest and asked for appointments. Soon Milchan was jetting around Europe signing representation contracts.

All defense-related deals at Milchan Bros. were conducted by the owner of the company personally – first the father, then the son. Israel began buying arms from the United States in 1962 with the approval of the Kennedy administration, but did not receive any military grant assistance until 1971 when Congress first earmarked a specific amount of aid for Israel.

As a result, Israel had to go deeply into debt in order to finance its economic development and arms procurements. However, since 1974, following the Yom Kippur War, Israel has received nearly $100 billion in US assistance, and to this day receives over $2 billion in military assistance annually. By law, the bulk of US military aid to Israel must be spent in the United States on procurement of US weapons systems.

Any company licensed to import and export defense systems to or from Israel, in addition to being capable of signing exclusive and very lucrative representation agreements with major US defense contractors, is going to succeed.

4 ‖ Six Degrees of Separation

Arnon Milchan is a man who knows how to create opportunities.

Israeli president Shimon Peres

When Arnon was twenty-one years old in the summer of 1965, he made his first direct foray into the strange world of Israeli politics. He became a contributor and "almost-candidate" for one of the strangest political parties in Israel's history.

The story begins when Arnon, newly flush with cash from his recovering business, became a close friend to Tel Aviv's nightlife king Rafi Shauli and a frequent patron of his club and restaurant, which at the time was the most prestigious and popular hangout for the who's who of Israeli high society. By all accounts, Arnon was an unrestrained party animal. "He was the kind of person who lived on the edge. He burns the candle from both ends," observed his personal assistant of thirty years, Ety Kanner.

The club, Mandy's, was named after Mandy Rice-Davies, Rafi Shauli's beautiful blond wife from England, who also happened to be a supporting player in the Profumo affair, a huge political sex scandal in 1963 in the United Kingdom, named after John Profumo, then secretary of state for war in Britain's conservative government.

Mandy Rice-Davies participated in a notorious sex ring involving a number of Britain's most powerful politicians at the time. The entire affair ended up a public spectacle in court, where Rice-Davies is well remembered for countering the testimony of powerful political figures denying their involvement, with the catchphrase, "Well, he would say that, wouldn't he?"

The expression stuck; it became a national joke and a cultural phenomenon in Britain. Rice-Davies traded on her newfound notoriety, comparing herself to Admiral Nelson's mistress, Lady Hamilton. She then converted to Judaism, married Arnon's new nightclub friend, moved to Israel, and became the famous hostess of the club. In the 1989 film about the Profumo affair titled *Scandal*, actress Bridget Fonda portrayed the nineteen-year-old Mandy Rice-Davies.

Arnon came to know the real Mandy, and as a young man was mesmerized. He spent many hours at the nightclub and it was there that he held most of his meetings, both business and social. That is where he also met socially for the first time a person whom he had known only from afar, one of Israel's most talented politicians both then and now: Shimon Peres.

The forty-two-year-old Peres was deputy minister of defense after having served for years as the director general of the ministry. Of course, these were positions that greatly impacted the business interests of Milchan Bros.

Peres told Arnon of his intentions to become a founding member of a new political party called Rafi (Israeli Workers' List, in no way connected to Rafi Shauli) shortly before the elections to the Sixth Knesset. The new party would be led by a number of breakaway members from Mapai, the country's largest political faction, which had ruled Israel from day one. Ironically, the leader of this rebellious faction was none other than David Ben-Gurion himself.

Since the day that he declared the establishment of the State of Israel, Ben-Gurion had been the dominant political personality in the country; as the first prime minister and minister of defense, he ruled the country with a firm hand.

The plan to challenge the only party in power since the establishment of the state was cooked up at Kasbah, a restaurant, and it intrigued Milchan greatly. Here was the vaunted "Old Man," David Ben-Gurion, passing the torch to the younger generation, Shimon Peres and company. Milchan believed that Peres would return to the Ministry of Defense as a representative of the new party and decided to concentrate on the upcoming election, emotionally, intellectually, and financially.

Beyond his personal interests, he quickly learned that Rafi was packed with some of Israel's top political talent, like Abba Eban, Israel's premier diplomat, Tzvi Tzur, a former army chief of staff, as well as forty-four-year-old Yitzhak Navon and forty-seven-year-old Chaim Herzog, both of whom would later become presidents of the country.

In the eyes of many young sabras,[1] Rafi represented a rebellious battle cry against the crusty old establishment, Mapai, whose time they felt had come and gone. Arnon was swept away with youthful fervor. He was captivated by Peres and company, who represented to him the new generation of competent, active professionals, more than capable of leading the country in exciting new directions.

There is no question that Rafi was the fashionable party, but whether it could translate its modern allure into votes was still an open question. Milchan claims that he was the second contributor to Rafi, and described a meeting with Ben-Gurion and Peres: "In those days they didn't actually take contributions, they took a 'loan' and gave you back a promissory note stating that the funds would be returned."[2] Of course, the funds would never be returned.

Milchan officially contributed $3,000,[3] but his contributions were certainly not limited to money. The party needed a new star and someone able to make connections.

---

1. A term used to describe native Israelis, so named after a cactus fruit that is sweet on the inside but hard and prickly on the outside.
2. Caspit, "The Flying Producer."
3. Tom Tugend, "Producer Arnon Milchan's Goal: Broker Mideast Peace," *LA Jewish Journal*, September 24, 2008.

His first task was to secure the backing and membership of former IDF chief of staff and legendary war hero fifty-year-old Moshe Dayan. Peres felt that the prospects for an electoral knockout were far more viable with Dayan on board.

Milchan knew Dayan from his dealings between Milchan Bros. and the Ministry of Agriculture, which occurred on a near-daily basis, similar to his contact with the Ministry of Defense. Dayan's office had issued licenses and permits for all of Milchan's agriculture-related businesses. Dayan walked out with Ben-Gurion, and was left without a job after resigning from the Ministry of Agriculture, a post he had held for five straight years.

But following the founding of Rafi, Dayan was not in a hurry to join the Peres bandwagon. He hedged his bets, sat on the fence, and played hard to get. At first he stated that he intended to stay in Mapai and oppose the breakaway faction. But later, as a result of his conversation with Milchan, Dayan was successfully convinced that if he stayed in Mapai, he would be marginalized and unable to advance his personal and political agenda.

"Set up the meeting," Dayan told Milchan. It was one of the first displays of Milchan's keen talent for brokering deals.

On a hot summer day in August 1965, only days before the election, Milchan arranged the crucial late-afternoon meeting between Moshe Dayan and Shimon Peres. Because of the summer heat, the three sat on the patio in the garden of Dayan's home in Zahala, a suburb of Tel Aviv, trying to catch a cool breeze coming in from the Mediterranean. They were surrounded by Dayan's legendary collection of antiques, which he "found" at various historic sites throughout the Holy Land. Any other person would have been thrown in jail for violating Israel's strict antiquities preservation laws, but Dayan didn't have to worry about little things like that.

Milchan told us that "with my passion for peace, I was able to help bridge the gap between them." Within the hour, Dayan announced that he would join Rafi. Both Dayan and Peres were very impressed with the successful new businessman's mediating skills, and after the two politicians reached their agreement, Dayan pointed at Milchan and told Peres, "You know what, Shimon? I want Arnon as minister of finance."

"OK," Peres replied with a sly smile.

Unbeknownst to the three participants in the meeting, there had been a security breach. A certain person was hiding behind a fence listening in on the entire conversation. He was an investigative reporter for *HaOlam HaZeh*, Israel's leading gossip tabloid. Within days, the paper came out with a loud headline: "Meet the Youngest Minister of Finance in the History of Israel." Following that publication, Milchan was invited to participate in an interview on Israeli TV.

"How can a young man like you feel like he is qualified to be the minister of finance of the State of Israel?" the interviewer asked in a snotty tone right off the bat.

At that very moment Arnon understood what he'd gotten himself into, and at that instant he made his decision: "Take a good look at me," he told the host. "Do I look like the kind of guy who will show up at 8:00 a.m. at an office in Jerusalem every day wearing a suit and tie for the next four years?"

He slammed the door on politics as an option for himself right then and there on national TV, for everyone to see. "I resigned before I was even nominated.… I understood that it was not for me," he later explained. What Milchan did not understand was that Dayan and Peres had in mind a completely different kind of "minister of finance," unelected, secret, far outside the country, and in service indefinitely.

Milchan, like every Rafi backer, was absolutely convinced that the party would score big on election night. He would be disappointed. In the elections for the Sixth Knesset, Rafi pulled about eight percent of the vote, translating into ten parliament seats out of 120, and went straight into the opposition.

Rafi's failure was so extensive that not only did it fail in coming close to the number of Knesset seats its backers had hoped for, but its rival Mapai actually increased in strength and was able to form a government without the need to invite Rafi to join in a governing coalition, even as a junior partner. It was a humiliating defeat that confirmed that what is fashionable among the elite doesn't always translate into popular votes.

One of the first things that Rafi did in its role as an opposition party was to attack Prime Minister Levi Eshkol for a large "defense-related failure," without specifying what it was. Today it is understood that the failure they were referring to was Prime Minster Eshkol's decision to slow the pace of development of the nuclear reactor in Dimona in exchange for military aid from the United States.

Shortly thereafter, on the eve of the Six-Day War, Rafi entered Eshkol's coalition government as part of the national unity government that was hastily formed in response to the growing crisis, which led to war on the morning of June 5, 1967. Sweeping politics aside, Moshe Dayan was appointed minister of defense and led the country to its unprecedented victory, turning Dayan into an even greater international celebrity.

A few months after that, all Rafi members returned to Mapai with their tails between their legs – with the exception of David Ben-Gurion, who continued to wander in a political wilderness until the day he died in 1973.

Together, Rafi and Mapai created what is known to this day as Israel's Labor Party. With that, the Rafi episode came to an end. Yet despite the ill-fated outcome of the fledgling party, the entire experience ended up being extremely beneficial for Milchan, who had gained credibility, notoriety, and important connections that lasted him for many years to come, and indeed would change his life forever. Dayan's idea of Milchan as an alternative kind of "minister of finance" would eventually materialize in unexpected and unconventional ways.

Many of Rafi's main players eventually went on to occupy the most senior positions in government and Arnon was now on a first-name basis with them all, and had developed real friendships and a deep trust with some.

Left to right: grandmother Esther, mother Shoshanna, father Dov, and grandfather Chaim Eliezer. Arnon and his sister Dalia outside his grandfather's house in Rehovot, Israel 1952.

Arnon Milchan and Shimon Peres, a close friendship and strategic partnership that has lasted since 1965. They are the holders of some of Israel's most significant secrets.

Arnon Milchan was one of the few men whom Minister of Defense Moshe Dayan could rely on, both for covert dealings and late-night socializing. Milchan was also one of the very few people to see Dayan's left eye without his trademark eye patch. In the picture are Milchan, Dayan, and the author of *Exodus*, Leon Uris, exploring a possible movie production of Dayan's life.

The Dimona nuclear reactor in the Negev, and the heart of Israel's nuclear weapons program (public domain photo).

Canadian Prime Minister Pierre Trudeau (on the left) and Arnon Milchan were
close friends, and both were single parents in the early '80s.

Arnon Milchan developed a close relationship with the
new minister of defense, Ezer Weizman, 1977.

Roman Polanski and Arnon Milchan announce their collaboration on the Polish
production of *Amadeus* at the height of the Solidarity protests, 1981.

Left to right: Robert De Niro, Roman Polanski, and Arnon Milchan in Poland,
1990, in front of a Solidarity sign (photo courtesy of Meir Teper).

Robert De Niro, Arnon Milchan, and Polish President Lech Walesa. The Polish president did not forget those who stood by the Solidarity movement in its early days; he extended to Polanski and Milchan an official invitation to Poland and hosted a Robert De Niro film festival (photo courtesy of Meir Teper).

Arnon Milchan and longtime lover Ase Thastrom greet their next-door neighbor at Montfort-l'Amaury, French President Jacques Chirac.

Liza Minnelli and Arnon Milchan shared a deep love for Broadway
and a close friendship with Canadian Prime Minister Pierre Trudeau.

On the set of *The King of Comedy*, summer of 1981 in New York:
Martin Scorsese, Jerry Lewis, and Arnon Milchan.

1981, Robert De Niro, Arnon Milchan, and Martin Scorsese. Lower center is Diahnne Abbott, De Niro's first wife, who played his character's love interest in *The King of Comedy.*

Arnon Milchan arranged for a VIP tour of Israel for Oliver Stone, escorting him to various military installations and meetings with the country's top leadership.

Yasser Arafat and Arnon Milchan during the height of the Oslo peace process.
One of multiple encounters.

Arnon Milchan introduced the original James Bond, Sean Connery, to Yasser
Arafat. Arafat was known to be a big Bond fan. He had little knowledge of
Milchan's covert activities.

Arnon Milchan and Bjorn Borg, 1993. An obsessively competitive tennis player, Milchan has been known to hold his own with some of the world's best.

The krytrons: "It's always that little thing that causes the most problems," Milchan told us. The smallest and least expensive item on Israel's shopping list blew up in everyone's face.

Arnon Milchan, his longtime friend Meir Teper and Warren Beatty.

Terry Semel, Michael Douglas, Joel Silver and Arnon Milchan.
Hollywood royalty on vacation.

It was Terry Semel who brought Arnon Milchan in to the studio system and the Hollywood establishment.

Married to Michael Douglas, Catherine Zeta-Jones co-starred in Milchan's movie '*Entrapment*' with Sean Connery.

Milchan squats to pose with Danny DeVito, who performed in his films
The War of The Roses, and *L.A. Confidential*.

5 ⫼ Don't Say a Word

We went for Dimona in order to reach for peace.

Israeli president Shimon Peres, February 8, 2010

Milchan's friendship with Shimon Peres and Moshe Dayan opened new worlds. Peres exposed Arnon to Israel's big secret, which only a few hundred individuals in the country, if that, were privy to at the time. "It was I who recruited him," Peres boasts.[1]

In those days Israel was a relatively poor developing nation, struggling under an extensive Arab economic boycott. It was a strange mixture of high-tech and low-tech, deeply religious and extremely secular, a mosaic of people from all over the world bringing different languages, cultures, and foods to the national table. Almost all were immigrants and most had family outside the country. The pool of potential intelligence assets was, and still is today, enormous.

Back in September 1957 (the year of Arnon's bar mitzvah), his future mentor and close friend Shimon Peres flew to Paris to put the final touches on a highly secret agreement. Peres had negotiated with France to build a full-scale Marcoule G2 nuclear reactor in Israel for, as far as Israel was concerned, the specific purpose of manufacturing the ultimate deterrent; another holocaust would be avoided at any cost. Of course, the entire deal

---

1. Personal interview with Shimon Peres, February 8, 2010, at the president's residence in Jerusalem.

would be packaged as a peaceful energy program, were it to be prematurely discovered.

The nuclear deal was part of the secret understanding between the two countries that led to Israel's agreement to participate with France and Britain in the 1956 Sinai Campaign to oust Egypt from control of the Suez Canal, one of the world's critical shipping arteries. Israel also agreed to help with the science behind France's own growing nuclear program.

The reactor would be paid for off the books, mostly by a group of twenty-five wealthy individuals from around the world, eighteen of whom were Americans. All were largely unaware of the specifics of how the money was spent and knew only that it was going to a vital security need.

This arrangement protected everyone's legal backside. They contributed approximately $40 million, which would be a quarter of a billion dollars today. The reactor was completed and went critical in 1962, became operational in 1963, and it had produced its first nuclear weapon by 1967. Since then, Israel is believed to possess the sixth (possibly the fifth) largest arsenal of nuclear weapons in the world – around two hundred – behind the United States, Russia, China, France, and Britain.

Israel's nuclear program, and the intelligence organization built to support it, was conceived by people from a generation that had witnessed the unimaginable horrors of the Holocaust firsthand, all of whom had lost many extended family members. Indeed, the words "Never Again" were welded onto the first Israeli nuclear bomb.

They deemed the project so important to the future security and survival of the tiny nation that no expense was spared and there was no boundary that would not be crossed in order to reach the final objective: a full-scale nuclear deterrent with every possible delivery system.

Aside from David Ben-Gurion, who made the ultimate decision to proceed with the project, there were three people who were secretly and primarily responsible for making the Israeli bomb a reality.

First was Shimon Peres, who handled the delicate diplomatic side of things with the French and was the senior hands-on person in charge. It was his baby. "Very little was known about our nuclear program; I wanted even less to be known about my own involvement. I felt that if I were exposed, the press would quickly destroy both me and the program. After all, I was politically controversial and known as a reckless fantasizer, and the program itself seemed so fantastic. For this reason, my name was never included in any formal committee created in the area of atomic energy. That did not prevent me from effectively running the entire program on behalf of Ben-Gurion, nor did it in any way impair my authority."[2]

However, in a personal interview with the authors of this book, for the first time Peres greatly elaborated on his basic motivation for spearheading Israel's nuclear program. His focus had been peace through strength: "In order to avoid the use of power, I calculated we must be powerful. I went for Dimona [the nuclear option] to reach for peace. Arnon filled an important role in the service of that mission."[3]

The second person to contribute to the development of the Israeli nuclear program was Dr. Ernst David Bergmann, rightly called the father of the Israeli bomb. He was a brilliant German-Jewish chemist who left Germany with the rise of Hitler in 1933 and ultimately joined Dr. Chaim Weizmann at his science institute in Rehovot. Bergmann was the senior scientist, or the *Oppenheimer*, of the program.

The third person was a mysterious man who was in charge of counter-intelligence and security for the Ministry of Defense until he was hand-picked in 1957 by Peres to handle all security-related matters to guarantee the success of the program. His name was Benjamin Blumberg.

Blumberg was not well known in Israel or anywhere else, but he became legendary in the small circle of Israeli intelligence as the High Priest of Secrecy. His closest counterpart in the Manhattan Project would have been Lieutenant General Leslie Grove.

Immediately upon embarking on the massive, covert Israeli version of the Manhattan Project, Peres (who is today a Nobel Peace laureate) realized that he would have to deceive people on a large scale to avoid early discovery and the predictable international pressure to put an end to the

2. Shimon Peres, *Battling for Peace: A Memoir* (New York: Random House, 1995), 117.

3. Authors' interview with president Shimon Peres, February 8, 2010, at the president's residence in Jerusalem.

program before it even got off the ground. He also realized that the pro-gram would need to gain access to material and equipment that was not easily obtainable on the open market, and that few countries would be willing to sell such material to Israel.

To overcome these complex and daunting problems, Peres decided to create a new top-secret agency, a unit so secret that even Israel's vaunted intelligence agency, the Mossad, would not be aware of its existence for years to come, even though it operated right under its very nose. When they did become aware of it, they did everything in their power to shut down the "rogue operation." Eventually, the Mossad came to accept it and even work closely with it.

For a while, the secret unit operated with no name out of small offices inside the Ministry of Defense in Tel Aviv. Later, it was given the vague label Office of Special Tasks, and was moved from the Ministry of Defense to an unremarkable commercial area, on the third floor of an unremark-able office building on Carlebach Street, at the corner of HaChashmonaim Street in Tel Aviv.

In the early 1970s, the unit would adopt the name Science Liaison Bureau, or LAKAM, its Hebrew acronym, and was nicknamed "Mossad II." Its original narrow mission was to secure the materials and the equip-ment that would make the production of nuclear bombs possible.

It was authorized to do so by any means necessary – by legitimate pur-chases on the open market if possible, by theft and deception if necessary, or by lethal force as a last resort.

Blumberg's job was to make sure that nothing would stand in the way of the scientists and workers at the reactor near the desert city of Dimona so that they could achieve their ultimate objective. In later years, LAKAM would take on much wider missions to seek out any technology related to nuclear weapons delivery systems, such as missile guidance, nuclear bomb miniaturization technology, nuclear triggers, centrifuges for uranium en-richment, solid rocket fuel, lasers, voice scramblers, night vision equip-ment, and many other sensitive scientific and technological materials, equipment, and designs.

A number of top-secret commissions were formed, including select and trusted representatives of Israel's entire military industrial complex and scientific institutions.

Every week these commissioners conducted a meeting in which lists of highly sensitive and unobtainable items needed for the various projects were presented to a "supplies coordinator" who was an undercover LAKAM agent.

The commissioners generally explained the materials on the list, what the materials were for, their level of importance, where the item might be found, and any other pertinent information that might be helpful in obtaining it. Of course, the representatives of these projects had no idea what the undercover LAKAM agent actually did; all they knew was that this was where one goes to request difficult-to-obtain items. Exactly how those items were obtained was none of their business. Sooner or later, the item would magically appear and the projects would move forward, no questions asked.

Ultimately, with its continued success, LAKAM would expand into a kind of overall contractor for international acquisitions – mostly by theft – of all the scientific and technological needs of what would become Israel's vast government-owned military industrial complex. As a group, these Israeli industries would evolve into the fourth largest exporter of defense-related systems in the entire world (behind the US, Russia, and France), involving annual sales in the multiple billions of dollars – in no small part because of LAKAM.

It was LAKAM, not the Mossad, that played the critical role in building the very foundation of Israel's nuclear deterrent capability. A report written by the CIA in 1976 illustrates just how successful LAKAM was at hiding its existence. The report carefully and meticulously surveyed and analyzed the entire intelligence community of Israel and all of its various branches, referring, in a general sense, to Israel's "high interest in science and technology" in Western countries. Curiously, however, the report never mentioned the Office of Special Tasks or the Science Liaison Bureau (LAKAM).

Instead, all the suspicions in the report fell on the Mossad, which served LAKAM just fine, and provoked more than a few smiles from those in the know. Despite its massive advantage in resources, manpower, budgets, and technology, the CIA was completely in the dark about LAKAM's existence and had been since 1957. It would only become aware of the organization under scandalous circumstances years later, in 1985.

Furthermore, the CIA's guard was down on this front because it generally relied on an official understanding between Israel and the United States that the two countries would refrain from meddling in each other's secrets – an agreement that both sides have repeatedly and egregiously violated, as evident in the recent unauthorized release of secret diplomatic cables by Wikileaks.[4]

LAKAM's ultra-secret status also relied on the work of legendary CIA counterintelligence chief James Jesus Angleton, who ran the Israel account at the CIA as if it were his private property. He was a stalwart friend who tended to look the other way as long as Mossad intelligence on the Soviet Union kept flowing in his direction.

* * *

During his first foray into politics on behalf of the Rafi campaign in the summer of 1965, Milchan met Benjamin Blumberg, a man who would become one of the most important and meaningful people in his life. He was introduced to him by his patron, Peres, who told us: "If there was a single value that I tried to instill in the young Arnon, it was that any person who serves his own ego is a small man. A real man must serve a cause larger than himself, and that is what will fill one's life with true meaning."

Unlike Peres, Blumberg himself was not publicly part of a political movement. He was a quiet man whose silence helped him maintain his position as the LAKAM chief even after Peres and Ben-Gurion left the Ministry of Defense. Blumberg is described by those who have encountered him, but likely do not know him, as a cold man with a formidable poker face. He fit the visual image of a mid-level government clerk, and it was hard for many to believe that this soft-spoken teetotaler created a global intelligence network of unprecedented daring, complexity, and

---

4. See appendix A.

secrecy. Milchan would become his recruit, his friend – and his boldest operative.

Their first meeting was casual and took place at the cafeteria in the Zionist Organization of America building on Ibn Gavriol Street. Later, meetings in the war room of LAKAM took on greater intensity. The recruitment process was gradual, but there wasn't a great deal of convincing necessary. "Despite the difference in their age, a difference of over twenty years, Benjamin Blumberg and Arnon Milchan developed a close friendship," a former LAKAM agent explained. "The only times that I have ever seen Blumberg smile was when he was in Milchan's company."[5] Milchan was basically the only one who was able to cut through Blumberg's façade and engage in small talk with the High Priest of Secrecy.

Blumberg's role in Israel's nuclear program was central. In 1958, the United States had taken photographs of the Dimona reactor from U-2 spy planes, and legendary US photo interpreter Dino Brugioni immediately identified the site as a probable French-designed Marcoule reactor complex.

Even though there was a strict policy of censure on every word regarding the reactor in Israel at the time, the information finally seeped out beginning on December 16, 1960. The *New York Times* broke the news in a front-page article, based on leaks from US government sources, in a concerted effort to force the Israelis to come clean about the operation.

At that point, David Ben-Gurion was compelled to appear on the lectern of the Knesset and publicly admit the existence of the nuclear reactor, which he promised was for "peaceful purposes" only. Of course, from the very beginning, Peres and Ben-Gurion had no intention of keeping any promises of a peaceful program, but Israel played the innocent. When the United States insisted on physical inspections of the reactor, Blumberg and his team kicked into high gear. The entire reactor was equipped with false walls, a fake control room, fake windows and passageways that led nowhere – the kind of props that would put any top Hollywood set designer to shame.

---

5. Yossi Melman, "Discreet," *Haaretz* (Israel), April 23, 2005.

As soon as the Americans departed, the elaborate sets were quickly dismantled and stored nearby for the next round. The inspectors walked away with no sense of what was actually happening at Dimona during multiple visits between 1962 and 1969. Finally, the Americans gave up.

During the entire 1960s, Blumberg personally escorted every major shipment of equipment and material that seemed to suddenly appear in Israel like magic to and from the reactor, with a hands-on approach and almost fanatical determination to see the project through. When any individual was found to be talking too much or needed to be set straight, it was Blumberg himself who would personally do the job. He would sit them down, look them in the eye, and caution them in his uniquely stern, quiet, and calm voice, almost whispering.

After such nerve-racking encounters, individuals rarely made the same mistake again.

By the mid-1960s, around the same time that Milchan was recruited, France, under the leadership of de Gaulle, made a strategic decision to "repair" their relationship with the Arab world, at Israel's expense. The close alliance between France and Israel, which had been in place since the founding of the state, began to dissolve, and Israel was forced to go it alone until it found a new backer.

If LAKAM had been important before, it became that much more important after the break with France. Israel would need additional equipment and material that would no longer be available from France. It was also clear that none of this material would be easily accessible anywhere else. Of course, it was LAKAM's mission to fill the gaps and it would look to Arnon Milchan to come through.

To that end, Blumberg spread a network of science attachés across the United States, Italy, Great Britain, Germany, and France, all of whom were selected from a pool of chemists, physicists, and engineers, and most of whom were connected at some level with the Israeli Atomic Energy Commission, or with different branches of Israeli defense industries. They were asked to have their ears to the ground in regards to any and all scientific and technological developments in the world, subscribe to every periodical and scientific journal, to develop professional and personal relationships with scientists in the countries that they were sent to and send back their reports.

The science attachés answered to Blumberg himself, and all of their reports landed on his desk. LAKAM personnel would privately give them their instructions before the science attachés departed overseas, and would debrief them upon their return. In some cases they would also serve as links to top universities and scientific institutes, and to the Israeli and Jewish scientists who may have worked there. These scientists were usually academics on a sabbatical abroad, and were asked to do favors for LAKAM. Very few refused. The scientific community in Israel has always been deeply connected to the establishment, and dependent upon it as well.

Slowly but surely, with experience, LAKAM became more confident, more daring, and over time took on more missions. It later added military attachés in Israeli embassies to its network as well. It was not long before Blumberg started to instruct his attachés to seek actual stolen material from the amateurs they handled at various scientific institutions – a research paper here, a technical drawing there.

Blumberg directed classic, cinematic methods of transfer and drop-offs of stolen material, from package exchanges underneath tables at public cafes to drop-offs at public bathrooms in airports. Eventually, the material would be put in diplomatic pouches, sent to Tel Aviv for analysis, and distributed to the various relevant scientific and defense entities that could use it most.[6]

One of the first LAKAM operations in the United States occurred in the early 1960s. John Hadden, the CIA station chief at the US embassy in Tel Aviv – who conducted an ongoing battle of wits with Blumberg, as well as a full-time program to spy on the activities around the reactor in Dimona – exposed a shipment that he estimated at about two hundred pounds of highly enriched uranium, which had already been absorbed into the Israeli nuclear program. Various leads led to the Nuclear Materials and Equipment Corporation, NUMEC, in Apollo, Pennsylvania. The owner of the factory was a chemist by the name of Dr. Zalman Shapiro. Years

---

6. Amnon Abramovich, "Kadish al ha-LAKAM," *Globes* (Israel), April 24, 2008.

earlier, Dr. Shapiro had worked on the Manhattan project, and he later
worked for the US Nuclear Regulatory Commission.

Hadden was convinced that the entire factory in Pennsylvania had been
established with money from Israel for the primary purpose of supplying
Dimona with enriched uranium. Even though Hadden was in possession
of damning evidence, at the end of the day the matter was settled with
a fine paid by the factory for "negligence." Shapiro was never charged,
the missing two hundred pounds of highly enriched uranium were never
found, and no conclusive proof was ever produced.

But there was a problem with the scientific attachés: they were not
professionally trained agents. In some ways, it was a daring and unconventional method and worked to Blumberg's advantage, but in other ways it
was risky. There were a number of incidents where only the tiniest of mar-
gins separated the operatives from a jail cell, as in the NUMEC incident.
Yet the demand for scientific intelligence continued to grow with every
small step toward achieving strategic objectives. Blumberg recognized that
he needed to expand his methods if he was going to continue to feed the
insatiable appetites of his organizations and of other defense-related entities as well.

That is how he came to seek out and recruit key players in the Israeli
and international business sector. That is what motivated Blumberg when
he later met with the young and impressionable Milchan, who, like the
scientists, was for the most part enthusiastic about the opportunity to serve
his country. With Milchan's assistance, Blumberg would develop a true
global reach.

In many ways, Blumberg's relationship with his recruits from the captains of industry was symbiotic. Everyone understood that they did not
officially work for the Israeli government; they received no salary and nobody paid their dental insurance. In exchange for their covert services they
would be treated as princes among their people. Milchan's initial years
with LAKAM would be some of the busiest in the organization's history,
and Milchan's creativity was a substantial asset.

His first taste of action came during two of the most well-known operations conducted by LAKAM, both of which took place after France im-

posed a complete weapons embargo on Israel following the Six-Day War. One was called Operation Cherbourg by the Mossad, while the LAKAM portion of the operation was named Starboat. The affair was a colorful illustration of how LAKAM recruited and worked closely with leading business figures from Israel's private sector, most of whom were glad to be asked to serve.

On Christmas Eve 1969, Israeli intelligence agents departed the French port of Cherbourg with five missile boats that Israel had already paid for, but that the French were refusing to release because of their newly imposed arms embargo. For this particular sting, LAKAM recruited a prominent Israeli businessman, Mila Brenner, one of the wealthiest men in Israel and the owner of a shipping company that primarily transported citrus from Israel to Europe.[7] Brenner's mission was to open a fictitious oil exploration company in Norway called Starboat, financed by LAKAM's secret accounts.

It would be listed as a Panamanian company and would approach the French government with a fictitious offer to purchase the boats in the Cherbourg harbor. The French government presented the offer to Israel, who engaged in "heated negotiations" with the "Norwegian company." Finally, following a week of pretend haggling, the Israelis would agree to sell the boats to the "Norwegians," who would not agree to the final purchase unless they were allowed to take the boats out to sea for a short test run to confirm their suitability. All sides agreed.

A contingent of blond Israeli Mossad agents posing as Norwegian sailors made for the open sea, with the full permission of the French government, for what was supposed to be a quick test run. The boats never returned to Cherbourg; instead, they headed straight for the eastern Mediterranean. By the time Paris figured out what was happening, the boats were already halfway to Israel.

LAKAM arranged for a number of secret, predetermined refueling rendezvous for the missile boats in the Mediterranean. This was achieved through one phone call to Israel's national shipping company, Zim. The French were stunned and embarrassed as word of the brazen sting went

---

7. His granddaughter is Hollywood actress Shirly Brenner.

public. They retaliated by expelling Israel's Ministry of Defense attaché in France, Mordechai "Mocha" Limon.

These were the Wild West days that followed the Six-Day War, when anything seemed possible and chutzpah was a virtue to be admired and celebrated. Business for LAKAM was booming and every imaginable defense-related material found its way to Israel. Another major success for LAKAM that would help propel Blumberg's reputation in Israeli intelligence circles to new heights was the brazen theft of the design of the Super Mirage fighter jet, France's premier warplane, from a Swiss jet-engine manufacturer, an operation that was also executed in 1969.

Colonel Dov Sion, Moshe Dayan's son-in-law, was Israel's military attaché in Bern, Germany. Sion identified and recruited a disgruntled worker at the Swiss firm, Alfred Frauenknecht, who was not Jewish but was a strong supporter of Israel. Frauenknecht was paid approximately $200,000 to hand over a complete blueprint of the Mirage fighter by putting documents into boxes on several separate occasions and delivering them to a German driver by the name of Hans Stracher, who transported them by car to Rome and then on to Israel in diplomatic pouches.

Eventually Swiss authorities noticed what was going on, but by that time Blumberg already had most of the designs at the LAKAM offices in Tel Aviv, which he quickly delivered to Al Schwimmer, CEO of Israel Aircraft Industries. Frauenknecht was arrested and he immediately confessed, declaring that he did it all for ideological reasons, because of his sympathy for Israel.

He was given a light sentence of one year in prison. The driver, Hans Stracher, narrowly escaped arrest and was smuggled to Israel, where he was given a new identity by LAKAM before moving to an unknown country to start his life over again. This LAKAM method would repeat itself in other cases when the organization was exposed.

On April 29, 1975, Israel showed off its newest "original" fighter jet, the Kfir, which looked strikingly similar to the Mirage. Frauenknecht flew to Israel to witness the maiden flight; also in the crowd were Benjamin Blumberg, Arnon Milchan, and other LAKAM operatives.

In November 1968, a German chemical corporation named Asmara, through a complicated web of subsidiaries, purchased two hundred tons of uranium oxide, or yellowcake. They produced an end-user certificate as required for any international transaction involving uranium, and had all the necessary documentation. The yellowcake arrived at the port of Antwerp in Belgium from a mineral mine in the Congo owned by a Belgian company called Société Générale de Minaro. From the port of Antwerp, the cargo was loaded onto a ship called the Scheersberg A, which flew a Liberian flag.

The ship reported its destination as Genoa, Italy. It never arrived. Instead of heading north as it entered the Mediterranean, it proceeded east. Somewhere in the eastern Mediterranean it rendezvoused with an Israeli ship owned by Zim, and the two hundred tons of uranium oxide were never seen again. A few days later the ship was spotted in Iskenderun, Turkey, without its cargo and under a new name.

This entire incident became known as Operation Plumbat. Plumbat is derived from the Latin *plumbum*, meaning lead, and is a reference to the labeling of the drums used to transport the yellowcake. The web of front companies and deception used in the operation was so complicated that European authorities were never able to actually figure out the entire plot.

* * *

It was during these operations that Milchan cut his teeth in the intelligence business. He learned how to be a man in the shadows from Benjamin Blumberg. He also learned why he should stay away from the media (one of the most stinging curses in Israel's intelligence community is "may I read about you in the paper someday"). Milchan learned how to remain silent and how to work in a strictly compartmentalized way. He learned why a double layer of secrecy was important: secrecy from the enemy abroad and secrecy from rivals from within – the Mossad, the Aman, the Shabak, and the Ministry of Foreign Affairs.

He learned how to create front companies using third-party identities, secret bank accounts, fake end-user documents, diplomatic pouches, and

mid-sea rendezvous for shipments. He learned how to recruit and motivate foreign nationals to do his bidding through lust, greed, or any other
weakness he could exploit. In short, he learned the art of the secret agent
from Blumberg, who had plenty of patience for the young man. When
Milchan spoke, Blumberg would slowly take sips from his cup of tea and
listen, mostly in silence.

The character of LAKAM appealed to Milchan's particular nature. The
organization was purposefully run on the fly, with little formal oversight.
The idea was to encourage a creative environment of daring, calculated
risk taking. Blumberg looked for aggressive operatives with an adventur-
ous spirit who thought outside the box, people who demonstrated just the
right balance between good judgment and the ability to improvise in the
field and assume responsibility for risks without having to phone home
every minute. LAKAM's creativity achieved unprecedented successes for
Israel, but it was that same mentality that led to disaster.

The close working relationship between Milchan and Blumberg was
exceedingly productive, and much of it will never be known. When
Blumberg rehashes in his mind with great satisfaction the details of the
global network that he established, Milchan's name makes frequent appearances. When Blumberg needed a thousand tons of ammonium perchlorate, Butarez, carbon-carbon, inertial-grade gyros and accelerometers,
precision tracking radars, and other such basic material required by anyone
seeking to develop a nuclear deterrent, it was Milchan he would call.

Milchan's constant movement between countries and continents made
him an elusive target for any counterintelligence effort against him, and
it made him the most productive asset for LAKAM and for the State of
Israel.

6 ‖ Dangerous Beauty

*The problems began when she learned Hebrew
and I really learned French.*

Arnon Milchan, *Los Angeles Magazine*, April 2000

For any normal person, political activism, running a chemical and fertilizer consortium, and becoming an intelligence asset might be enough to keep sufficiently occupied. But for a person like Milchan, even in his early twenties, it wasn't nearly enough. Since his earliest years he had been fascinated by movies and celebrities; he began hanging around the sets of the few films produced in Israel, and the idea of participating in the business began to grow on him.

One day in February 1965, on his way to a conveniently scheduled meeting in the lobby of the Tel Aviv Hilton, the largest and most luxurious beachfront hotel in town in those days, he noticed a gorgeous young woman who happened to be a French fashion model. She reminded him of Brigitte Bardot, another French bombshell who was an icon of popular culture at the time. The young woman had been invited to Israel in an effort to extend a bit of European glamour to the isolated country's first large fashion show. It was to take place at the same hotel that week and was something of a local media sensation.

With typical determination, yet carefully and tactfully, he established contact and discovered her name, Brigitte Genmaire, and that she was a distant relative of former French prime minister Pierre Mendès. Within hours, all inhibitions were dropped and a passionate romance developed.

Arnon fell for her head over heels; he took a room at the hotel, and even though they could barely communicate – he only learned French years later, and she spoke no Hebrew and very little English – the sudden couple couldn't get enough of each other in the international language of physical attraction.

In the following days he was completely consumed. He called his friend Rafi Shauli and arranged for his nightclub, Mandy's, to be shut down for the night to impress Brigitte with an exclusive evening there. He would invite only his closest friends. Naturally, Tel Aviv's top bohemian society, the so-called beautiful people, the cream of the crop, were all there.

Shauli brought his trophy wife, the real Mandy, and for the occasion Arnon also booked one of Israel's up-and-coming rock bands, the Lions. The group was considered to be the first Israeli band to experiment with reggae music, and in 1968 they became the first Israeli band to produce a song ranked at the top of the British charts with "Our Love's a Growing Thing." They hailed from lower-class neighborhoods of the type with which Arnon was neither overly familiar nor comfortable.

The bass player for the band was a penniless, unknown, long-haired hippy, who later in life would become a multi-billion-dollar media tycoon in the United States and one of the largest donors to the Democratic Party: Haim Saban, the man who introduced every American child to world-famous characters like the Teenage Mutant Ninja Turtles and Power Rangers. He also owns Univision, the largest Spanish-language media company in the United States, and was eventually to become a business partner of Arnon Milchan, co-owning Israel's Channel 10.

Saban and the Lions were used to playing in seedy nightclubs in tough neighborhoods, and the fact that they were suddenly invited to perform at Tel Aviv's top nightclub was a major breakthrough for them. Haim Saban remembers very clearly the day his band received an invitation to appear at Mandy's: "We were excited as if we had finally arrived. At last, we would be able to rub elbows with the who's who of Tel Aviv, the country's cultural capital. All the beautiful people would be there. Arnon closed the deal with us on two sets of three songs with a brief intermission in the middle. This was certainly the kind of break we were looking for. It would be the first opportunity for long-haired people like us to interact with the cultural elite and gain some legitimacy."

Four workers were needed to carry the band's heavy equipment up onstage, including a large organ. Everything was ready to go. The Lions began to perform and things went very well; the crowd seemed to get into the performance. But after the third song at the end of the first set when they were supposed to take a break, things took a turn for the worse: "Instead of allowing us to mingle with the crowd during the break, Arnon instructed that we be moved to the kitchen," Haim Saban remembers. "We could only peek through the kitchen doors like lowly servants. We then went up and finished our second set and were escorted immediately from the club through the back door. That's the way it was in those days, uppity Ashkenazim here, lowly Sephardim there. That's how I met Arnon Milchan for the first time."[1]

Arnon, who claims to have an elephant's memory, recalls it differently: "The deal was three songs for $200. Later, after some negotiations, another three songs were added. During the second song, I'm dancing with Brigitte, and suddenly I hear behind my back a conversation in French. I turn around and I see Haim Saban, the bass player, chitchatting in French with Brigitte from the stage. Some kind of connection was made and I don't understand a word of French, and she's talking back to him and he seems to be charming her – the person I'm dancing with! Basically, he was hitting on her from the stage. So after the set I sent them to the kitchen. That was the farthest place from Brigitte that I could think of. If Haim Saban hadn't hit on her, he would have stayed with all the 'Ashkenazim.' It's that simple."

As if an exclusive evening at Mandy's wasn't enough, at the same time Arnon also moved the Milchan Bros. offices from the grungy Agricultural Wholesale Market to a nicer location on Carlebach Street nearby. The move was made in great haste, just in time to host a short visit by Brigitte, who was completely unaware of all the earlier commotion on her behalf.

---

1. Caspit, "The Flying Producer."

Coincidentally or not, Milchan Bros.' new location was right next door to the most secretive intelligence organization in Israel, LAKAM.

Arnon made an impression on Brigitte. She fell for him in return and decided to stay in Israel. On her part, Brigitte made an impression on Arnon's new friend, Shimon Peres, who was taken by her beauty and appreciated her connection to former French prime minister Pierre Mendès; Peres also enjoyed showing off his fluent French.

Within ten days Arnon and Brigitte were married[2] in a civil ceremony in Paris, and within a few months her stomach began to show. Arnon then suggested a traditional Jewish marriage;[3] Brigitte had no problem abandoning her career or her Catholic roots for a Jewish life in Israel. Arnon asked Brigitte to convert, a long and difficult process that can take over a year due to the fact that in Israel, only Orthodox conversions are officially recognized. It was a desperate race against time because without a conversion certification, the child would not be born Jewish. But Arnon was confident in his ability to exercise influence over Israeli bureaucracy, including rabbinical authority. As her pregnancy advanced, her expedited conversion studies culminated in a ceremony at the rabbinical court.

According to Arnon, when Brigitte arrived at the *mikveh*[4] she was accompanied by his sister and mother as witnesses, and was already nine months pregnant. The *rabbanit* (wife of a rabbi) asked her, "Do you swear that you are a virgin?" Without blinking an eye, with her bulging stomach, standing naked on the edge of the pool, she answered loudly: "Yes."

When she told Arnon of this he couldn't help but burst out laughing.

The low-key Jewish wedding took place only days before the bulging Brigitte was rushed to the hospital to deliver their first child, a boy, whom they named Yariv. As a noun it means adversary, opponent, or rival. As a verb it means "he will fight." A typical interpretation of the name is that God will fight (*yariv*) against those who would want to harm the nation of Israel.

Beyond the initial infatuation, Brigitte saw in Arnon a man who could protect her and provide for her, and introduce her to an exciting world well

2. Dutka and Citron, "A Mogul's Bankroll – and Past."
3. Bardach, "The Last Tycoon."
4. A small ritual bath, in this case used for the purpose of immersion into Judaism.

beyond her narrow horizons. Arnon saw in Brigitte a passionate, beautiful foreign woman, who in those days in Israel would certainly be considered something of a status symbol.

According to Arnon years later, "The trouble started when Brigitte began to understand and speak Hebrew and I learned to speak French." He is quoted as saying: "When we started to really communicate, that's when the trouble began."[5] They were both young, quick to anger, and inexperienced in relationships.

Arnon Milchan was not built for a single business, a single home, and at that time of his life, he was not built for a single relationship either.

As he testified of himself: "I fall in love all the time. I fall in love with the spirit, the face, and through the eyes."[6]

"He has a Scandinavian in every port," claims director Terry Gilliam.[7] Yet with all of that, Milchan describes himself as a one-woman man.

* * *

The process of Milchan's recruitment to LAKAM was gradual, but the time had come for him to sit down with Peres and Dayan to discuss the most effective ways for him to contribute to the cause.

Milchan had an idea. He had already made initial connections with various defense contractors and aerospace companies seeking to represent them in Israel. If the Ministry of Defense would gently encourage these companies to work through him as their exclusive representative in the country, he would then funnel the commissions earned back to Israel, to finance off-the-record operations.

That, in fact, was the direction that Peres and Dayan had in mind when they thought of Milchan as a potential "minister of finance" back during the Rafi campaign. They were impressed by his ability to grasp the larger picture, reach the solution on his own, and offer up his services as an act of patriotism.

---

5. Bardach, "The Last Tycoon."
6. Ibid.
7. Ibid.

The plan that came together was similar to the original plan that financed the Dimona nuclear reactor itself. Funds would be generated from outside the country, deposited in accounts outside the country, and used to finance missions outside the country that are better left undisclosed – in short, a parallel system that couldn't be traced back to Israel itself.

But Milchan took it even a step further. He offered Peres and Dayan the use of his company as a front in order to open subsidiaries wherever LAKAM or the Mossad deemed necessary for their activities.

Milchan would open accounts and front companies for the State of Israel, essentially putting him in charge of the mechanisms and the resources to finance the special needs of the entirety of Israel's intelligence operations outside of the country. This is how Milchan gradually became the indispensible man in the middle.

Such off-the-books accounts would give the Israeli prime minister the ability to execute decisions beyond Israel's borders without the need for the formal budgeting, cabinet approvals, petty internal politics, or leaks to the press that might endanger the operation. With one phone call to Milchan, events were set in motion and resources were made available.

Arnon was now ready to conquer the world. Peres suggested that his new French wife, Brigitte, could be a helpful bridge. France was still the country's primary weapons supplier in the mid-1960s and was therefore Milchan's initial stop; he cooked up his first deal when visiting what is today Aérospatiale.[8]

He had already been informed that a group of high-ranking Israeli Air Force personnel had recently visited the factory in Marignane, near Marseille, and had been very impressed with their new heavy-transport helicopter, the Super Frelon. He convinced Aérospatiale that they needed a facilitator to help them move the deal forward, and after a short investigation, they were sufficiently impressed by the young Milchan's confirmed connections to Peres and Dayan to appoint him their official representa-

---

8. Sud Aviation merged with Nord Aviation in 1970 to form Aérospatiale. Aérospatiale formed several large-scale international consortia, such as with British Aerospace and Messerschmitt-Bölkow-Blohm to form Airbus, and ultimately merged into European aerospace company EADS in 2000.

tive in Israel. The deal was consummated as quickly as Arnon's new marriage, and the first commissions for the secret accounts were earned.

In response to an Egyptian blockade of the Straits of Tiran, on the morning of June 5, 1967, at 7:45 a.m., the entire Israeli Air Force (IAF) fleet, save a mere twelve aircraft, left Israel and attacked all of Egypt's airfields simultaneously, and later those of Jordan, Syria, and Iraq, in what became known as the Six-Day War. The Super Frelons brokered earlier by Milchan transported Israeli paratroopers to Sharm el-Sheikh, enabling them to capture the southern tip of the Sinai Peninsula in a lightning strike and end the blockade.

The Super Frelon deal was quickly followed by twelve light-transport helicopters, known as Alouette. These aircraft, also manufactured by Aérospatiale, were used primarily for rapid deployment of infantry in hot pursuit of terrorist infiltrators, and for evacuation of the wounded throughout Israel's War of Attrition.

Milchan played a key role in the growth of Israel's entire modern helicopter fleet. To accommodate these deals, he opened Heli Trading Ltd., a sister company to Milchan Bros. Within only a few months, he also signed up the German aircraft company Dornier, and brokered the sale of a number of surveillance planes for the IAF.

Through his LAKAM sources, Milchan learned of a huge HAWK deal in the works with Israel and he immediately headed for the 1967 Paris Air Show, only days after the Six-Day War. The HAWK, which stands for Homing All the Way Killer, is a medium-range, surface-to-air guided missile that provides air defense coverage against low- to medium-altitude aircraft. It is a mobile, all-weather, day and night system, effective against the electronic countermeasures of the time.

Standing just outside the Raytheon pavilion, he sent his stunning new Swedish "companion," Ulla,[9] whom he had met only days earlier, to deliver the first impression. Within moments, she was surrounded by Raytheon salesmen with offers of champagne. She alluded to her "boyfriend," a leading Israeli businessman who was working the show and looking for new

---

9. The authors were unable to learn Ulla's last name, and suspect that she was a LAKAM recruit.

deals. Israel, of course, was basking in the glow of its recent military victory, so when Arnon arrived a few minutes later he was a major source of
curiosity. Milchan presented himself as deeply familiar with the "troubled"
HAWK deal, leading Raytheon representatives to believe that the transaction was in jeopardy because of cost issues.

Within moments, frantic phone calls were made from Paris to Raytheon
headquarters in Massachusetts, and from there to Israel. Milchan mentioned his friend, Minister of Defense Moshe Dayan, who also received a
phone call. Dayan, of course, played along according to the plan, stating
that Milchan could be a good facilitator for them. Raytheon got the hint.
Within days, Milchan became their exclusive representative in Israel and
the new HAWK deal was consummated to the tune of $900 million. It
was the beginning of a long and lucrative relationship.

Milchan's official commission from the new HAWK deal was $45
million, which was deposited in the secret Israeli offshore account. The
HAWK was by far the most sophisticated and expensive antiaircraft system in Israel's arsenal. Over time, Milchan would broker more deals involving improved versions of the HAWK. And of course every missile fired
in anger, or in training, had to be replaced, translating into more orders
and more commissions. Over time, the HAWK system in Israel shot down
thirty-six enemy aircraft.

It took years before the lucrative connection between Raytheon and
Arnon Milchan became publicly known. As reported in the *Washington
Post* following a federal review in the United States, suspicions arose that
Milchan had received an inappropriate commission of $300,000 from
a Raytheon subsidiary. Nothing ever came of it, and the matter was
dropped.[10]

Thirteen years later, in 1988, the connections between Milchan and
Raytheon became a matter of public record when British director Terry
Gilliam, who had just finished directing Milchan's movie *Brazil*, described
how he walked with Arnon and his eldest son Yariv into the Raytheon

---

10. Robert Windrem, co-author along with William E. Burrows of *Critical Mass: The
    Dangerous Race for Superweapons in a Fragmenting World* (New York: Simon and
    Schuster, 1994).

pavilion at the biannual Paris Air Show. "It was wonderful to see how the whole arms business worked," Gilliam said. "Arnon was very psyched about the video games. He brought his son with him to play the games, which can replicate the destruction of the planet." In Gilliam's words, "He took me to the Raytheon booth, and it was all showmanship. He was obviously a big star to Raytheon."[11]

* * *

During the Six-Day War, much larger territories came under Israeli control and it became clear that the IDF would need the ability to deliver rapid-response forces over much greater distances. General Motti Hod, commander of the IAF at the time, sought to purchase an entire fleet of Agusta-Bell 205 Iroquois, better known as Hueys, planes that had achieved a level of fame in Vietnam. They would become the workhorses of the Israeli helicopter fleet well into the 1990s.

The Hueys were officially bought from the Italian firm Agusta to bypass the Arab boycott, which in the early days was greatly feared by many US companies. Highly lucrative Arab markets were, at least theoretically, off-limits to any company doing business with Israel, and it was up to people like Arnon Milchan to facilitate creative ways to purchase these systems for Israel without damaging the suppliers' business interests in cash-rich markets like Saudi Arabia or Kuwait.

With helicopters and many other items, Milchan arranged for front companies to purchase the products in a third country, then have them shipped on to Israel. Eventually the Arabs caught on to these methods and established a secondary boycott, punishing companies doing business with companies that were doing business with Israel.

Milchan solved that problem by simply creating an additional foreign shell company, which the first shell company would sell to, before shipping to Israel. The Arabs upped the ante with a tertiary boycott, and a third-level shell company sometimes became necessary. If it weren't real it would be comical.

---

11. Bardach, "The Last Tycoon," 74.

Eventually the Arabs realized the futility of the effort and the boycott slowly lost its effectiveness. By 1977, the US Congress passed a law that then president Jimmy Carter signed, with the encouragement of Milchan's friend, DuPont chairman Irving Shapiro, mandating that fines be levied on any American companies cooperating with the Arab boycott. To enforce the law, the Office of Antiboycott Compliance was opened. By the 1980s, companies like PepsiCo and McDonald's, which had adhered to the Arab boycott for decades, entered the Israeli market openly, as did US defense contractors.

It was the resourcefulness of Milchan and others that kept Israel from being brought to its knees. They played a substantial role in keeping Israel supplied during the more effective years of the boycott. On the other hand, as with the Arab-Israeli conflict itself, the Arab boycott made Milchan's services crucial. Following the Six-Day War, America's view of Israel as a potential strategic asset in the region began to grow, and with that perception, a line of credit for the purchase of US weapons systems began to grow as well.

Over the coming years, Israel would become the largest single recipient of direct military assistance from the United States since World War II. Large lines of credit would gradually turn into massive grants in the form of military aid worth billions of dollars. As illustrated by the events at the Paris Air Show, Milchan would be in the thick of it like no one else, charming his way through a maze of potential land mines, representing many elite European and American defense and aerospace manufacturers in indirect negotiations with the Israeli Ministry of Defense.

In late 1967, Israel received its first squadron of McDonnell Douglas A-4 Skyhawks from the United States, which would become its primary ground attack aircraft. A few short years later, on September 5, 1969, it received its first squadron of F-4 Phantoms, also made by McDonnell Douglas.

Milchan did not represent McDonnell Douglas, but he did represent the company that would supply its primary weapons systems, advanced avionics, radars, infrared, guidance, and navigation systems. Over the years, Israel has purchased thousands of Sidewinder ($84,000 per unit) and Sparrow ($125,000 per unit) missiles and other air-to-air and air-to-ground weaponry for the Skyhawk and Phantom platforms, and later for its squadrons of F-15s and F-16s. Unlike the planes themselves, missiles and bombs were constantly depleted, either through training or actual military engagements, and needed to be regularly replenished through Milchan, inflating Israel's secret offshore accounts, and by extension its covert capabilities around the world.

One example of such covert activities is familiar to many moviegoers from the 2006 Steven Spielberg action thriller *Munich*. The movie tells the true story of Israeli Mossad agents from the Kidon (Spear) unit, dispatched to Europe to assassinate those responsible for the 1972 massacre of Israeli athletes at the Munich Olympic Games.[12] Spielberg depicts the operation as being financed by the Israeli government, with one laughably unrealistic scene involving a government clerk in Israel loudly demanding that the assassins provide receipts for every expense, generating a paper trail of all of their activities.

What was realistic, however, was a scene in which the lead agent, Avner (played by Eric Bana), opens a safety deposit box at a Zurich bank to get the cash to finance his mission.

Without Spielberg knowing it, he had stumbled upon the exact kind of offshore account that Israel used to finance these and similar operations. The fictitious Norwegian company that "purchased" the Cherbourg boats, the fictitious company that bought the two hundred tons of uranium oxide that "disappeared" in the Mediterranean, the covert purchase of the top-secret plans of the French Super Mirage – all are examples of operations financed through these covert accounts.

It was not unusual for an Israeli agent to win over senior corporate executives and government officials in key sensitive sectors, through their identification with Israel, through money, or both. But these accounts were not only used for cloak-and-dagger operations. For the most part, they were used for the straight purchasing of access to forbidden technolo-

---

12. Kidon is the assassination unit of the Mossad; it is part of the Caesarea Department, the operational wing of the Mossad, and is considered the most elite branch of the organization.

gy, or even such activity as maintaining the widow and children of a fallen spy, such as Nadia, the widow of fallen Israeli master spy Eli Cohen.[13]

One typical method of operation, giving plausible deniability to the perpetrator, would be to convince an executive to "innocently" leave designs in an exposed area at a predetermined time. One or two hours was more than enough for a well-trained crew to photograph and document the material, before its "forgetful" owner returned it to its rightful place.

* * *

"No matter what the accomplishment, the journey to the goal has always been more satisfying than the accomplishment itself," said Arnon.[14]

That was certainly the case in his relationship with Brigitte. Within a short period of time, Arnon had formed an attachment with Ulla, an equestrian from Gothenburg, Sweden, whom he had met in Paris before the Air Show. He "adopted" Ulla and her young boy, and rented them a house in Cyprus, a thirty-minute flight from Tel Aviv, where he opened a local office. He then proceeded to live a double life.

Almost every week, the Milchan Bros. office in Tel Aviv received an "urgent" telex requiring Arnon's presence at a pressing business engagement in Cyprus, prompting him to fly off to spend time in the arms of his new lover. Within a year of flying back and forth, Arnon decided to bring Ulla to Israel, where he set her up in a comfortable small house in a Tel Aviv suburb, and bought her the best horse in Israel that he could find. He then spent his days between his wife, his business, and his secret lover. It was not a sustainable situation, and something had to give.

---

13. Eli Cohen was publicly hanged in the central square in Damascus, Syria, on May 18, 1965.

14. Personal interview with Milchan, November 2009.

7 ||| The Client

> *[Iran?] I only received a contract to remove*
> *weeds from the airport's runway.*
>
> Arnon Milchan, *Los Angeles Times*, February 28, 1992

Milchan's fertilizer and chemical businesses kept the cash flowing; it was a good cover, but nothing like his low-profile, ever-increasing defense systems transactions through Milchan Bros., and the multiple front companies and bank accounts created to handle them.

The legend of the rehabilitation of his father's fertilizer business spread, making him a mysterious semi-celebrity in Tel Aviv. Milchan gained strong inroads into the political elite, and was now a real mover in the behind-the-scenes world of Israeli security and armaments. Those who needed to know, knew.

He was married to a beautiful woman and was the father to a new son, while maintaining a Swedish beauty on the side. But none of that would bring inner peace – only a relentless restlessness. He had yet to make a mark on the world in a way that came even close to satisfying his aspirations, and he was constantly on the lookout for new and unconventional challenges. By the late 1960s those challenges began to arrive. "From my point of view, I stumbled into things," Milchan said.

Surprisingly, in the late 1960s Iran supplied ambitious and well-connected Israelis with their most interesting international business opportunities, and one of those opportunities was delivered to Milchan on a silver platter. Once again he would make the most of it.

From the day of Israel's creation until the Iranian Revolution in 1979 (during the time Iran was led by the shah, Mohammad Rezā Shāh Pahlavi), the two countries enjoyed a very special and close relationship. Iran was actually the second country in the world to recognize Israel as an independent nation, just behind the United States, and was considered its closest friend in the Muslim world.

Like everyone else, the shah was especially impressed by Israel's lightning victory during the 1967 Six-Day War, and within a few short years the two countries were developing a wide range of joint projects – military, agricultural, and commercial. Iran supplied Israel with much of its energy needs, and Israel paid Iran back with know-how. To help secure and maintain the shah's precarious internal position, Israel trained Iran's secret service, SAVAK, one of the largest and most ruthless internal security forces in the world at the time.

The two countries even developed a joint energy distribution company called Trans-Asiatic Oil. With the Suez Canal closed following the Six-Day War, Iran would ship oil to Israel's southern port of Eilat, transfer the oil by pipeline to its Mediterranean port in Ashdod, and ship to Europe from there, bypassing the Suez Canal altogether. For Israel, the main players in the Iranian-Israeli arms trade were its military attaché in Teheran, Ya'akov Nimrodi, and Israeli American businessman Al Schwimmer, a former aircraft smuggler during Israel's War of Independence who was the founder and chairman of Israel Aircraft Industries (today Israel Aerospace Industries, IAI), a state-owned company and one of the largest employers in Israel with annual sales of about $3.5 billion. Both Nimrodi and Schwimmer quietly pioneered and cultivated the Iranian-Israeli relationship at the highest levels over a period of years. Their big breakthrough finally came in the aftermath of the Six-Day War, elevating Israel's reputation in the eyes of the shah and leading him to sign many lavish security-related contracts with the Israelis.

By the late 1960s and early 1970s Nimrodi and Schwimmer were reaping the substantial fruits of their labor; no one was better connected in

Iran than they were, not the CIA and not MI5. Both of these men opened the door to Iran for the young Milchan and other Israelis. In 1982, the *New York Times* reported that over half of all weapons systems bought by Iran, all the way up to the revolution in 1979, either came from, or were arranged by, Israel.

With the approval of Shimon Peres, Schwimmer and Nimrodi presented the shah and his top generals with the idea of constructing a sophisticated network of remote mountaintop early-warning stations and listening posts capable of intercepting communications and radar signals from Iran's neighbors. Israel maintains a similar electronic ring around its own borders for early-warning purposes and to eavesdrop when necessary, and they shared some of that data with the shah and with the commander of the Iranian air force, General Mohammad Khatami, to impress upon them the importance of such intelligence.

But Iran is more than sixty times the size of Israel, and Schwimmer quickly realized that the project would cost well over a billion dollars and was probably beyond Israel Aircraft Industries' capabilities at the time. He felt confident that IAI's electronics division, ELTA, could supply the antennas and some of the electronics, and that Israeli crews could manage installation, which would amount to about twenty percent of the project, but many of the other elements were beyond IAI's scope.

A larger company would have to serve as the senior contractor, with IAI as its subcontractor. There were only a small number of companies in the world with which Israel felt comfortable that were capable of executing such a project. One of those companies was North American Rockwell.[1] Israel Aircraft Industries already had a modest relationship with Rockwell, amounting to about $10 million annually in joint projects, mostly related to the Westwind business-executive jet, a non-military aircraft manufactured in Israel. But even this came at a risk for Rockwell in potential lost revenue from oil-rich Arab countries that continued to adhere to an economic boycott of Israel, so the relationship was deemed classified.

---

1. The name was changed to Rockwell International in 1973; it was later bought out by Boeing.

Rockwell's board was growing restless as Saudi oil seemed more alluring than business with Israel, so they decided to send their newly appointed vice president and regional business development representative to Tel Aviv to see if the joint venture could be restructured to lower the profile, or be dissolved altogether.

The regional representative they sent was a senior engineer by the name of Dr. Richard "Dick" Kelly Smyth. Smyth, in his early forties, was an unusual character – a scientist and mathematician with business ambitions. He grew up in rural Oklahoma and had struggled financially over many years to put himself through school, ultimately obtaining a BS in physics from Caltech, and an MS and PhD in electrical engineering and mathematics from the University of Southern California (USC). Along the way, he'd gotten married and fathered five children. Smyth rose through the ranks, coming to play a pioneering role in the development of advanced missile guidance and automatic flight control systems. He gained a solid reputation among his peers and was appointed to various defense-related boards and commissions at the Pentagon, NATO, and NASA.

Smyth landed at Israel's international airport and got in the long line for passport control. Suddenly he felt someone place a hand on his shoulder from behind, and, as he turned around, a young man extended his hand and introduced himself as Arnon Milchan. The two exchanged pleasantries. Smyth was stunned to see how young Milchan was. He had first heard of him from his daughter Gretel, who worked in Rockwell's accounting department, and assumed that he was a major player in Israel's growing aerospace industry. The image in his mind didn't conform to the person standing in front of him.

Arnon smoothly navigated Smyth around the crowd at passport control and quickly bypassed immigration formalities. They exited the airport and proceeded toward Arnon's illegally parked red Chevy convertible, which, strangely, no one had towed or ticketed.

In truth, to say that Arnon represented Rockwell or any other defense-related company in the traditional sense is a bit misleading. Arnon represented the State of Israel, he represented himself and his company, and then he represented Rockwell – in that exact order. To what extent

Rockwell – or for that matter Raytheon or Beechcraft, or any of the other defense contractors he worked with – was aware of this reality is not clear. Richard Kelly Smyth had originally assumed that the young Arnon was a simple state employee assigned to facilitate Rockwell's presence in Israel, and he naïvely wondered how a young civil servant could afford to be driving around in an imported American convertible, a rarity in Israel at the time. Only later did he realize how much he'd underestimated Arnon, and he began to grasp the complex nature of the relationship between Arnon and the State of Israel, yet he never did come to fully understand it.

As long as plausible deniability for the US contractor was built into the deal, what Arnon actually did with the money that exchanged hands was not of Rockwell's concern; they were only interested in the results that Arnon would produce, and on that front there were few complaints. Unaware of Israel's unique method of operation and Arnon's unique role in it, when US defense contractors approached the Israeli Ministry of Defense for a possible sale, they were routinely advised to go and talk to Arnon; some were confused as to why the state preferred to work with a middleman rather than directly. For a country in a constant state of war since well before its inception, dedicating about eight percent of its entire GDP, a growing percentage of its exports, and about sixteen percent of its entire budget to defense-related expenditures necessary for survival, this was not an insignificant pool to swim in – and it was expanding quickly.

When it became clear that Israel Aircraft Industries needed Rockwell to sign on to the Iranian surveillance project with IAI as its subcontractor, Milchan was brought in for a briefing at LAKAM to strategize and devise a plan for how the tail would wag the dog. This was to be his first real foray into a large, covert international project that didn't involve a sale to the Israeli Ministry of Defense but rather an export from Israel to a third country. From the beginning it was made clear to Arnon that if things went well with his client Rockwell, there would be more worldwide opportunities for him in addition to Iran. It was also understood that deals Arnon brokered that did not involve shipments to Israel meant commissions went to him and not to Israel's covert accounts. A man has to make a living.

After explaining the importance of the project, Blumberg instructed Milchan to size up Richard Kelly Smyth, give him the VIP treatment, wine and dine him, learn his weaknesses, and look for personal vulnerabilities. Most important of all, he was tasked with getting Smyth committed to the Iranian project.

Milchan immediately proceeded to set up a series of meetings for Smyth with Israeli VIPs – not because these VIPs' input was technically necessary for the project, but because it was necessary to make it abundantly clear to Smyth, and by extension his bosses at the Rockwell headquarters in Los Angeles, the level of connections that Milchan brought to the table. But there was also another motive: to make Smyth perceive that he was trusted enough to join an elite inner circle in Israel that ordinary outsiders didn't enjoy, and to gauge how he'd respond.

Following their initial encounter at Ben-Gurion Airport, Milchan drove Smyth to the Tel Aviv Hilton on the beach for an initial briefing. The warm sunshine, the gentle cool breeze, the blue Mediterranean, and the smooth sound of the crashing waves were intoxicating, as was the view of the long sandy beach that stretched all the way south to Jaffa, where, Milchan explained to Smyth, his grandfather had first arrived in the previous century. In the distance he could clearly see the hill where the whale had disgorged Jonah in the famous biblical tale that he learned about as a child. Like so many before him, Smyth was quickly hooked on Israel.

After a good night's sleep, Milchan paraded Smyth in and out of the offices of generals and famous politicians, briefed in advance, who explained the importance of the relationship with Rockwell in general and of the project in Iran specifically. Smyth had come to Israel to gently discuss downgrading Rockwell's profile because of concerns over the Arab boycott. Instead, he found himself in a whirlwind of meetings and presented with a massive opportunity for Rockwell in Iran. It was an immediate game-changer. Smyth sensed that the Israelis had already been briefed by someone in advance about the purpose of his mission to Israel, and were fully prepared to counter with a deal that Rockwell would have difficulty refusing.

That evening, Milchan took Smyth to the Alhambra restaurant just south of Tel Aviv. Alhambra was one of Israel's first gourmet restaurants and was certainly one of the most expensive in the country at the time, offering non-kosher French cuisine. It was the in-place for Israel's elite. Minister of Defense Moshe Dayan maintained a permanent private table, and happened that night to be hosting a couple of foreign visitors accompanied by two gorgeous women.

The married Dayan was a notorious womanizer and half the country knew it. He was also an international celebrity who had graced the covers of *Time* and *Newsweek*, instantly recognizable thanks to his famous eye patch. Milchan casually introduced Dayan to Smyth, who was immediately starstruck, surprised, and impressed by the warmth between Milchan and Dayan.

Over dinner, Smyth expressed his concern about whether Rockwell would be able to obtain the necessary US export licenses to Iran for such sensitive technology. It would require approval from multiple layers of competing agencies and egos. Milchan assured him that a solution was already in the works. Smyth was puzzled by Milchan's confidence.

Indeed, the Israelis had already considered every obstacle and had arranged a negotiating posture that they felt would be sure to lure the American government in with an offer they couldn't refuse. Of course James Jesus Angleton with the CIA, who controlled the Israel file, had already been partially briefed by the Mossad and had given a tentative thumbs-up, but the CIA under director Richard Helms was hardly the last word – this was just the beginning. Milchan filled Smyth in on the game plan: As coordinated with the shah's negotiating team, Iran's position would be that they were only interested in surveillance sites along the borders of Afghanistan, Pakistan, the Persian Gulf, and Iraq. They would make no mention of their vast border with the Soviet Union to the north.

When the Pentagon and the US State Department would predictably hesitate to authorize the execution of such a sensitive deal involving the Iranians spying on US allies like Saudi Arabia, Iran would then sweeten the deal by offering two surveillance sites along its border with the Soviet Union, one at Bushehr and the other at Kapkan. The additional cost would be minimal, and paid for by Iran.

The US was warming up to the idea but was still hesitating.

Iran would then extend an invitation to the CIA and the Pentagon to directly access all of the intercepted data and communications gathered from the Soviet southern frontier via the Iranian surveillance stations. Israel, predictably, had its own interest in the intelligence generated from neighboring Arab countries.

The United States had a problem with Iran obtaining the latest US encryption technology. A Swiss company that provided all of the encryption for the secretive Swiss banking system would be brought in instead, Milchan explained.

Bingo. The Americans were in.

The US government would obtain cost-free, direct electronic intelligence (ELINT) from the southern Soviet border, and an American contractor got a billion-dollar deal. The Americans would later call the project Dark Gene for the aviation elements, and Ibex for the stationary electronic surveillance outposts. Ibex is the name of a rare mountain goat found in Iran, and was the shah's favorite wild animal to hunt.

Milchan assured Smyth that as far as the Iranians were concerned, the deal was already done. He informed him that Rockwell's Iranian representative for the project would be General Mohammad Khatami, commander of the Iranian air force and the shah's brother-in-law. Khatami would appoint a key contact to act as his front person, but it was Khatami who was the man behind the man. And it was the shah who stood behind him.

Smyth was stunned and dazzled by the young Milchan's charm, his grasp of the situation, his sophisticated presentation, the magnitude of the project, the potential geostrategic implications, and the sheer audacity of the concept. Milchan gave him the party line about inheriting a failing fertilizer business from his father and turning it into a powerhouse. Smyth didn't fully understand that behind this fresh face stood LAKAM, Benjamin Blumberg, Ya'akov Nimrodi, Al Schwimmer, and ultimately the intelligence machinery of the State of Israel. But what he did grasp was that Milchan was not some small-time civil servant as he'd originally suspected. Finally he thought he was beginning to understand the big picture.

For his part, Milchan sensed that he was succeeding in making an impression on the older American engineer. He also felt that Smyth was the kind of person he might be able to recruit. He observed in Smyth a strong taste for the good life, an affinity for money and women, even though he was a married man and decently paid by Rockwell. He noticed a rather inflated ego – the man insisted on using his "doctor" title at every opportunity – and a feeling that he and his talents were somewhat under-appreciated.

Smyth was indeed a talented electronics engineer with a depth of knowledge about weapons systems, materials, and technologies, and where to obtain them. These were talents that Milchan and LAKAM could use. Smyth seemed to have a strong interest in history and responded with enthusiasm and awe to his meetings with important figures in Israel.

When casually and gently questioned about his understanding of the Arab-Israeli conflict, he consistently took a pro-Israel position. Some of it may have been to please his hosts and could be discounted, but Milchan sensed a strong degree of authenticity in his expressions of support. As planned, Smyth had no idea he was being sized up.

Milchan clarified that as far as Israel and the Iranians were concerned, the project was a go, so long as IAI secured from Rockwell twenty percent of the project as subcontractor. He assured Smyth that he would be able to navigate Rockwell through the Iranian system. Milchan would rely on Nimrodi and LAKAM for that guidance, but that was not Smyth's concern.

Milchan knew that Rockwell could do the job; his primary concern was how to steer the project through American bureaucracy to get the necessary export licenses and multiple agency approvals. That was the biggest obstacle, and he sought Smyth's reassurance that he was up to the task. Smyth did not hesitate to give it, knowing that he would have an entire department working on it.

Later that night, Smyth made an urgent phone call from his hotel room to the CEO of Rockwell to update him on the turn of events, and was given the green light to pursue the opportunity.

The next day included a business breakfast at the Hilton and some sightseeing. Smyth mentioned that he was interested in purchasing a diamond for his wife and had heard that the Tel Aviv Diamond Exchange was where good deals could be had. Milchan called a contact and within moments arranged for a backroom meeting at the Diamond Exchange where Smyth would be offered a great wholesale deal on a one-karat diamond for his wife. Every hour seemed to bring a new opportunity for Milchan to impress Smyth with his connections.

Following diamond shopping, the two headed for the Church of the Holy Sepulcher in Jerusalem, the Church of the Nativity in Bethlehem, and Masada overlooking the Dead Sea. Milchan lectured Smyth on the history and politics of each of these sites with great knowledge and an infectious enthusiasm. Smyth's impression of this young man became more and more favorable. He was particularly moved by Masada and the simultaneously tragic and heroic stand taken by Jewish zealots in their final moments of battle against the encroaching Roman soldiers before they ultimately committed mass suicide rather than subject themselves to slavery.

The next day, Milchan took Smyth to the airport and personally escorted him through security and to the VIP lounge to await his flight. The two departed with a binding handshake and promises to stay in touch and work closely together to see this project through. Milchan had done his job; Smyth left Israel that day armed with a potential large project, a newfound admiration of Israel, and what he felt was a solid friendship with Rockwell's representative in Israel.

Upon returning to Rockwell headquarters in Los Angeles and briefing company leadership, a tentative go-ahead was given. Technical teams were assembled and the complicated process of designing the project and ushering it through monstrous American bureaucracy began.

But there was another routine meeting that Smyth had upon his return to Los Angeles, the kind of meeting that most high-level US defense contractors have upon returning from overseas business as a condition for maintaining their top-secret clearance: a meeting with a CIA agent who debriefs defense-related executives about their encounters with foreign officials during their overseas trips, to learn as much as possible about intentions and methods, and to evaluate if recruitment or infiltration attempts were made.

Defense contractors like Smyth helped supplement the CIA's eyes and ears around the world, and despite agreements not to spy on each other,

Israel was certainly one country that the CIA was focused on. Richard Kelly Smyth casually disclosed all of his contacts and activities in Israel during the trip, naming Milchan, among others, while the agent quietly took notes as he had during their previous meetings. This was not the first time that a CIA agent had taken note of the name Arnon Milchan.

From back in Israel, Milchan followed Smyth's progress with diligence, and with the behind-the-scenes help of Israel's military attaché in Teheran, Ya'akov Nimrodi, he was able to guide Rockwell through the complicated and corrupt world of Iranian arms procurement. Nimrodi's hidden hand made sure that General Khatami's "broker" was brought in.

A complicated and lengthy contract written up by Rockwell's legal team was signed by the Iranians within months. And a few months after that, Rockwell's director of security personally flew on the company's Sabreliner jet with a stack of papers over ten feet tall representing the entire billion-dollar project, including every design and specification, to the Pentagon's Office of Munitions Control for an extensive review by the Pentagon, NSA, the CIA, and the State Department, all of which needed to give their approval before the project could move forward. Six months later – in record time, in fact – the project was approved, and by early 1969, construction was underway. Milchan was twenty-four years old.

* * *

In 1968, Motti Bloch was a thirty-three-year-old construction specialist for the Israeli Air Force and Navy, specializing in communications and radar facilities. In his memoirs he describes returning one day sweaty and dirty from the Sinai Peninsula after working on a large project. Upon arriving home his wife informed him that somebody had been trying to reach him and that he was needed at an urgent meeting in Tel Aviv.

Being the constant professional, he arrived dutifully. "We are sending you to Iran in three days," he was informed. Bloch was not entirely happy and tried to learn who was behind this sudden assignment; "If we tell you that Benjamin is behind this, would that be enough for you?" he was asked without the slightest expectation of an answer.

"Blumberg was a holy name," said Bloch. "I have never met him but everybody in the know knew that he was the final word when it came to national security." That was how Bloch learned that he was off to Iran not only for commercial reasons, but in the interest of national security. "They asked that we keep our eyes open and report."

Before his departure, he was briefed on the fact that in Iran he would be working for a company called Sarik-Iran. Within three days of returning from the Sinai, Motti had landed in Teheran. He joined a team that included fifteen Israelis and two Americans from Rockwell, and they hired about 750 Iranians for the job, or 150 Iranian workers for every Israeli supervisor:

> We built the communications structures in fourteen different locations, and each location included two radar domes, four antennas, and a communications tower with giant dishes that were used for operational communications – we called them "the monsters." The locations were spread out from the southern border with Pakistan, to Bandar Abbas at the entrance to the Persian Gulf, northwest toward Bushar, through the center of the country, Shiraz, Isban, and Teheran. In those days Israeli and Iranian officers and businessmen would cross boarders regularly, share knowledge, and invest in joint projects. The Americans would bring the equipment, the Israelis would bring the know-how, and the Iranians would bring the money. There were many Israeli companies operating there, and Israelis were dominant players in the country.[2]

Motti Bloch kept LAKAM informed of his observations in Iran; he was one of the first to raise the alarm about the growing strength of radical Islamists in the country, and predicted an imminent revolution. This information would serve Milchan well.

Milchan enjoyed his activities in Iran, and spent many an evening in the nightclubs along the glamorous Pahlano Boulevard in Teheran. His role

2. Davida Ginter, "An Israeli Hand in the Iranian Nuclear Reactor," *Ma'ariv* (Israel), August 26, 2007.

in the Iranian electronics surveillance project, Ibex, was a breakthrough for him, the consequences of which would be far-reaching. He earned a personal audience with the shah himself at the grand palace, and charmed his way into many additional agricultural and military contracts throughout the 1970s. He created a number of companies in Iran to service those contracts, including the construction of a major new air force base, which he later claimed was simply a contract for "clearing the weeds around the runway." His company Farm Medicine became the largest agrochemical company in Iran.

Milchan's client Raytheon was not neglected. Raytheon sold improved medium-range surface-to-air HAWK missiles to Iran in the 1970s, and sophisticated, top-secret electronic systems were installed in the shah's personal plane by Raytheon's low-profile subsidiary, E-Systems. General Khatami ordered hundreds of Raytheon Sidewinder, Phoenix, Sparrow, and Maverick missiles for the Iranian air force. For these transactions, as with all transactions outside of Israel, Milchan pocketed the commissions.

By 1973 the construction phase of the Ibex project wound down and Israeli involvement was phased out. As the Israelis and Milchan moved on to other projects in Iran, Ibex and Dark Gene evolved and expanded throughout the 1970s into a top-secret, ongoing US operation on the Soviet Union's southern border.

Rockwell continued with various upgrade projects. On August 28, 1976, three Rockwell employees working on Ibex were assassinated in Teheran by suspected Soviet agents or Muslim extremists; the incident was never conclusively solved. Rockwell itself became embroiled in multiple bribery scandals relating to Ibex, the details of which journalist Bob Woodward happily splashed all over the front page of the *Washington Post* on January 2, 1977. It was the first time the world had ever heard of Ibex, but by then Milchan was long gone. He had other fish to fry in Iran and other parts of the world.[3]

In 1975, the shah's brother-in-law and closest confidant, General Mohammad Khatami, who acted as Rockwell's de facto representative in

---

3. Bardach, "The Last Tycoon."

Iran, died in a mysterious paragliding accident as the country became increasingly unstable. The radical Islamist group Tuda was the usual suspect. As a result of the Iranian Revolution in 1979, the listening posts' self-destruct mechanisms were activated to avoid allowing them to fall into hostile hands.

One person who came to resent Milchan's success in Iran was Ya'akov Nimrodi. Nimrodi quickly tired of watching Israel's elite, particularly someone as young as Arnon, get rich off of connections in Iran that Nimrodi himself had cultivated over a period of many years. By 1970, Nimrodi resigned as Israel's military attaché in Teheran and started his own successful arms trading business, eventually earning millions in transactions in Iran and elsewhere. (Nimrodi was later implicated in the Iran-Contra affair along with Al Schwimmer, while Milchan steered clear of that mess, even though it also involved the sale of Raytheon HAWK missiles from Israel.)

In 1978, Milchan understood that the shah had reached the end of his rope, and that it was only a matter of time until the collapse of his regime. He quickly moved to sell Farm Medicine, which had become the largest agricultural conglomerate in Iran, and all of his other interests in the country, at a substantial profit. A year later, Ayatollah Khomeini and the Islamist radicals had taken full control of the country. Milchan had dodged a bullet by following his instincts and leaving the scene before it was too late.

By the early 1970s, Milchan Bros. had opened companies in many countries, including several with which Israel did not maintain diplomatic relations, and in some cases countries with which Israel was at war. Through subsidiaries in Greece and Cyprus, he opened branches in Egypt, Sudan, Ethiopia, Jordan, and Turkey, among others. These companies, more often than not, served as fronts for the various needs of the State of Israel. At the height of these activities, Milchan controlled over thirty companies in seventeen countries. "I gave Israel free rein to use my companies to help in the defense and survival of my country."[4]

---

4. Ibid.

But Iran was his first financial windfall on an international scale, and perhaps the most consequential outcome of the Iranian surveillance project was Milchan's growing relationship with Richard Kelly Smyth at Rockwell. The two worked closely together throughout the development of the Ibex project, both in Israel and Iran, and had developed a level of trust. Milchan had many opportunities to plant the seeds for the next stage, and by late 1972 Milchan and Smyth sat down once again for dinner, this time at the Kasbah restaurant in north Tel Aviv during one of Smyth's routine visits as part of his business development responsibilities.

Milchan was feeling comfortable enough to drop more than a few hints about his intentions, and suggested that perhaps this was the moment for Smyth to consider making some "real money" in his own procurement business. By now, he knew Smyth well enough to know that he felt underpaid and underappreciated at Rockwell. He knew that Smyth was not a fan of corporate culture where all of his time was structured and managed by others, and that he was accountable to people whom he perceived as doing less yet earning more.

But it was a risk for Smyth. Matters like health insurance, retirement pension, and job security weighed heavily on his mind. He thought hard about the long road he had traveled from rural Oklahoma to his present position at the highest levels of his profession: years of expensive education, family, children, and mortgages. He was deeply enmeshed.

Milchan sensed a degree of hesitation from Smyth. He emphasized that the idea was to work legally and openly, and that he could supply him with all of the orders that he could possibly handle from a long list of items needed for various programs. Smyth was enthusiastic about the idea of being in the loop on some of Israel's most covert programs, but the prospect of being his own man, making his own schedule, and enhancing his lifestyle was the cherry on top. Milchan knew what buttons to push, and certainly greed was the big one.

The offer was tempting, the seeds had been planted, and Smyth was already imagining how he could tell his wife Emilie that she could quit her teaching job. His mind was filled with images of beachfront properties and yacht club memberships.

8 ||| The Man Who Knew Too Little

Arnon Milchan was the Chuck Norris of LAKAM.

Amnon Abromovich, *Globes* (Israel), April 24, 2008

Richard Kelly Smyth enthusiastically suggested that the company be called Milco, which put a nervous smile on Milchan's face.

Smyth assumed that he would like the name, but for Milchan it was too close for comfort and he mildly objected. He would have preferred something a little more generic, but he didn't want to seem disrespectful, and he also didn't want Smyth to think that he was distancing himself for any reason. Smyth explained that the name was short for military, not Milchan, and stuck with it. Later, when Blumberg heard of the name, he reprimanded Milchan, but by that time it was too late.

Despite his enthusiasm, Smyth had procrastinated for weeks before giving his answer to Milchan's enticing proposal. After all, he'd reached his position at Rockwell following years of personal struggle, attaining the status of senior executive at one of America's premier aerospace companies. He'd gained experience that went well beyond his professional training as an engineer. He dealt with contracts worth hundreds of millions of dollars, sums that he could never dream of obtaining as an employee or even as a senior executive. He knew who was making the money, and he knew that he was not among them, and would likely never be.

He'd come to deeply admire Milchan and in many ways was both jealous and in awe of him. Arnon represented the good life; he was swimming in money and youth, with a seemingly endless ability to obtain whatever he wanted; he was independent, confident, and unconfined by life's constraints, social or economic. With every day that passed, Smyth became more attracted to the opportunity that Milchan had gently, and later not so gently, laid at his feet. In his mind, Milchan knew how to make money, and he was the kind of guy Smyth should stick with and emulate if he wanted to break free of the grey shackles of an employee in order to live the lifestyle that he felt he deserved.

When Smyth agreed to Milchan's proposition he had no idea how Milco would work, or what the arrangement between them would be. He had hesitated, as had his wife Emilie. But to his surprise, when he gently broached the subject with his bosses at Rockwell, they were delighted; it represented a solution to the constant pressure that they felt from the Saudis to cut ties with Israel.

Instead of ordering from Rockwell directly, trade with Israel could be funneled through Milco, and Rockwell could pretend that it did little or no business with Israel at all. Milchan could place his Rockwell orders through Richard Kelly Smyth, who would then forward orders to Israel, or if necessary through a third company controlled by Milchan.

According to Smyth, Rockwell even offered him a position on the board to maintain his top-secret clearance, so that he could remain up-to-date on the latest classified developments in aerospace technology. Milchan made many promises of his own, according to Smyth, that he would place all of his orders from Rockwell and from elsewhere in the US through Milco.

Smyth also realized that if he operated free from Rockwell, he could do other things as well. He sat on various commissions for NATO and NASA, dealing mostly with missile guidance and control systems. He was on the Scientific Advisory Board (SAB) of the Pentagon, and had a civilian protocol rank of a three-star general. He could order USAF transport aircraft to take him anywhere he wanted to go. He was convinced that he would be able to secure a few consulting contracts from these institutions. Milchan naturally encouraged that line of thinking.

Milchan knew that licensing would be Smyth's primary obstacle and it was one of the reasons for his interest in Smyth to begin with: his proven ability to move things though the vast system of American bureaucracy was clearly showcased during the entire Ibex project. Unlike in Israel, where Milchan could cut through layers of bureaucracy with one phone call to Blumberg, bureaucracy in the US was a different animal. Highly sensitive missile components, complex electronic systems, and guidance systems would all theoretically require munitions export licenses, although every effort would be made to avoid the hassle.

Many items would simply get standard export approvals from the US Department of Commerce, and in some cases wouldn't even need that. Milchan knew that most dual-use items, bought and shipped separately, would not be perceived as having a military application. In most cases, a special license would only be necessary if an item was assembled or had an exclusive military function.

Over the years, the United States has clamped down significantly on the dual-use market, but in the early 1970s it still fell into a convenient grey area, with wide gaps that someone like Milchan could drive trucks through. As Smyth describes it, the two discussed the structural makeup of the company: Milco would be owned entirely by Smyth, who would be its president and CEO, and Milchan would have no interest in the company. However, since Milchan would be providing Milco with almost all of its orders, he demanded that the profits should be divided sixty percent to him and forty percent to Smyth. Despite the agreement, Smyth was unaware that the sixty percent profit Milchan claimed would in fact be going to Israeli covert accounts under Milchan's control. Smyth quickly convinced himself that the unequal distribution of profit was fair but that expenses were another matter, and Milchan agreed that Smyth should deduct all his reasonable expenses from the company's revenue.

Seed money was the last obstacle. Since Smyth didn't possess that kind of cash, Milchan agreed to front the first order to capitalize the business. Smyth was satisfied. This was his opportunity to break away from the confines of corporate America; he was effectively liberated from progress reports, performance evaluations, strict schedules, and time sheets.

He would be his own man, and most important, it was his opportunity to share in the "real money."

In reality, Milchan had subtly dictated the terms of Milco's structure and its method of operation. He created a company free of his finger-prints and recruited a highly respectable and knowledgeable agent, who was completely dependent upon Israel's willingness, through Milchan, to place orders. In exchange for this dependence, and in exchange for the opportunity to work for Milchan and by extension Israeli intelligence, Richard Kelly Smyth would have his expenses taken care of and a forty-percent share of the profits.

The method of operation agreed upon was simple and straightforward. Milchan's office manager, Dvora Ben Yitzhak, working directly with Benjamin Blumberg, would send a coded telex to Smyth listing sensitive items that any number of Milchan's companies wished to order. Milchan himself would fade into the background and make contact only when nec-essary.

In late December 1972, Smyth departed North American Rockwell. Few at Rockwell knew that Smyth had already informally opened Milco, which he ran out of his house in the City of Orange, south of Los Angeles. He conducted business during off hours, in order to cater to business hours on the other side of the world in Israel.

On January 19, 1973, Smyth, now forty-four, officially opened Milco International Inc., and registered the company in Orange County, California. Dvora forwarded long lists of items for him to purchase. At this early stage, almost all of the items ordered were for the Jericho II nuclear ballistic missile system, and as an engineer specializing in missile guidance systems, Smyth could very quickly deduce what the items were likely for, and from whom he might obtain them.

He tried, to the maximum extent possible, to abide by US export laws and to obtain munitions export licenses where necessary. Many dual-use items required no license at all. The end-user declared for most shipments was Rehovot Instruments Ltd., a company closely affiliated with the Israeli Ministry of Defense, whose address was close to the Weizmann Institute of Science in Arnon's hometown of Rehovot. Rehovot Instruments Ltd.

was run by a genius chemist by the name of Professor Joseph Yaffe, who had left the Weizmann Institute to establish the company.

If there was an item deemed too sensitive for telex, it would be sent in predetermined code, or forwarded to Smyth by courier. Smyth would obtain the items, mark them up according to Dvora's instructions, and pay upfront with money forwarded by Milchan's companies. Smyth then shipped the items to Israel.

Sometimes the items were sent to another company in Houston, Texas, according to the *Washington Post*,[1] and then shipped on to Israel. Sometimes they were shipped through a third country or by Israeli diplomatic pouch. Smyth would invoice Milchan's companies the agreed-upon sum and they would transfer the money to Milco's bank account in the United States. Milchan's sixty percent would end up in one of his covert bank accounts. The system worked smoothly and efficiently.

By the time Milco International Ltd. began to operate in full gear in the United States, Milchan was well aware and well briefed on a long list of Israel's top-secret programs: the atomic bomb factory in Dimona, the push for the neutron bomb, the bomb miniaturization program, the heavy water research facility, the Jericho II ballistic missile production at Be'er Tuvia, the Zachariah missile silos, the Tel Nof nuclear squadron, the chemical and biological weapons research at the Israel Institute for Biological Research in Ness Ziona. Milchan was made keenly aware of the missing elements in all of these programs, which Israel desperately needed in order to move them forward, and was depending on him to make it happen.

According to information publicly revealed by former Israeli nuclear technician Mordechai Vanunu, one of Israel's top priorities at the time was to manufacture nuclear bombs containing four kilograms of plutonium, capable of 120 to 160 kilotons of explosive power, or about ten times the force dropped on Hiroshima and Nagasaki by the United States at the end of World War II. Although Israel's nuclear arsenal had grown exponentially since the two primitive bombs manufactured on the eve of the Six-Day War in 1967, the strategic arsenal was still perceived as insuf-

---

1.   John Goshko, "LA Man Indicted in Export of Potential Nuclear Bomb Component to Israel," *Washington Post* series, May 14, 15, 17, 1985.

ficient, and in many ways it did not meet the complex range of Israel's deterrence needs.

Peres, Blumberg, and Dayan calculated that Israel would need approximately fifty bombs to create a viable, long-term, region-wide deterrent, but even that was not enough for their wider strategic objectives.

Israel needed to let the Soviets know that Moscow itself was not immune. Without question, the Soviets had the capacity to destroy Israel a thousand times over, but as long as they understood that such a move potentially involved an unimaginable price, then Israel would have achieved its larger strategic objective. That meant not only large bombs but the capacity to deliver them over much greater distances.

Yet that was only the beginning. Israel felt it needed much smaller battlefield nukes, only five to ten percent the size of the Hiroshima bomb, capable of being fired from cannons at a range of about seventy kilometers (forty-three miles). It needed miniaturized "suitcase" nukes as deterrents to those who may have thought they were out of range. And given the short distances between Israel and its enemies, it felt the need for the neutron bomb – small thermonuclear weapons that produced minimal blasts and heat and released large amounts of lethal radiation, confined to an area with a radius of only a few hundred yards. Because of its short-range destructiveness and the absence of long-range consequences, the neutron bomb is highly effective against tank and infantry formations on the battlefield but would not endanger cities or other population centers only a few miles away.

The short distances in Israel's theater of operation and the close proximity of its own population made the neutron bomb a high priority. LAKAM had its work cut out for itself.

During various meetings with Blumberg and Peres, Milchan came to know and understand the Samson Option, Israel's nuclear weapons doctrine: publically, Israel would not be the first country to introduce nuclear weapons into the Middle East and would neither confirm nor deny their existence.

What is not openly acknowledged, but is generally assumed, is that Israel maintains the sixth (possibly the fifth) largest stockpile of nuclear weapons in the world and will use them only if faced with physical annihilation with nothing left to lose. Of course, the term *Samson Option* refers symbolically to the biblical story of Samson, a prisoner who brought the Philistine temple down on his tormentors and upon himself after declaring, "Let me die with the Philistines."

As Milchan's covert activities accelerated and his work for the "big secret" expanded, Blumberg and Peres felt it was time to bring him into the club. He would be taken to the Dimona reactor for an all-day tour that only the most trusted and informed members of Israel's leadership have ever been privy to. The tour was conducted by the chief of operations of the reactor complex at the time, Yossef Tuipman.[2]

The first thing that Arnon was impressed by, upon arriving at the gate following the long drive, was the peaceful atmosphere, like an oasis in the middle of the desert. The landscape was carefully manicured and the entire facility was lined with friendly palm trees gently swaying in the breeze. At the time of his first tour, it was a much smaller complex, with only six *machonim* (institutes), compared to the current ten.

Arnon was systematically escorted through the various sectors. He quickly learned that the reactor had a 150-megawatt capacity and employed roughly 2,700 people in highly compartmentalized tasks. He and half the country already assumed that the primary objective of the enterprise was the production of plutonium, a by-product of uranium for the purpose of manufacturing a nuclear weapons arsenal. Arnon learned that on average, Israel needed no more than four kilograms of plutonium to produce a single bomb of the kind the country was currently focused on.

Machon-1 was the dominant structure in the complex with a containment dome reaching up about sixty-five feet and clearly visible from the main road that ran between Beersheba and the Arava Valley. It was, and still is, the instantly recognizable symbol of Israel's nuclear program, and that's where Arnon's tour began. He learned that uranium oxide enriched to three to four percent was fabricated into pellets, then inserted into fuel rods.

2. Detailed descriptions in this book of the Dimona reactor were derived from Israel's Channel 10, which based their information on revelations by Mordechai Vanunu, an Israeli nuclear technician arrested for revealing details about the facility to the UK press. Ironically, Israel's Channel 10 was partially owned by Arnon Milchan at the time.

These rods were neutron emitters and, in close proximity with each other, began a self-sustaining chain reaction releasing energy and producing new elements by the fission of the uranium and producing plutonium (^{239}Pu).

That plutonium was collected for bombs, but it was a slow and agonizing process. Arnon's quick mind absorbed the process with little need for further explanation. From there he was escorted to Machon-3, skipping Machon-2, to which he would return at the end of the tour.

Machon-3 was used mostly for the processing of natural uranium for the reactor and conversion of lithium-6 into a solid, for use in thermonuclear warheads, his guide casually explained. They quickly moved toward Machon-4, dedicated to the treatment of radioactive waste products, which included a waste treatment plant and high-level waste storage. Low-level waste was mixed with tar, then canned and buried in a secret location, assumed to be outside the country.

Machon-5 dealt with uranium from Machon-3, which was made into rods and coated in aluminum before being sent to the reactor at Machon-1. From there it was on to Machon-6, which essentially acted as a maintenance facility for the entire complex. Arnon felt privileged to have been allowed access to a world that any number of top intelligence agencies would literally kill for. The tour reached its climax upon arriving at a simple, windowless, two-story rectangular structure, known as Machon-2, the crown jewel of the entire Dimona complex. Of the many employees associated with Dimona, only about 150 were permitted access to Machon-2. Beneath the innocent-looking two-story building were six expansive floors, deep underground, unseen by any satellite or uninvited guest. This was the holy of holies, where Israel set up a large plutonium separation facility with one goal: manufacturing nuclear bombs. They entered the second level, which was actually the eighth floor.

When US inspectors visited Dimona throughout the 1960s, they visited Machon-2 many times, seeing the offices and even eating lunch at the cafeteria there, completely oblivious to the profound secrets right under their feet. Because of the fake wall put up by Blumberg in front of the "forbidden elevators" leading from the cafeteria to the entire underground complex, the American inspectors couldn't possibly imagine the magnitude of Israel's deception.

Arnon was mesmerized. His guide pushed the button for the fourth level, and the elevator door opened at a large balcony that overlooked a huge space below and above. This was the famous Golda Meir balcony, named after Israel's prime minister who stood at the very same spot numerous times, receiving briefings and inspecting the process. "From what I have seen here, no Jew will be led defenseless to the slaughter as occurred during the Holocaust," she is reported to have said.

Arnon was stunned by what he was witnessing and felt a sense of pride and empowerment that overwhelmed any similar feelings he had experienced in the past. Standing on the Golda balcony he received a detailed briefing on the manufacturing process of nuclear weapons. The briefing included many technical terms, procedures, and materials, which Arnon quickly committed to memory as he watched, amazed by the process unfolding in front of him.

Arnon learned that special trucks brought in processed uranium rods from Machon-1 to the seventh floor, which was at ground level. A crane grasped the rods and lowered them to the workspace below. The rods were dipped in nitrous acid tanks and "cooked." A system of pipes drained the water containing the uranium and plutonium through a chemical process and the materials were separated and baked in an oven, producing a small, 130-gram plutonium ball, resulting in 1.7 kilograms per week; 4 kilograms were needed for a bomb.

Arnon quickly calculated that Israel could produce a nuclear bomb every two and a half weeks, or about twenty bombs a year. In other underground labs, Arnon was told that additional critical materials are produced, such as tritium for thermonuclear bombs, lithium, and deuterium. Within a few moments, he was in a room with a small group of technicians, watching them assemble a nuclear bomb. As they went about their task, the room was eerily silent, with only occasional whispers, as if they were in a library or a church.

Arnon then followed his guide into the next room, which was an employee recreation room especially for the bomb assemblers. The idea was to create as stress-free and comfortable an environment as possible for the assemblers. It would not be a good idea to have people with that kind of a job unrested, uncomfortable, or unhappy in any way.

In the recreation room, Arnon received a key briefing on Dimona's material needs.

A long list of items was required and Arnon now began to understand that this was one of the critical missions that Peres, Dayan, and Blumberg had groomed him for – to take Israel's nuclear program to the next level. Naturally, the biggest concern was a steady supply of uranium. Israel had hoped to extract enough uranium from its potash resources in the Negev, but the results were disappointing.

Arnon learned that the reactor was operating by the seat of its pants, dependent on imaginative and daring LAKAM operations to keep it going. Most of the items needed were exotic and unfamiliar to him: green salt, a crystalline solid compound of uranium tetrafluoride; krytrons, cold-cathode gas-filled tubes intended for use as very high-speed switches for detonating nuclear weapons; and centrifuges, devices that use centrifugal force to separate substances. A centrifuge could be used for many things, but it was not well known at the time that it could also be used to enrich uranium to weapons-grade quality. And uranium deuteride was also on the list, a substance that had no possible civilian or military use other than the production of a nuclear bomb.

Milco and other fronts that Arnon was in the process of establishing were set up precisely for the purpose of acquiring these materials. The tour of the reactor had achieved Peres and Dayan's objective: Arnon was more motivated than ever to do his part.

He wanted to come through as a matter of deep patriotism. He thought of his late grandfather, Chaim Eliezer Milchan, who escaped the pogroms and left his family in Poland at the tender age of fourteen to arrive alone on the shores of a desolate land, with a big dream, where he carved out a prosperous life with his own hands. Chaim instilled in his grandson a fierce love of country and a willingness to do whatever it takes, including sacrificing his life if necessary. "I love Israel, and any way I can help, I will. I'll do it again and again," said Arnon.

One of his many objectives was to secure the design for centrifuges, a new and highly secret method of enriching uranium. The primary manufacturer of centrifuges in the world was Urenco Ltd., a firm based in Jülich, Germany, and owned by a consortium of Dutch, German, and British companies.

According to Dr. Avner Cohen, a leading expert on nuclear proliferation, Israel started experimenting with centrifuges in the early- to mid-1960s, "but it took a while, at least a decade, to master the technology."[3] In fact, Israel never entirely mastered centrifuge technology on its own. Only after secretly obtaining the Urenco centrifuge blueprints in the early 1970s, from a senior Urenco executive, did Israel finally take command of the technology. Money was exchanged, the blueprints were "misplaced" and later found, but not before copies were made, which miraculously appeared on Benjamin Blumberg's desk in Tel Aviv. Mission accomplished.

Within a few years of Milchan's first Dimona visit, an entire new *machon* at Dimona was devoted to enriching uranium, more efficiently and quickly, through centrifuges manufactured entirely in Israel based exactly on the Urenco blueprint. Machon-8, with its thousands of spinning centrifuges, might justifiably be called Machon Milchan.

Later, an additional facility, Machon-9, would be added to Dimona to accommodate a newly developed laser technology.[4] Milchan was the key figure in securing much of the sensitive material and equipment that the scientists needed in order to develop this unique Israeli method of uranium enrichment.

It's noteworthy that shortly after Israel secured centrifuge technology from Urenco, Dr. Abdul Qadeer Khan, the father of the Pakistani bomb, who then worked at one of Urenco's affiliated labs in Holland, also secured the same designs for Pakistan, and later sold them to Iran and North Korea. Dr. Kahn's theft and later proliferation represented the single worst

---

3.   Dr. Avner Cohen, author of *Israel and the Bomb* (New York: Columbia University Press, 1999), in written communications with the authors. Dr. Cohen is a senior fellow at the James Martin Center for Nonproliferation Studies at the Monterey Institute of International Studies.

4.   Even later, Machon-10 was established in order to manufacture depleted uranium for tank and artillery shells.

security breach relating to nuclear weapons technology since the dawn of the atomic age.[5] It also explains why Israel and Iran are operating "virtually identical nuclear centrifuges," a fact that Israel would take advantage of at a later stage.[6]

US intelligence analysts knew about Dimona's purpose, and its needs, as well as other secret Israeli programs to develop delivery systems, such as the Jericho II missile.

They knew about Milco's role as a new supplier for Israel's military requirements, primarily because of Richard Kelly Smyth's regular reports to the CIA as a condition of maintaining his security clearance. None of this bothered Milchan because he understood that the greater risk in the United States would be to operate outside the system. It was better to operate in broad daylight, within the boundaries of legality, right under everyone's nose, and push the envelope to the max from within, and then claim ignorance, an innocent mistake, or a misunderstanding lost in translation if things went wrong. The good news was that if push ever came to shove, Milchan had no stake in Milco.

In any event, in 1973 the CIA and the United States in general had bigger problems to tend to than little Israel scrounging around the globe for materials. Things weren't going well in southeast Asia. Israel was an ally in the Cold War and delivering crucial intelligence, mostly from the Jewish community inside the Soviet Union. Israel was a primary testing ground for US weapons, it had a growing influence in the US political establishment that coincided with the growth of the pro-Israel lobby AIPAC, and it had powerful friends throughout the government, including in the intelligence community.

That kind of environment allowed Richard Kelly Smyth to feel comfortable moving forward with shipments to Israel that pushed the limits of legality. In 1973 he shipped barrels of butyl, a compound used to bind explosive powders into solid rocket fuel, to another company in Houston, where it was shipped on to an end-user that eventually turned out to be Israel.

---

5. Jack Burston, *Nuclear Engineering Magazine* (August 2004).
6. William J. Broad, John Markoff, and David E. Sanger, "Israeli Test on Worm Called Crucial in Iran Nuclear Delay," *New York Times*, January 15, 2011.

It was a crucial component for the Jericho II. Smyth had come through in a big way and it was only the start – ammonium perchlorate, Butarez, gyroscopes, neutron generators, high-speed oscilloscopes, high-voltage condensers, and hundreds of other dual-use components, totaling in the tens of millions of dollars. All were shipped by Smyth to the end-user Rehovot Instruments Ltd.

As Milchan expanded his operations in the United States, he was also consumed by operations in Iran and standard defense procurements for Israel. He was jetting around the globe, cutting deals, meeting with the high and mighty, and generally living the kind of life that the average person could only dream of – with one problem.

Over time, Ulla had grown to be the dominant love of his life¸ and he began to think of ways to separate from his wife. He promised Ulla that he would take that step. A year earlier, in 1971, Brigitte had informed Arnon that she was pregnant with their second child, their daughter Alexandra. It was no time for talk of separation. A few months after Alexandra's birth, however, Arnon finally mustered the courage to break the news of his intentions to Brigitte. That evening, he walked through the door, nervous but determined. He called Brigitte to the living room for the discussion, but before he could begin, she interrupted him with the news, "I'm pregnant again."

Once again, Arnon backed away from the talk with Brigitte, and informed Ulla of the situation.

On the day that his third child and second daughter Elinor was born, Arnon rushed to the hospital to accompany his wife. As he waited outside the delivery room with family members, he noticed a nurse directing two stern-looking policemen in his direction. As they approached him, one asked, "Are you Arnon Milchan?" When the surprised Arnon replied in the affirmative, the next question was, "Do you own a horse?"

Ulla had finally cracked. She packed her bags, and before departing for the airport she had released the horse that Arnon had bought her. The spooked horse then proceeded to rampage through the streets of the suburbs of Tel Aviv, causing mayhem and property damage to a number of street vendors and cars. After the police had finally corralled the beast, they tracked down the negligent owner.

As Brigitte gave birth to Elinor, Arnon was escorted down to the police station, and was ultimately forced to pay a fine and cover the damage the horse had caused. When Brigitte learned of the incident, all hell broke loose in their relationship. It was a giant wake-up call for Arnon.

Now that Ulla was out of the picture, he was determined to salvage his marriage. The couple agreed to make a drastic change in their lives in hopes that it would bring them closer. Their answer, and what they hoped would be the solution, involved moving to France as a family, where Brigitte would feel more at home and closer to relatives.

Arnon decided to purchase a large, eighteenth-century chateau on the edge of a small lake, twenty-five miles sothwest of Paris. The fifty-acre estate was just outside the historic, picturesque town of Montfort-l'Amaury, on the edge of the Forest of Rambouillet, and had once served as a hunting lodge for numerous French kings. His neighbor, who lived in a much humbler dwelling, was future French president Jacques Chirac.

Arnon's greatest hope was that the picturesque country environment, with its horses and every imaginable luxury, would rekindle his troubled relationship.

9 ‖ Under Siege

*Success is the ability to go from one failure to
another with no loss of enthusiasm.*

Winston Churchill

On October 6, 1973, the Yom Kippur War broke out, the most difficult
and costly of Israel's post-independence wars. The surprise was complete.
In a coordinated and simultaneous attack, Syrian forces rushed across the
Golan Heights and Egyptian forces crossed the Suez Canal on the holiest
day of the Jewish calendar.

The fear was that enemy forces would overwhelm Israel before it was
able to mobilize its reserves, and by that time it would be too late. Terror
and a sense of real danger, death, and destruction hung heavy.

Milchan was stunned to hear his mentor, Minister of Defense Dayan,
in a moment of despair describe the situation as being "on the verge of
the destruction of the third temple,"[1] and the end of the State of Israel.
Israeli losses were unprecedented, eventually in the thousands, and were
especially felt in the armor corps and the air force.

In response to the dire situation, Prime Minster Golda Meir activated
the first phases of the Samson Option. Israel's "nonexistent" nuclear weapons were prepared for use, and Meir informed President Nixon that if

---

1. Seymour Hersh, *The Samson Option: Israel's Nuclear Arsenal and American Foreign
   Policy* (New York: Random House, 1991), 223.

Arab forces continued to advance without Israel being resupplied and able to defend itself, it would have no alternative but to resort to its nuclear option to halt the assault. Without the Samson Option, and those who made it possible, Israel might never have survived the 1973 onslaught.

The message to Washington was loud and clear, and was passed on secretly to the Soviet Union, who informed Egypt and Syria, who in turn ordered their forces not to proceed beyond Israel's red lines.

The Arab hesitation, especially over the Golan Heights, allowed Israel time to mobilize its reserve forces. President Nixon ordered an all-out resupply of Israeli forces over the objections of his advisors, including Henry Kissinger and James Schlesinger, who suggested sending only a few planes to mute the Arab response. Nixon would have none of it: "You let me worry about the politics. If we send them three planes or three hundred planes, the response will be the same... Send them everything that can fly."[2]

Within days, giant Galaxy aircraft, the largest transport planes in the American fleet, were landing almost nonstop at Ben-Gurion Airport, packed with weapons systems and ammunition, which were immediately sent off to the front.

Resupplied with fresh reserves and new equipment, Israel turned the tide of the war, crossing the Suez Canal, surrounding the Egyptian Third Army, and driving to within sixty-three miles of downtown Cairo. In the north, Israeli forces retook the entire Golan Heights and pushed to within sight of the Syrian capital of Damascus.

The Soviet Union then threatened to physically intervene on behalf of its Arab allies. In response, President Nixon placed the United States on DEFCON 3, and certain nuclear units were put on DEFCON 2, the highest level of preparedness for nuclear forces reached during the Cold War. Finally, a ceasefire took hold on October 26, 1973.

The Yom Kippur War was traumatic for Israel, and it exposed great weaknesses in its defenses. Particularly effective on the Arab side were the Soviet-supplied AT-3 Sagger antitank missiles, which proved to have a longer range than Israeli tanks and were effective in putting a stop to multiple

---

2. Jason Maoz, "Thirty-Six Years Ago Today, Richard Nixon Saved Israel – but Got No Credit," *Commentary Magazine* (October 2009).

Israeli counterattacks. Soviet surface-to-air heat-seeking missiles wreaked havoc on the once-invincible Israeli Air Force and deprived Israeli ground forces of effective close air support, which they had come to take for granted.

Bitter recriminations reverberated throughout Israeli society as soldiers coming home described how the enemy was better equipped, and how the Israel Defense Forces had been utterly unprepared for the onslaught. Milchan understood that an entire revamping of the IDF was necessary. At the Pentagon, initial Israeli losses were viewed as a failure of Western weapons systems against Soviet technology, and the United States was to make sure that such a situation would not be repeated.

In the aftermath of the war, an unprecedented weapons-buying spree commenced in order to modernize and reequip the IDF. As the difficult year of 1973 faded, the United States extended to Israel $972.7 million in loans and $1.5 billion in an outright grant for military equipment purchases from US companies.

This was the beginning of a massive military aid program designed to deter Israel's enemies, and to secure and maintain Israel's long-term technological qualitative military edge in the region, which would become official American policy, with Congress earmarking annual funds for that specific purpose.

Suddenly, Israel was flush with cash as never before for defense purchases from the exact kind of companies represented by Milchan, who, with all of the unfortunate circumstances that led to the need for such systems to begin with, found himself at the center of the revamping effort.

One of Israel's first priorities following the war was to strengthen its antiaircraft capabilities. Until then, it had relied almost exclusively on aging HAWKs. Now Milchan would introduce a new system, the MIM-72 Chaparral surface-to-air missile.

Raytheon was eager for the Chaparral to prove itself in combat, and Israel quickly provided the opportunity. Shortly after absorbing the system, on May 16, 1974, a Chaparral battery shot down a Syrian MiG-17 that had strayed over the Golan Heights. Once again, it was the first confirmed kill for an American weapons system, and was further proof of

Israel's role as the leading testing ground for sophisticated Western military equipment. Milchan was delighted.

Another priority for Israel in the aftermath of the Yom Kippur War was the need to find a solution to counter large, fast-moving armored columns, of the kind that surprised and overwhelmed Israeli defenses both in the Sinai Peninsula and in the Golan Heights. The solution was a tank-busting helicopter, the Cobra, which could rapidly deploy to the theater in a matter of minutes.

The Cobra platform brought more work for Milchan, because the primary missile it deployed was the AIM-9 Sidewinder, manufactured by Raytheon. Every missile fired needed replenishing.

Although Milchan mostly focused on high-ticket, high-tech aerospace platforms and weapons, he also worked with IDF ground forces. The Soviet Sagger missile was a deadly wake-up call for Israeli armor during the Yom Kippur War, picking off Israeli tanks almost at will. There was nothing like it in Israel's arsenal and no serious defense against it. The response was Raytheon's BGM-71 antitank guided missile called TOW, which stands for tube-launched, optically tracked, wire data link.

To this day the TOW is the most widely used antitank guided missile in the world, at a cost of about $180,000 per unit. It quickly became Israel's primary antitank weapon system, and infantry brigades formed TOW platoons called *Orev*, which nicknamed these units "Tank Hunters."

In 1982, Israel made devastating use of the TOW on Syrian forces in Lebanon. In one famous battle on the eastern slopes of Mount Baruch, a jeep-mounted Israeli TOW antitank unit destroyed ten Syrian T-72 tanks in a matter of moments with no Israeli casualties. Again, every missile fired needed to be replenished through Milchan Bros.

Another missile Milchan introduced to the IDF was the M-47 Dragon by Raytheon. The M-47 was a surface-attack, wire-guided, man-portable, shoulder-fired, medium antitank weapon system. It could defeat armored vehicles, fortified bunkers, concrete gun emplacements, and other reinforced targets. Every Israeli infantry battalion formed a Dragon Squad. Each missile cost approximately $13,000, but the units with night tracking systems cost $51,000. As usual, every missile fired during training or in combat was replaced by Milchan Bros.

Almost every imaginable system in the IDF, on the ground, on the sea, and in the air, was upgraded through Milchan's companies with new technologies. Throughout the process, the IDF evolved into one of the most modern fighting forces on the planet. The latest night vision equipment, the latest smart bombs and guided missiles, the latest radars and avionics systems, many of which are highly classified to this day, flowed like a river into Israel through Milchan's companies.

Commissions generated from the post-1973 modernization and resupply greatly boosted Israel's secret accounts fronted by Milchan and, with this increased revenue, Israel's global intelligence capabilities.

With the expansion of his defense deals, Milchan understood that for his company to continue on the path of success and influence, and as a matter of good business practice, he needed to hire a retired IDF general. The person he found was forty-six-year-old General Shlomo "Chich" Lahat. As it turned out, his choice was a little more popular than expected.

Only months after joining the company, Milchan invited Lahat to join him for a European League professional basketball game in Tel Aviv. When they entered the arena on their way to the VIP section, Lahat received a standing ovation from the crowd. Israelis love their war heroes.

It was at that moment that Milchan turned to General Lahat and suggested, somewhat in jest, that he should run for mayor. The idea stuck, and within months, Lahat threw his hat in the ring after Milchan promised him that his job was safe should he lose the election. Milchan also agreed to design his campaign strategy and back it financially. In February 1974, Lahat not only won the election but remained the city's popular mayor for almost twenty years. Milchan's second foray into politics had paid off.

* * *

Israel's unconventional weapons program moved forward with added urgency. There was little left to hide. In August 1974, about the same time that President Nixon was forced to resign and Vice President Gerald Ford assumed command, CIA chief William Colby issued a report confirming that Israel not only possessed nuclear weapons, but was an active proliferator of nuclear technology to its friends and allies, such as Iran and South Africa. The Colby memo, titled "Special Intelligence Assessment: The Risk of Nuclear Proliferation," was top secret:

> Israel is actively assisting a number of countries to develop nuclear weapons technology, and in one case is doing so in exchange for the acquisition of uranium for its own nuclear program. All over Israel are scattered numerous manufacturing facilities designated almost exclusively to the development of a missile capable of delivering nuclear warheads. Original missile designs that were acquired in France have been improved upon in Israel. Our assessment includes knowledge of Israeli acquisitions of large quantities of uranium, its ongoing program to enrich uranium, and its program to develop nuclear weapons delivery systems. We do not expect Israel to use nuclear weapons unless its existence is deemed in jeopardy. Without question, Israel will continue to develop and improve on these capabilities with longer range ballistic missiles, aircraft delivery, and a wider assortment of nuclear capabilities.

When Richard Kelly Smyth received his first list of items from Milchan, he quickly understood what the Israelis were focused on at the time. They wanted solid-fuel rocket components, and they wanted instruction manuals for manufacturing and anything else they could get their hands on.

The advantage of a solid-fuel rocket is that it can be fueled a long time in advance. It can be taken out of hiding and launched almost immediately, before being detected and before countermeasures can be taken.

Liquid-fuel rockets, on the other hand, require a slow fueling process on the launch pad immediately preceding launch, a time-consuming process that could potentially expose the launch prematurely and invite countermeasures.

Finally, solid-fuels themselves tend to be safer and easier to work with than those in a liquid form.

Israel's Jericho nuclear-tipped missiles were solid-fuel rockets that could be launched immediately if need be, and were constantly being upgraded and improved. Milchan, Smyth, and Milco were drafted to supply the billion-dollar Jericho II project and played the key role in obtaining its crucial components.

One of the most mysterious periods of the Milchan-Smyth relationship occurred shortly after Smyth left Rockwell, ostensibly to focus on Milco full-time. Instead, Smyth suddenly took a job for a short period of time, between February and June 1974, with the Martin Marietta Corporation on the other side of the country in Orlando, Florida, leaving his family behind in California.

Martin Marietta is the designer and manufacturer of the Pershing nuclear missile system, the first and only solid-propellant nuclear MRBM (medium-range ballistic missile) deployed by the US Army. Israel had sought to purchase the Pershing missile off the shelf from the United States as part of the Yom Kippur War ceasefire agreement, but the United States did not agree to the sale.

A few years later, on September 24, 1975, Soviet minister of foreign affairs Andrei Gromyko confronted Israeli minister of foreign affairs Yigal Allon at a chance meeting at the United Nations, asking him why Israel felt that it needed medium-range missiles. Allon was too diplomatic to give Gromyko the straight answer, which likely would have been "so that we can target Moscow for deterrence purposes."

The Pershing remained in US service for almost thirty years and was upgraded a number of times. In 1974 when Smyth rushed to take the job at Martin Marietta, the company was in the process of developing the Pershing II, a vast improvement in both range and accuracy over the Pershing I. Coincidentally or not, shortly following Smyth's mysterious short stint at Martin Marietta, Israel suddenly began to make great strides in the development of its Jericho II program using technology that was remarkably similar to the Pershing II.

What was also remarkable was that upon returning to California from his short employment with Martin Marietta, Smyth suddenly had the funds to move Milco's operations out of his house to new offices in

Huntington Beach, California, widely known as Surf City, USA. Clearly, Smyth's time at Martin Marietta in Orlando was very productive for him, for Milco, and for Israel. Smyth had passed his baptism by fire.

* * *

Milchan heard the word *krytron* for the first time during his briefing at the Dimona nuclear reactor. The krytron is a small, inexpensive, innocent-looking cold-cathode gas-filled tube intended for use as a very high-speed switch. In the real world, krytrons can be used to trigger large flash lamps in photocopiers, lasers, airport landing lights, and scientific apparatus in a number of fields including medical equipment. The fact that this little device is the most efficient trigger for a nuclear bomb was a tightly kept secret. Only one company in the US manufactured the device, EG&G in Massachusetts, a corporation involved with some of the US government's most sensitive technologies. The sale and distribution of krytrons was carefully monitored, particularly when it came to the export market.

In the summer of 1975, Israel, through Milchan's assistant Dvora Ben Yitzhak, sent a request to Smyth to purchase four hundred krytrons. In the purchase order, as usual, Dvora listed the name of the item, the intended use of the item – "remotely located instrument detectors" – and the name of the end-user, Rehovot Instruments Ltd.

Smyth located the manufacturer, got a quote of $75 per krytron, and verified the necessary licensing requirements, which in this case was a munitions export license from the US State Department. He had secured such licenses many times in the past. On October 30, 1975, he submitted to the US State Department a standard munitions export application for the krytrons. A few days later, the US embassy in Tel Aviv submitted a warning to the Israeli Ministry of Defense regarding the attempt to purchase krytrons. Smyth claims that he was unaware of the rejection or the warning to Israel on the matter, until he received a phone call from Dvora canceling the order. Smyth didn't think much of it and continued with business as usual.

Yet the krytrons continued to be a critical component for Israel's nuclear weapons program and somewhat risky attempts to obtain them would have to be made down the road. Behind the scenes, diplomatic inquiries were made at the State Department and the Department of Commerce, and the Israelis made the case that they needed the krytrons for a long list of civilian purposes. Once they felt they'd made headway on the matter in Washington, they signaled to Blumberg that he should try again. In March 1976, Blumberg again added krytrons to the shopping list.

Smyth submitted a munitions license application to the State Department again, and again he was rejected. The order was canceled. This time, however, the CIA took note of the activities of Richard Kelly Smyth.

Israel decided to drop the krytron matter for an extended period. Smyth had successfully executed many sensitive orders and there was no point in exposing the operative to further risk, at least not for now. For Smyth, his relationship with Milchan was everything. Well over eighty percent of all of Milco's business for Israel was done through Milchan Bros. satellite companies like Heli Trading Ltd. Although on paper Milco was a modest, struggling company, Smyth had learned some of the tricks of the trade, namely that it didn't necessarily pay to show a profit but was far better to show lots of expenses.

He maintained two waterfront properties in Huntington Beach and an apartment on Catalina Island. He joined the local yacht club, and by 1977 he'd reached the membership rank of commodore. He also purchased a 150-acre ranch in Oklahoma from his father. Life was good.

Eventually, his wife Emilie left her teaching position and joined Milco as the office manager, whose primary responsibility was to interact with Milchan's assistant Dvora Ben Yitzhak. The two developed a warm friendship over time. Smyth made occasional trips to Israel for briefings and consultations and he'd occasionally bring Emilie or one of his children with him to enjoy the fun and the sun, while he huddled with Milchan and eventually with Blumberg as well.

As Dvora later testified, "Dr. Smyth, his wife, and his children became good friends of my husband and me. We met many times in Israel and in Los Angeles when we came over for the wedding of his daughter. From many years of close acquaintance, I feel that I know Dr. Smyth well."[3]

---

3.   Schiller, *Irrational Indictment and Imprisonment*, 219.

Over the years, Smyth also employed three of his children at Milco, in accounting and IT for the office computers. One of his sons became an Olympic medalist in sailing, and a daughter, after attending university in Madrid, Spain, became an anchorwoman for Univision, the United States' largest Spanish-speaking television channel, owned by Milchan's friend Haim Saban.

Smyth's operations were mostly successful, but his efforts to obtain consulting contracts with NATO, NASA, and the Pentagon proved frustrating and not very fruitful. He was only able to obtain a few small contracts worth not more than $25,000 each. It's entirely possible that Smyth was quietly blacklisted because of the krytron incident in 1975, even though his security clearance remained unchanged.

In his efforts to expand the reach of the company, Smyth began to offer Israeli-made defense items to the US government and private companies. For that purpose he printed up fancy brochures promoting a long list of Israeli defense-related products that could be exported from Israel to the United States without any burdensome licensing process. These attempts were no substitute for Milchan's regular flow of sensitive orders from the United States. In any event, no known Israeli export deals were closed through Milco.

Milchan's orders for sensitive materials continued to pour in, and slowly, over time, Milco became known as a key purchasing agent for Israel's military needs in most quarters that needed to know – at the State Department, the CIA, the Pentagon, and the Department of Commerce. This was not entirely unanticipated by Milchan. After all, the idea was to operate in plain sight, quietly pushing the envelope, mostly in concert with the United States. He was not, however, happy with the higher profile that the company had assumed, and he was growing more uneasy with the company's name, which pointed directly at him. After all, his idea of a good profile was no profile at all.

Neither Milchan nor Smyth could possibly imagine how significant the order for the tiny, inexpensive little krytron would become in their lives.

* * *

As Arnon immersed himself in an ever-growing web of businesses and extracurricular activities, his relationship with his wife reached the end of the road. The move to France didn't make the difference they had hoped it would, and the original love was never rekindled. They made the decision to divorce.

Within months, a new Swedish woman, Ulrika, had entered his life. During their first night together, Arnon was surprised to learn that she was from the same town as Ulla and had lived right down the street from her in Gothenburg. They didn't know each other, but Arnon could not help but wonder.

He purchased a comfortable apartment for Brigitte and the children in the center of Paris, walking distance from the Eiffel Tower, and a place for himself nearby. He then spent much of his time in Paris to be close to the kids, and conducted all business from there while frequently traveling back and forth to Israel, the United States, Iran, and other business destinations.

One of those destinations was Las Vegas, where he had become a high roller, so much so that Caesars Palace would on occasion fly him and his entourage in a private jet for weekends of high-stakes gambling and fun. On one occasion, he gave his leftover poker chips, amounting to $30,000, to an unknown, small Israeli developer, Meir Teper,[4] whom he had met only hours before. "I bugged him next to the poker table until he agreed to invest in a scheme of mine. I think he gave me the money just to get me off his back," Teper told us.

Teper invested the money in a clothing store, Ted Lapidus, in Caesars Palace. He then surprised Milchan six months later with a $60,000 check for his share in their partnership, which Milchan had forgotten about. It was an act that cemented a close friendship that has lasted to this day.

---

4. Meir Teper would later produce the movies *Mistress*, *Crazy in Alabama*, and *What's Eating Gilbert Grape*. He and Robert De Niro co-own Nobu, an international Japanese restaurant chain.

10 ‖ The Devil's Advocate

*I will fight the rest of my life against racism
and apartheid.*

Arnon Milchan, *Los Angeles Times*, February 28, 1992

In June 1975, Arnon Milchan was invited by his friend Shimon Peres, then minister of defense in Prime Minister Yitzhak Rabin's government, to one of the strangest meetings in his life. He was asked to participate in a tempting scheme, ostensibly to help his country. If he played along, an entire new world of potential profits would present itself.

Following the Yom Kippur War, twenty-five African states severed diplomatic relations with Israel. Until then, the country had maintained good relations across the continent of Africa, providing training and aid to many up-and-coming nations and getting raw materials in return. The Israeli advisers, who fanned out across Africa, didn't carry with them the baggage of past colonialism like those from France or Britain, and the Africans were truly impressed with the egalitarianism shown by the Israelis, who had no problem getting their hands dirty along with the Africans.

Jerusalem consciously kept relations with South Africa quiet to avoid offending friendly black-majority African states and there was genuine opposition within Israel to the philosophy of apartheid. The two countries didn't even maintain full diplomatic relations at the ambassadorial level. But none of that was enough for African countries to overcome Arab pressure, with its accompanying petrodollars, to sever relations with the Jewish state following the Yom Kippur War. Israel's isolation in Africa was virtually complete by the end of 1973.

For South Africa the situation was just as bleak. Anti-apartheid sentiment was on the rise around the world and widespread violence had broken out at home. By November 30, 1973, the United Nations had declared apartheid to be a crime against humanity; economic boycotts and arms embargos would ensue. Even South African athletes were to be prohibited from international competition. The process of South Africa's international isolation had reached unprecedented levels and was about to get worse.

Contrary to the general African abandonment of Israel at the first real test of their relationship, South Africa came to Israel's aid in its desperate hour in 1973, even though the two countries did not maintain full diplomatic relations. Minister of Defense P.W. Botha (who would later become president) looked for any way possible to provide moral and even material support. Over fifteen hundred South Africans (mostly Jews) rushed as volunteers to fight for Israel, and the Pretoria government permitted over $30 million in aid to be sent to Israel.

Following the war, as the harsh reality of international isolation had set in for both countries, as a matter of self-preservation it was inevitable that they would drift together.

In June 1975, Oscar Hurwitz, a prominent Jewish South African businessman and architect, and a secret collaborator with South Africa's intelligence community, facilitated a meeting whose primary objective was to cultivate a new relationship with the State of Israel.

The South African delegation arrived under a heavy fog of secrecy. At the head of the delegation stood minister of the interior Dr. Connie Mulder, who was a rising star in South African politics and considered heir-apparent to Prime Minister John Vorster. He was accompanied by General Hendrik van den Bergh, head of the South African Bureau of State Security (BOSS), and maverick secretary of information Eschel Rhoodie. The mission circumvented South Africa's Ministry of Foreign Affairs, which they all viewed as lazy, bureaucratic, and ineffective.

Their mission was to lay the groundwork for a previously unthinkable meeting between their prime minster, John Vorster, and Israeli prime minister Yitzhak Rabin.

They candidly discussed South Africa's difficult predicament and revealed a top-secret five-year plan, approved by Prime Minister Vorster, to attempt to influence world opinion in favor of the South African apartheid regime, and asked for Israeli participation in a consultative role.

Specifically, they asked Rabin and Peres to appoint an individual to join a secret group known as the Club of Ten. This group consisted of ten key individuals from ten different countries, who would do everything possible to undermine embargos and boycotts, and enhance the image of South Africa by purchasing or influencing media outlets.

These men were carefully chosen for their cupidity, connections, drive, competence, and proven ability to get things done. They would operate in secret collaboration directly with Eschel Rhoodie's Department of Information. Rhoodie had already established a front company called Thor Communicators to coordinate and fund their activities. This included planning and overseeing Operation David,[1] which included everything from South African cultural and sports exchanges with Israel to secret defense deals and nuclear collaboration.

The entire project was designed as a fully funded psychological war in which no government oversight or regulations of any kind would be applied. "You should keep your paperwork to an absolute minimum and anything not necessary should be destroyed. In fact, where you can do without documentation, you should do so,"[2] Prime Minister Vorster told Eschel Rhoodie, whom he assigned to oversee the entire operation. The secret enterprise would be funded to the tune of hundreds of millions of US dollars.[3]

---

1. Operation David was a coordinated plan put together by Eschel Rhoodie to strengthen South African-Israeli relations, and soften South Africa's Jewish community's opposition to the apartheid regime. From Eschel Rhoodie's *The Real Information Scandal* (Pretoria: Orbis, 1983).

2. Rhoodie, *The Real Information Scandal*, 83.

3. The exact number has never been conclusively established because of an intentional avoidance of accounting records.

As with the Israelis, the ambitious covert project would be funded off the books, without parliamentary approval. The funds would come from South Africa's vast gold reserves in London, and a large shipment of gold bars was transferred under heavy security from London to a Zurich bank vault. Unlike Britain, Switzerland's banking secrecy laws at the time were far more suitable to serve South Africa's covert goals.

In exchange for assistance from Israel in military technology and covertly run public relations, South Africa would be willing to open up an entire world of possibilities in defense contracts and access to its vast natural resources, especially uranium. Somebody in Israel would need to be the designated point man, joining the Club of Ten. That somebody would receive contracts and other potentially lucrative transactions in the pipeline.

Following the meeting, Prime Minister Rabin and Shimon Peres considered the matter carefully, weighing the risks and potential rewards. As relations with most African countries were now shattered, the need to maintain appearances vis-à-vis South Africa had all but disappeared, and US secretary of state Henry Kissinger had asked that Israel act as the US proxy in support of South Africa's battle against Communist forces in Angola.[4]

Having just experienced the trauma of the Yom Kippur War and the very brink of destruction, the prevailing winds in Israel were that survival should take precedence over any other consideration. South Africa represented a large and wealthy market for potential Israeli arms sales to keep the crucial and growing domestic defense industry humming, and most important, the prospect of a steady supply of uranium and nuclear testing locations was deeply seductive.

The facts that apartheid was an unpopular and unappealing philosophy, that South Africa's prime minister, John Vorster, had been imprisoned as a Nazi sympathizer in his youth,[5] and that a voluntary UN arms embargo against South Africa had been in place since August 7, 1963, were all troubling, but didn't outweigh the potential benefits of a secret strategic alliance.

---

4. Benjamin Beit-Hallahmi, *The Israeli Connection: Who Israel Arms and Why* (New York: Pantheon Books, 1984), 166.
5. He claimed that he was not pro-Nazi, only anti-British.

Every choice is between two imperfect alternatives, Peres reasoned with Rabin. The movement of black South Africa was with Arafat and with the Soviet Union, and against Israel. "But we shall never stop denouncing apartheid. We will never agree to that," Peres said.

Rabin and Peres decided to sign on to Mulder and Rhoodie's scheme and they already knew who their operative would be: a dynamic individual who knew how to keep a secret, operate behind the scenes, and was not afraid of danger or averse to getting his hands dirty. That man was Milchan, and Peres moved immediately to arrange the meeting.

When Milchan arrived he was greeted warmly by Peres, who introduced him to Mulder, General van den Burgh, and Rhoodie. David Kimche, a Mossad superagent who specialized in African affairs, was also present, and no introductions were necessary. They all exchanged pleasantries and sat for a quiet talk.[6]

Peres started things off by informing his guests that Milchan was an independent businessman, trusted by the Israeli government, who owned a fertilizer and agrochemical company. He explained that he had completed a number of important joint US-Israeli projects in Iran, and was handling a sizable portion of Israel's defense procurements – a real go-getter.

Mulder and Rhoodie were surprised to see that Milchan was just thirty years old. Rhoodie began to pepper Milchan with questions about his views on South Africa and the world in general. Milchan quickly disarmed the three South Africans with his trademark charm, wit, surprising worldly knowledge, and youthful enthusiasm. Like most people who met him, they all took an instinctive and immediate liking to him.

The feeling was mutual. Although Eschel Rhoodie was in his forties, they quickly discovered that they shared a similar temperament. They were both athletic with a passion for tennis, and indeed would meet on the tennis court for years to come. They both appreciated the good life, fine wine, fine foods, women, and gaming. Both had a vivid imagination and a flair for pushing the limits of whatever they were involved in.

6. By the late 1970s, David Kimche, born in the UK, would rise to become second in command of the Mossad. He was implicated in the Iran-Contra affair, along with Nimrodi and Schwimmer.

Rhoodie invited Milchan to South Africa to formalize the relationship, and thus began Milchan's great South African adventure. Most is shrouded in secrecy, but enough is known about these activities to conclude with confidence that they were deep, extensive, covert, highly profitable, and, in hindsight, highly controversial.

Milchan was never ideologically attracted to apartheid. "If only I knew! I was young, uninformed, and naïve, and I thought it would be fun," he told us in a pained voice. His involvement was initiated by his own government in the larger interests of his country, as a matter of patriotism, and his activities can be divided into three primary categories: defense procurement, the propaganda war, and nuclear collaboration.

When Milchan arrived in South Africa for the first time, to his surprise he was greeted like a head of state. "Eschel Rhoodie put on quite a show, and you couldn't help but be impressed," said Milchan. Happy Africans were dancing to traditional drumbeats, and little children presented him with traditional gifts; it was all picture-perfect, and in great contrast to the realities of apartheid.

After the formalities, Milchan was whisked away to a luxury hotel in Johannesburg. During dinner, Rhoodie extended to him an item to study. It was Milchan's crisp new South African passport, Rhoodie's way of telling him that he was one of them now. Just like that.

Over dinner, Rhoodie filled him in on the game plan. Their mission was to identify important opinion shapers in Western media and entertainment, such as journalists, cultural icons, and politicians, and target them for subtle recruitment to the South African cause through gentle persuasion, through bribery, or even by buying controlling interests in entire media outlets if necessary.

The need for secrecy was obvious. The objective was not to promote apartheid directly, which they understood was a losing proposition, but rather to stress the strategic value of South Africa in general to the free Western world – a country rich in minerals and threatened by the spread of Communist totalitarianism from within, and by its surrounding neighbors who were directly supported by the Soviet Union during the height of the Cold War.[7]

The following morning, Rhoodie and Milchan flew south toward Port Elizabeth. As the plane reached the waterline of the Indian Ocean it banked west and flew along the beautiful Garden Route, on the southern edge of the continent. They landed near the picturesque little town of Plettenberg Bay, with its golden white beaches. This was the South Africa that Rhoodie wanted Arnon to see – isolated, idyllic, peaceful, and safe.

Rhoodie informed Arnon that he had arranged for a permanent luxury apartment for him in Plettenberg Bay, and that he should consider it his home in South Africa. As they lounged around in the new apartment, they delved deeper into the plan.

In essence he would play the same financial role for South Africa that he played for Israel. He would open secret bank accounts and spread the money around as directed by Eschel Rhoodie, with no South African fingerprints on it. They came to an understanding and the play moved forward.

Things kicked into high gear quickly after Prime Minister Vorster's official visit to Israel in 1976. At the core of his discussions with Rabin and Peres was the trade of Israeli weaponry and nuclear technologies in exchange for South African capital and raw materials. The sale of mortars, electronic surveillance equipment, anti-guerrilla alarm systems, night-vision equipment, radars,[8] patrol boats,[9] Bell helicopters,[10] and armored vehicles and Howitzer artillery pieces[11] were agreed to immediately. Israel would also supply South Africa blueprints for its Kfir fighter jet, which were themselves based on stolen blueprints of the Dassault-manufactured Super

7. The African National Congress (ANC) maintained a historic alliance with the South African Communist Party (SACP), and was perceived as a Communist threat allied with the Soviet bloc at the time.

8. James Adams, *The Unnatural Alliance* (London: Quartet Books, 1984), 86.

9. Jonathan Broder, "Israel Grows Sensitive over Links to South Africa," *Chicago Tribune*, April 2, 1977.

10. William E. Farrell, "Israeli Tours South Africa as Arms-trade Furor Grows," *New York Times*, February 10, 1978.

11. Michael Hornsby, "Pretoria Shows Off Its Military Might," *Times* (London), September 14, 1984.

Mirage. The result was the South African Cheetah fighter jet.[12] Somebody had to supply the missiles for the Cheetah platform, and Raytheon, through Milchan, stepped up to the plate with the latest systems.

November 4, 1977, brought more news. The UN Security Council adopted Resolution 418, imposing a mandatory arms embargo on South Africa. Until then, the arms embargo had been voluntary; now the UN acted with uncharacteristic firmness, which meant that the United States and European countries would have to abide, or at least pretend to abide.

That put Israel and Milchan in the ideal position to act as the covert middleman. Of course, on the surface Israel would officially abide by Resolution 418, but secretly, primarily through the services of companies established by Milchan, it would act as South Africa's primary defense systems supplier, funneling millions upon millions of dollars for purchases from third parties and through direct sales of its own military industries. The timing of the embargo could not have been better for Israel and Milchan. He was already deeply involved in the rapidly emerging Israeli-South African alliance as its representative in the Club of Ten, and just as he'd enjoyed being part of the elite inner circle in Israel for years, he'd now operate similarly in South Africa, an even larger environment. Like a night flower, Milchan flourished in the dark.

Western countries knowingly used third-country middlemen from around the world to trade with the lucrative South African market while publicly maintaining a posture of vocal opposition to apartheid. Virtually every diamond purchased in the Western world was mined in South Africa and helped to comfortably finance the South African military machine. Oil from Arab countries flowed freely without regard to any embargo.

Israel feared the political and mostly symbolic implications of the embargo and found it advantageous to secretly undermine it. If the West could be pushed into endorsing an embargo against South Africa, no matter how ineffective, it might also be pushed into one against Israel. Therefore Israel would not adhere to it as a matter of policy, although publicly it would pay it full lip service.

---

12. Beit-Hallahmi, *The Israeli Connection*, 124.

Every imaginable weapons system needed by South Africa that could not be purchased directly from Israel was purchased on the international market, and instead of ending up in Israel as indicated on the end-user documentation, it was diverted to South Africa. Milchan's company quickly became the largest defense procurer for the South African government.

But as important and lucrative as defense systems were, uranium was Israel's primary obsession in their relations with South Africa. The initial feedstock for the Dimona reactor had come from France and later from a series of covert LAKAM operations. Blumberg facilitated the purchase of the first fifty-ton shipment of uranium oxide from South Africa, but they were looking for something even more serious than that: a nuclear testing ground. Israel was confident in the reliability of its first generation of nuclear weapons, which were French tested. But following the Yom Kippur War, Israel had developed the neutron bomb involving much more sophisticated technology, which would require at least one test.

In exchange for the transfer of sensitive nuclear technology, South Africa would finally agree to allow Israel access to the wide-open space of the Kalahari Desert and the South Atlantic for the purpose of a nuclear test.[13] The nuclear transfer came in the form of tritium. General van den Bergh was eager to procure thirty grams of tritium from Israel, enough for twelve atomic bombs. Tritium was used to increase the power of nuclear weapons by creating fusion for thermonuclear bombs.

In an operation codenamed Teeblare ("Tea Leaves" in Afrikaans), Israel delivered twelve shipments of tritium manufactured in Dimona to South Africa in tiny capsules, which contained 2.5 grams each. Benjamin Blumberg, Eschel Rhoodie, Milchan, and others served as escorts on the special C-130 Hercules flights carrying the capsules. These deals secured both the testing site and, over time, an additional five hundred tons of uranium for Israel.

By August 1977 Israel was ready for an underground test at the new Kalahari Desert test site, but a few days earlier, on July 30, a Soviet recon-

13. Thomas Reed and Danny Stillman, *The Nuclear Express: A Political History of the Bomb and Its Proliferation* (Minneapolis, MN: Zenith Press, 2009), 174.

naissance satellite noticed the test preparations for what they assumed was a South African bomb. The Soviets forwarded their concern to Washington. Seven days later, a US satellite confirmed the Soviet finding. Immediate protests were issued to South Africa by the US, British, French, and West German governments, and the test was abruptly scrapped at the last minute. It was a setback, but one that was not impossible to overcome.

September 22, 1979, was just another evening. There was, however, a terrible storm circulating in the extremely remote southwest region of the Indian Ocean, nothing unusual for that time of year. Thousands of miles away, the world's largest radio telescope at Arecibo in Puerto Rico suddenly detected an anomaly, an electromagnetic ripple on the lower surface of the ionosphere emanating from the South Atlantic and Indian Ocean region.

At the same time, an American Vela satellite detected a distinctive double flash. A few commercial fishermen in the area reported a large flash in the distance coming from the direction of Prince Edward Island, located about fifteen hundred miles southeast of Plettenberg Bay. Infrared sensor data indicated what looked like a nuclear explosion, probably an enhanced-radiation neutron bomb. The device was likely exploded on a barge located near a ship-borne command post. It was probably detonated inside a steel container like a commercial vault.[14]

The minds behind the operation had cleverly waited for the onset of a major storm before proceeding with the detonation. This would quickly wash radioactive evidence into the sea. By the time snooping US planes arrived on the scene to conduct atmospheric tests, the storm had already cleansed the evidence and it would take days before a properly equipped ship would arrive on the scene with little if anything to find.

The sea was rough and the command ship maintained radio silence. It was packed with sophisticated electronics and sensors and was pitching violently. On board were numerous Israeli and South African scientists and technicians, and the key facilitators of the secret nuclear relationship. They witnessed the flash with a little trepidation, but mostly with a sense of excitement.

---

14. Ibid., 177.

It was a substantial coup and one of the most secret operations ever conducted by Israel and LAKAM, the details of which only began to emerge publicly years later, after the fall of the apartheid government of South Africa in 1995. Israel got its test. It was a small two- to three-kiloton neutron bomb, which demonstrated a high level of sophistication.[15]

United States security experts desperately scrambled to decipher the data, an effort that started immediately and lasted for months to come. Arguments over the interpretation of the data continued for years; most scientists and nuclear experts concluded with certainty that it was a nuclear explosion. President Carter was in a difficult bind. By US law, if the United States publicly confirmed that Israel was linked to a nuclear test, the president and Congress would be forced by the US Foreign Assistance Act of 1961[16] to prohibit US military and economic assistance to Israel.

The law clearly states that countries acquiring or transferring nuclear weapons, material, or technology outside of international nonproliferation regimes (such as the Nuclear Non-Proliferation Treaty, which Israel did not sign) would be prohibited from receiving any military or economic aid from the United States. That is the reason the United States has never publicly acknowledged Israel's nuclear arsenal, and that is the reason that the 1979 test has remained shrouded in mystery.

* * *

If there was one key financial facilitator in South Africa's covert global propaganda campaign to improve the image of South Africa, it was Milchan.[17] "I acted at the request of my own country," Milchan told us. Eschel Rhoodie directed a steady flow of funds from the Department of

---

15. The mere size of a nuclear explosion is not necessarily representative of the level of scientific sophistication it embodies. The ability to construct small nuclear devices yielding smaller explosive power with greater radioactivity is an indication of highly sophisticated capabilities.

16. As amended by the Symington Amendment of 1976 and the Glenn Amendment of 1977.

17. Beit-Hallahmi, *The Israeli Connection*, 155, and L. Rapoport, "Out of the Shadows," *Jerusalem Post*, March 8, 1986.

Information's front company Thor Communicators, through European accounts controlled by Milchan, who created multiple front companies to purchase key media outlets critical of South Africa.

He and South African operatives David Abramson and Stuart Pegg focused at first on African media such as *West Africa*, an important magazine published by Afrimedia International Ltd. He purchased administrative control over *African Development*, a quarterly magazine. He was involved in the purchase of *EurAfrique*, a monthly magazine read in all of the French-speaking African states. He then spearheaded an effort to gain control of the British publishing giant Morgan-Grampian, which was to be the crown jewel of the operation.

Through Morgan-Grampian, the plan was to take control over several prominent newspapers and magazines in the West, including the *Observer* in England, *L'Expresse* in France, and the *Washington Star* in the United States. "What better vehicle than Morgan-Grampian to be in charge of such takeovers?" Eschel Rhoodie wrote in his 1983 book *The Real Information Scandal*.

In November 1977, Rhoodie released $1.8 million for the purchase of enough shares to assume control of the *Investors Chronicle* in the UK, a deal that failed to materialize. Essentially, Rhoodie and Milchan, acting as partners, coordinated all of these activities using the secret funds. It would explode in their faces.

11 ‖ Mud

I can't be a painter or a writer, so I decided to
become a film producer.

Arnon Milchan

Milchan is an individualist, a lone hunter in many ways, but he has a weakness for grandiose displays of coordinated human activity, be it in war or in entertainment. He wants to be a part of it, but at a slight distance, on his own terms.

As always, he needed a new toy to keep him interested in the game. He realized that he was now financially secure enough to take a few risks outside his comfort zone and began to actualize a lifelong fantasy of getting involved in entertainment and movie making. He had always loved cinema and idolized the actors he saw on the screen. He admired the screenwriters who created and structured the stories, and the directors who somehow managed to coordinate and orchestrate the entire project. He was fascinated by the creative and logistical forces that converge to produce a successful motion picture, and he was also fascinated by the business of movies.

Initially, he began to drop by movie sets to observe the process. His daughter Elinor recalls how her father would sit with his children and watch movies endlessly during his visits: "All of our family is addicted to motion pictures; from the age of five I became obsessed with film through my father."[1]

---

1. Yehudit Haspel, "My Dad Is My Best Friend," *Globes* (Israel), August 8, 2007.

In 1976 Milchan made his first investment in the entertainment industry. The door was opened for him by producer Elliott Kastner, who quickly
identified the financing potential of the millionaire with youthful enthusiasm for the glamorous industry. Kastner was a Jewish-American talent
agent before becoming a producer. He moved his operations to Europe
in the 1960s, and though his film career failed to impress the critics, he
managed to produce a number of popular movies that did well at the box
office, including *Where Eagles Dare*, a World War II action drama starring
Richard Burton, who led a team of commandos deep into Germany.

Kastner systematically introduced Milchan to substantial players in
Hollywood. Milchan described how he met a genuine Hollywood star for
the first time:

> I was in a restaurant in Tel Aviv one night when a guy walks in and
> says his name is Elliott Kastner. Unreal! The guy who just produced
> *The Missouri Breaks*. I was just another fish, but he charmed the hell
> out of me. He was producing *A Little Night Music* with Elizabeth
> Taylor in Austria then. He said, "You know, I'm sure Elizabeth
> would love to meet you." I said, "Are you serious?" He said, "I'm
> going up there tomorrow, come along."[2]

Arnon immediately called his mother, Shoshanna: "You won't believe
what's happening to me – I'm going to meet Elizabeth Taylor!"[3]

By then, Elizabeth Taylor's superstardom was dimming; she'd gained
weight and was no longer doing cutting-edge material, but she was a
Hollywood legend in the truest sense and Arnon respected that greatly.
Following the highly anticipated dinner with Taylor, Arnon was sold. "I
got into it consciously, I wanted to be exploited; I volunteered to be the

---

2. Cited in Jack Mathews, *The Battle of Brazil: Terry Gilliam v. Universal Pictures in
    the Fight to the Final Cut* (New York: New York Theater and Cinema Books, 1987),
    31.
3. Ibid.

next sucker in the movie business. I told Elliott that I just want to be in the vicinity. Suddenly we are doing business together producing movies."[4]

A number of episodes illustrate Milchan's sudden enthusiasm for the film industry and how it mixed with his other endeavors. For example, British writer Anthony Samson became famous for his active opposition to South African apartheid and later was the official biographer of Nelson Mandela. Samson's opposition to apartheid and his role as an influential journalist and writer did not go unnoticed by Eschel Rhoodie, Connie Mulder, and the South African intelligence services.

Samson had just published a book titled *The Arms Bazaar: From Lebanon to Lockheed* that dealt with many of the spectacular arms deals of the mid 1970s, particularly focusing on South Africa. Of course, in hindsight Samson didn't know a fraction of it. Shortly after publication, Samson received a call at his London apartment from Elliott Kastner suggesting he wanted to make a movie based on his new book, and explaining that the financier of the project would be an Israeli by the name of Milchan, who was new to the movie business and was the most impressive person he had ever met. He assured Samson: "The man moves at the speed of light, he has no office and no secretary; his office is in his head. He courts danger and travels around the world with a suitcase full of cash in different currencies." Samson was suspicious but agreed to talk.

Shortly after his conversation with Kastner, Samson received a series of quick phone calls from Milchan, who asked to meet with him immediately. A few hours later, Samson opened his door to greet Milchan, who was dressed in a sweat suit and tennis shoes, carrying a black briefcase with a six-digit combination.

"He looked more like a movie star, handsome, upbeat, and charming," Samson later described. "He explained that he made his money from a fertilizer and chemical company that he had inherited from his father."

"I mostly want to create," Milchan said. "I can't be a painter or a writer, so I decided to become a film producer and I want to make a movie about the arms trade," a subject close to his heart. Samson had no idea that

---

4.   Bardach, "The Last Tycoon."

he was meeting with a primary mover on behalf of South Africa, a person who could easily have been the main subject of his new book.

The two talked for a while, first about a potential movie and then more generally. Milchan quickly understood that he was dealing with a highly knowledgeable person whose views on South Africa were persuasive. He never opened that briefcase, and the two agreed to continue discussions. No movie ever came of it, but seeds of doubt in Arnon's mind about his activities on behalf of South Africa had been sown.[5]

Yet his real awakening to the realities of apartheid occurred on subsequent, routine visits to South Africa, when he was no longer greeted upon his arrival at the airport with an elaborate ceremony or accompanied by government minders. It was during those trips, when he took the opportunity to rent a jeep and explore well beyond the isolated areas of white privilege, that his eyes were opened.

> I found myself face to face with the most extreme poverty that I had ever seen; I visited townships and little villages. The inequity that I witnessed was a life-changing experience. I was free to go wherever I wanted, and I realized that was not the case with the people I met along the way. It was a growing burden on my conscience. But there was one incident that broke the camel's back. One day I visited a local zoo. At the entrance, I noticed a sign that stated "No Blacks or Asians Allowed." It wasn't the first sign like that that I had seen, but it suddenly occurred to me that I am an "Asian" and I took it personally in a way that I previously had not. I knew that it was more of a racial statement than one of geography, but I simply could not bring myself to enter.
>
> I couldn't help but think of the racism that my own immediate family had escaped from, or all of those who stayed behind in Europe and were murdered because of this type of prejudice.[6]

---

5. Confirmed by Milchan during a personal interview with the authors, and also published by *African News Service*, May 24, 2001.

6. Personal interview with Milchan, November 2009.

That same night, he couldn't sleep.

In the morning, he packed his bags and headed for the airport. He had made a personal decision to never step foot in that country again until apartheid was abolished, and that he'd do everything in his power to undermine it.

* * *

During this period, Kastner and Milchan went on to collaborate on a movie called *Mud* (later changed to *The Stick-Up*, starring David Soul). Milchan says the film was so bad that he had his name removed from the credits, but he refused to get discouraged. Winston Churchill's observation that the sign of a successful person is the ability to move from one failure to the next without any loss of enthusiasm is classic Milchan.

For his next film project, he worked with a producer from New Zealand, Martin Campbell,[7] on the 1976 film *Black Joy*, a musical comedy adapted from a play about a young black man who arrives from the Caribbean to the tough, unforgiving neighborhood of Brixton in London, and goes from one comedic disaster to the next. "Life is for living" was the film's slogan; "leave us out of politics" was the subtext.

Many people were surprised when they learned that *Black Joy* would be prominently featured at the prestigious Cannes Film Festival and that director Anthony Simmons was nominated for the Golden Palm award.

Keeping up appearances, Milchan rendezvoused with a starstruck Eschel Rhoodie in Cannes that year, where Milchan introduced him to his friend Roman Polanski and others in the film industry. Also at the table were David Abramson and Stuart Pegg, the two South African financiers who served as collaborators for the South African Department of Information, and worked through Milchan's front companies to purchase targeted media outlets. They were unaware of Arnon's change of heart and that he was already beginning to undermine their efforts.

---

7.   Martian Campbell later directed a number of James Bond movies, including *Casino Royale* and *GoldenEye*.

But it wasn't only movies that Milchan began to dabble in. On December 28, 1976, he opened the Broadway musical *Ipi Tombi* ("Where Is the Girl?" in Zulu) at the Harkness Theater in New York City. *Ipi Tombi* was an original South African musical about a young African tribesman whose village is poor and suffers from drought. He journeys to the big city in hopes of finding wealth so he can save his people. Instead he finds greed, corruption, and con artists. Disillusioned, he returns home just in time to prevent his village from going to war.

A fish-out-of-water plot not dissimilar to *Black Joy*, the musical lasted for only thirty-nine shows through February 1977. That same year, Milchan and Kastner co-produced their second movie together, *The Medusa Touch*, with the legendary Richard Burton in the starring role.

The Medusa Touch is typically described as a seventies "devil conspiracy" movie, like the popular *The Exorcist* and *The Omen* series combined with disaster movies like *Earthquake* and *Airport*. Richard Burton plays an obsessed psychic who tries to convince a psychiatrist of his demonic power to kill people and to cause disasters just by the strength of his thoughts.

The movie was based on a novel by Peter Van Greenaway. The cover of the novel portrayed a large passenger airliner crashing into a skyscraper. Years later, the coincidence would trigger the imagination of 9/11 conspiracy theorists.

Milchan had invested a total of $400,000 in his first two movies, *Mud* and *Black Joy*. For *The Medusa Touch* he put up more than half of its $4 million budget.

Soon he received a call from Lord Lew Grade, a British tycoon who invited Milchan over for lunch to discuss *The Medusa Touch*. According to the *Los Angeles Times* entertainment reporter Jack Mathews, the meeting lasted for no longer than half an hour, with Lord Grade buying the film's foreign rights for $5 million. No matter how badly the film might do, Milchan was already ahead a million dollars. "It's like a game. It's Monopoly; two million, five million, one hundred million. In the business world I come from, a million dollars is a lot of money. With movies, you're lopping off or adding millions in the same sentence," Milchan said.[8] The film received generally good reviews in the UK but did not do well in the United States.

Following *The Medusa Touch*, Milchan felt that Kastner didn't share his vision for the kind of films he dreamed of making; he also felt that Kastner had a weak track record in the US market, where Milchan ultimately intended to plant his flag. Milchan had learned the basics from Kastner, and it was time to move on. The two parted ways.

* * *

Perhaps it was inevitable, but by 1978 Eschel Rhoodie and Connie Mulder's secret information war was in jeopardy. Prime Minister Vorster announced his retirement on September 20 and serious jockeying for his position had begun. Mulder threw his hat in the ring against Minister of Defense P.W. Botha, yet he couldn't get Vorster to support him.

But another Botha, no relation to P.W., would ultimately determine the outcome of the elections. The longtime minister of foreign affairs Pik Botha, a relentless self-promoter and schemer, had no love for Rhoodie and Mulder, whom he viewed as the Tweedledee and Tweedledum of South African politics. He'd been personally undermined for years by the two of them, as they kept him and his ministry out of the loop one time too many.

Removing Mulder as a credible candidate would help strengthen Pik Botha's position with P.W. Botha, who had a reputation for rewarding loyalty, and Pik Botha intended to help P.W. Botha win the prime minister's office, reaping his revenge against Mulder and his reward at the same time.

There was one good way to undermine Dr. Connie Mulder and make his candidacy instantly unviable: a gigantic financial scandal involving the disappearance of millions upon millions of rand during Mulder and Rhoodie's rogue information war.

Rhoodie assumed that Pik Botha was handed the lethal ammunition against him by a former close friend who had stabbed him in the back and who was also a close collaborator with the operation. His name was

8. Mathews, *The Battle of Brazil*, 31.

Retief van Rooyen and, according to Rhoodie, he was the deep throat who systematically, and behind his back, gave Pik Botha all the goods on the covert information war.

What Rhoodie didn't know was that Milchan, not Retief van Rooyen, was the ultimate source of the leaks. Milchan was in fact the deep throat of the great South African Information Scandal, which was the single biggest blow to the apartheid regime since it was instituted.[9]

Immediately public questions about the purchase of various international media outlets began to surface in the press: Where did the money come from? What exactly was it spent on? Who was accountable? Who actually now owned these media outlets? It was an immediate and unmitigated disaster for Mulder and Rhoodie. The entire operation was compromised, and because it was covert from the outset, little documentation had been generated, and they were left holding the bag. Nobody wanted to come forward and volunteer that they were aware and had approved of the entire operation, including Vorster.

Within weeks, the affair was labeled Muldergate and it exploded in the press, not only in South Africa but around the world. Rhoodie was humiliated and forced to resign. Mulder lasted a little longer, but left in disgrace as well. That is how Milchan brought the covert South African information war to an abrupt and embarrassing end.

One day at his Paris apartment during the height of the scandal, Milchan received a surprise visit from someone who presented himself in a heavy South African accent as a representative from Pretoria. The individual then informed Milchan that they were well aware of his leaks and that if he knew what was good for him and his children, he'd "better keep your big kaffir-lover mouth shut." Milchan claims that he didn't report the incident to the Mossad or LAKAM so that he could continue with his private agenda, undermining the entire enterprise.

Eschel Rhoodie read the tea leaves and fled the country, first to Ecuador, and finally to Cannes in the south of France, where he proceeded to write a book exposing much of the affair. While in France, Rhoodie received a visit from General van den Bergh, who advised him to avoid going over-

---

9. Personal interview with Milchan, November 2009.

board in his exposures, especially as it related to the sensitive aspects of the South African-Israeli connection. Rhoodie took his advice and eliminated references to the key secret collaborator from the entire book. But for some strange reason, he forgot to remove one name from the index: Arnon Milchan.

On July 19, 1979, at 10:15 a.m., Rhoodie rose and kissed his wife. He was going to take a short walk up to the corner to see if a friend had arrived. He took the keys to the apartment. He didn't even bother to say goodbye since he expected to be back in a matter of minutes. He even left his wallet behind.

He walked out of the apartment, went down the stairs, through the front door and into the strong sunshine. He had barely walked fifteen steps when a voice from behind asked, "Mr. Rhoodie?" He turned. Two other men closed in on him. They grabbed him by the arms and hustled him into a car parked in front of the building. All three wore plain clothes. The eldest of the three said in a heavy French accent: "You are under arrest." He was relieved because he had imagined much worse than that.

For the first time in his life Rhoodie felt handcuffs enclose his wrists. He was numb and shocked. He asked if he could inform his wife. They refused. He asked to leave the apartment keys with the janitor. They refused. He asked what it was all about. They didn't answer. He was taken to police headquarters in Nice to be fingerprinted; they locked him up in a dirty cell, without a bed, a chair, or running water – just a hole in one corner for a toilet.

After many hours, he was informed, still in handcuffs, that there was a warrant out for his arrest and that he was to be deported immediately to South Africa. He requested to contact his family to inform them but was told no. He requested an attorney but was told no. As it turned out, his French lawyer, informed of his disappearance, suspected that he was picked up for immediate extradition and filed an injunction on his own initiative. The police, who were on a mission to get him out of the country before that could happen, were stunned when a judge issued an emergency stay. A long and difficult extradition process would commence while Rhoodie remained in a filthy French prison cell.

In the end, Rhoodie was extradited to South Africa and stood trial for his involvement in the affair. He was convicted and sentenced to twelve years in prison, but the conviction was overturned by an appeals court that ruled that he was acting in his official capacity under the instructions of higher-ups who were fully aware of his activities. He left South Africa a bitter man, and began a new life in the United States, where he became an advertising agent in the Atlanta, Georgia, area. On July 17, 1993, while playing his beloved game of tennis, he collapsed on the court and died of a heart attack at age sixty.

The South African Information Scandal was a worldwide sensation that detailed a campaign involving dozens of projects to cow the opposition press at home and buy friendly coverage abroad. Rhoodie took the brunt of the blame in the scandal while the key financial figure, Arnon Milchan, dodged the bullet. It would not be the last time. Shortly before the fall of apartheid, South Africa transferred almost all of its nuclear material to Israel, including the tritium and its six existing bombs. The South African government then reported to international agencies that it had "dismantled" all of its nuclear weapons.

While ambivalent toward apartheid at first, Arnon gradually grew to oppose it in an active way. By 1991, three years before the dismantling of apartheid, Milchan produced the film *The Power of One*. Directed by John G. Avildsen, of *Rocky* and *The Karate Kid* fame, the film was adapted from a Bryce Courtenay novel about the coming of age of an anti-apartheid activist during the years of World War II in South Africa. Seven-year-old P.K. is a white South African raised on his family's farm by his Zulu nanny. When his mother takes ill, he's sent away to an Afrikaner boarding school, where he's picked on and nearly killed by the school bully. He later befriends a German musician, and a former black boxer (played by Morgan Freeman), who teaches P.K. how to use his fists to defend himself. By the time he's eighteen years old, P.K. is becoming the Great White Hope for the black Africans, boxing his way into their hearts and minds. He joins up with an old boxing foe, and takes up the anti-apartheid struggle.

The Power of One represents a remarkable transformation for Milchan, considering all that had occurred in the preceding years. "I will fight the rest of my life against racism and apartheid," he said.[10]

As far as Milchan, South Africa, and tennis are concerned, there's more to tell. In 1988, Israel played host to an international tennis tournament to which South African players were invited. South African athletes were boycotted internationally, so they jumped at any opportunity to play abroad. As part of the special relationship between the two countries, Israel agreed to facilitate such sporting competitions involving South Africa. It was at that tournament that a seventeen-year-old tennis star would make her international debut. Her name was Amanda Coetzer of Hoopstad, South Africa, and she would become the third highest ranked female tennis player in the world, defeating powerhouse players like Steffi Graf and Martina Hingis. Much later, she would also become Milchan's second wife, and the mother of his youngest child.

Among other places, the two maintain a house in the beautiful Plettenberg Bay, the place that Arnon fell in love with so many years ago. In August 2003, Arnon and Amanda attended Shimon Peres's eightieth birthday party at the Tel Aviv Hilton. Like most people seeking anonymity, they rode the service elevator. On the way down, another guest seeking anonymity joined them by chance. It was former South African president F.W. de Klerk, a Nobel Peace Prize laureate who oversaw the dismantling of the apartheid system. He recognized Amanda immediately, but was unsure of the man standing next to her. As Amanda recalls, when she introduced her companion as Arnon Milchan, de Klerk immediately recognized the name, raised an eyebrow, smiled, and said, "You did important things for South Africa."[11]

10. Dutka and Citron, "A Mogul's Bankroll – and Past."
11. Amanda Coetzer to the authors, November 2009.

12 ‖ Guilty by Suspicion

Let's assume that there's nothing that Israel and the United States do separately.

Arnon Milchan, *Los Angeles Magazine*, April 2000

The money was pouring in. Business in Iran continued to hum along. Milco and other operations continued on their mission to provide technology and material support for Israel's nuclear and ballistic missile programs. Milchan's moves on behalf of Israel in South Africa were bearing substantial fruit, defense imports and exports were booming with annual US congressional earmarks for military aid, and Milchan Bros. continued in its lucrative fertilizer and chemical distribution activity. Meanwhile Arnon was in a steamy relationship with the Swedish beauty Ulrika.

While in Israel, and away from his Paris base, Arnon spent much of his time in meetings at a new private club opened by his friend Rafi Shauli in April 1977, in north Tel Aviv. The new club was simply named The Club.

If Mandy's was the epicenter of Israel's bohemian society, The Club went well beyond that. Isolated and exclusive, its members were selected carefully from the social, economic, and cultural elite, with a rigid membership committee. It created a secretive atmosphere where members were expected to use their influence to take care of each other.

* * *

On Friday, December 10, 1976, three F-15 fighter jets landed at the Tel Nof Air Force Base outside of Rehovot, making Israel the first country other than the United States to possess the F-15. However, because of headwinds that the planes encountered on their long flight over, along with mid-air refueling, they landed late in the day, just as the Sabbath was about to begin.

As a result, a number of religious ministers were unable to return home from the welcoming ceremony in time, and were forced to violate the sanctity of the Sabbath. This was the last straw for some politicians, and religious Knesset members walked out of the governing coalition, causing the collapse of the first Rabin government and new elections to be called.

The surprise that rocked Israel following the elections to the Ninth Knesset on May 17, 1977, shook the country to its political foundation. The conservative Likud party, under the leadership of Menachem Begin, came to power for the first time, ousting the Labor Party, which had controlled all political power in the country in one form or another since its inception. Suddenly, Benjamin Blumberg's standing as head of LAKAM was on shaky ground. Milchan's operator and mentor was at serious risk of losing his position as the incoming administration sought to place its own people in key posts. The new minister of defense, Ezer Weizman (a nephew of Israel's first president Chaim Weizmann), was looking to dump Blumberg for a party loyalist.

Blumberg was not one to give up easily, and he went directly to Prime Minister Begin. He made the case that his membership on the Israeli Atomic Energy Commission, his responsibility for the reactor complex in Dimona, his leadership position within the nuclear weapons program, and his direct handling of Israel's network of informal secret agents around the world meant that he answered directly to the prime minister and not to the minister of defense.

Begin was no political hack, and unlike many of his ministers, he wasn't quick to purge talented people because of their political affiliations. Begin was convinced, and issued an order to cancel the replacement of Blumberg. Begin clearly understood that Israel's nuclear program, its de-

velopment of ballistic missiles, and its intelligence activities were not political toys to be tampered with.

Milchan quickly adapted to the new political leaders in town; Shimon
Peres was a real soul mate, but soon Arnon would develop close friendships with others, including incoming minister of defense Ezer Weizman.
His friendships and contacts were deep and spanned the entire political
spectrum, which placed him as a bridge between the intelligence establishment and the new government – a role that he has continued to play ever
since, with almost every Israeli government.

In the years to follow, Israel received 120 F-15s, and by 1980, following the fall of the shah in Iran, the F-16 took its place in the Israeli
Air Force arsenal. Originally these F-16s were meant for Iran but were
diverted to Israel after the downfall of the shah in 1979.

Indeed, two events around that time converged to motivate an increase
in US military aid to Israel: one was the Iranian Revolution, which put an
end to Milchan's interests in Iran, and the second was the Camp David
Accords signed on September 17, 1978. The shah's fall, although a strategic defeat for both Israel and the United States, had the silver lining of
solidifying Israel's status as the United States' only reliable ally in the entire region; and part of the Camp David Accords stipulated a substantial
increase in US military aid in exchange for Israel's agreement to withdraw
from the Sinai Peninsula.

For the first time, Milchan's activities would benefit from a peace agreement, although the primary vehicle for the profits remained sophisticated
defense systems. The IAF's new F-15s and F-16s were state-of-the-art platforms, but they'd need the latest missiles to reach their full potential. That
is where Milchan and his clients came in with a potent cocktail that gave
the IAF the technological qualitative edge over any of its adversaries in the
region.

The AIM-7 Sparrow medium-range semi-active radar homing air-to-
air missile, valued at $125,000 per unit (at 2009 prices), was a good fit
for the IAF. The Sparrow and its derivatives were the West's principal
beyond-visual-range (BVR) air-to-air missile well into the 1990s. The
AIM-9 Sidewinder, a heat-seeking, short-range air-to-air missile valued at

approximately $85,000 per unit was also in the mix. Systems brought in by Milchan Bros. and its satellite companies proved themselves time and again, with multiple high-profile downings of enemy aircraft. On April 28, 1981, an AIM-7 downed a Syrian, Soviet-made Mi-8 helicopter and on July 14 of the same year, another AIM-7 destroyed a Syrian MiG-21.

Millions of dollars in commissions to Milchan generated from these sales substantially inflated Israel's secret bank accounts, and greatly expanded the reach and scope of Israel's covert activities around the world.

A month before that, on June 7, 1981, a sixteen-plane Israeli strike force launched from Etzion airbase in the Sinai Peninsula. The flight profile was low altitude, across the Gulf of Aqaba, southern Jordan, and then across northern Saudi Arabia. Two F-15s remained circling over Saudi Arabia as a communications relay back to Israel.

The remaining six F-15s and the F-16s continued on to al-Tuwaitha, the site of Iraq's Osirak nuclear reactor. Each F-16 carried two two-thousand-pound Mark 84 bombs with delayed fuses. These bombs were unguided, and required maneuvering close to the target. The strike force arrived near Osirak undetected at low altitude and circled around at predetermined points to begin their bombing runs, while the F-15s patrolled the theater to intercept any Iraqi fighters that might materialize.

At least eight of the sixteen bombs released struck the containment dome of the reactor and completely demolished it. This was one of the first examples of a precision attack; it was certainly the first recorded attack to destroy another country's nuclear facility. All Israeli aircraft returned safely to the base.

Iraqi nuclear weapons ambitions were reduced to a pile of rubble, never to recover. Israel's own program proceeded aggressively.

* * *

The krytron, that little, innocent-looking electrical tube that also serves as the most efficient device to trigger a nuclear explosion, made a comeback in 1979, tucked away at the bottom of a long list of sensitive items that Dvora Ben Yitzhak sent in coded form directly to Richard Smyth at Milco.

Money was certainly not the concern, as the devices were only $75 per unit, probably the smallest and least expensive item ever ordered by any of the companies affiliated with Milchan Bros., who were by now ordering materials and technology in the hundreds of millions of dollars. The entire issue was the incredibly sensitive nature of the tiny item and the ability to get it past those pesky US export controls.

Apparently Blumberg felt enough time had passed that it might be worth trying once more to see if they could slip it through the system. Instead of ordering a large quantity, Smyth would try for multiple shipments of only thirty to forty krytrons in hopes of flying under the radar. Smyth said that Milchan personally called to confirm that he understood the objective and the urgency. Smyth depended on Milchan Bros. and he was eager to please.

Smyth researched the Department of Commerce export rulebook and found that gas-filled electronic tubes had many commercial uses. He noticed the paragraph called "Diodes, Triodes, and Pentodes" under the heading "Gas-Filled Tubes." Such items, he concluded, could be shipped without a munitions export license. Smyth was in possession of the manufacturer's brochure, which showed a hand-drawn picture of a krytron, and it looked exactly like it had five wires leading out of it, making it a pentode. He then decided to use the Department of Commerce's rulebook on pentodes as a cover, and the source of his "confusion" if US authorities ever discovered the shipments of krytrons to Milchan's company without a munitions license.

It seemed like quite a risk, given that Milco had already been turned down for export licenses for krytrons in the past. If the previous export attempt came up, the second fallback position would essentially be, "Oops, I forgot." The krytron shipments were to be sent to Heli Trading Ltd., a Milchan Bros. subsidiary, primarily used for helicopter transactions. The end-user was listed again as Rehovot Instruments Ltd. The shipments were designed to avoid suspicion and declared to be cold-cathode gas-filled tubes. The word *krytron* was not mentioned. It was the first of thirteen shipments, totaling at least 810 nuclear triggers, sent by Milco every few months between the years 1979 and 1982.

Although Milchan had originally promised to funnel most of his projects with major US defense contractors through Milco, Smyth came to understand and except that his role was more of the boutique operator, securing the exotic items not easily obtainable, and that Milchan used other options for more routine operations. Perhaps without realizing it, Smyth had become another LAKAM agent.

Smyth was able to ship Israel long lists of sensitive products: training simulators for air defense missiles, voice scramblers and lasers, computerized flight control systems, thermal batteries, gyroscopes for missile guidance systems, and almost everything else a country might need to turn itself into a high-tech, nuclear armed powerhouse.

Although absent minded, Smyth was a smooth operator, well connected, with a top security clearance that enabled him to research, procure, and ship critical components to Israel in broad daylight. He was diligent about briefing the CIA of his activities and presenting himself as an American patriot. But the devil was in the details.

As long as the orders came in, Smyth's bank account grew along with the company itself. Aside from his wife and children, numerous other employees came on board, and two small satellite offices were opened in the Washington, DC, area, primarily to help secure the various licenses for his exports, and to maintain relations with suppliers, many of whom had offices in the area. Milco hired a bookkeeper and corporate treasurer, Smyth's daughter Gretel Siler, and she too was very aware of transactions involving the purchasing of krytrons and many other items.

Smyth recruited a number of highly talented professional colleagues to join Milco's board of directors: Robert Mainhardt, a respected nuclear scientist; Arthur Biehl, a former director of hydrogen bomb design at Lawrence Livermore National Laboratory; and Ivan Alexander Getting, a physicist and electrical engineer credited with inventing the Global Positioning System (GPS). When they joined the board, they claimed they were under the impression that they were joining a company that dealt with the development of avionic systems for the US Air Force and NASA.

They knew and respected Richard Kelly Smyth from the various boards and commissions they served on together at the Pentagon. Like Smyth, they all had top-secret security clearances and access to much of the United States' latest military and aviation-related technology, and were well qualified to sit on any aerospace company's board.

During the same year, Milco secured a contract to supply all of the control systems for the Laví, Israel's ambitious multi-purpose advanced fighter jet, which was meant to replace its aging Skyhawk fleet and become its primary fighter plane, a project that was later aborted in 1987 under US pressure on Israel to purchase the F-16 instead. To amortize the cost of the Laví, up to the date of its cancelation, Israel sold designs to Taiwan, and later to China, who went on to develop the Chengdu J-10 advanced fighter jet based on the Laví.

Israel didn't formally maintain diplomatic relations with China until the early 1990s, but in the 1970s and early '80s Milchan focused on Taiwan as a natural marketplace. According to Smyth, twenty percent of all Milco business was with Taiwan. Taiwan, not China, benefited most from defense technology transactions involving Milchan and Milco. As with South Africa, Israel acted, in essence, as a US proxy, supplying Taiwan with weapons systems and nuclear technology since the United States felt uncomfortable doing so due to its relationship with the People's Republic of China. And as with South Africa, Milchan helped facilitate that relationship.

Eventually the Chinese wised up to the system and opened their own bilateral relations with Israel, which led to a dramatic decrease in Israeli defense shipments to Taiwan and an increase in sales to China, but for that there was little need for a middleman. By 1992, full diplomatic relations were established between Israel and the People's Republic of China, and Milchan's covert sales to Taiwan dried up almost entirely.

In addition to supplying foreign governments with what they needed, Milchan encouraged Smyth to create a respectable and legitimate image for Milco as a company that served the interests of US defense needs by working with the Pentagon. But, of course, his larger mission was to secure supplies for Israel's defense needs. According to Milco's board members

Ivan Getting and Arthur Biehl, from very early on in their involvement with Milco they noticed that Smyth spent most of his time and energy procuring duel-use material and equipment for Israel, including nuclear-related material. Smyth was relentlessly seeking to purchase a uranium by-product called green salt that could be processed into weapons-grade uranium. "I had no evidence that anything improper was going on," said Biehl. "I just thought it was a strange way to do business.... I wondered why the Israelis were paying fees when they could get the same equipment directly using US foreign aid money."[1]

If the United States had no problem with Israel receiving these items, why did Israel feel the need to pay a fee to a middleman? When he was asked years later by a *Washington Post* journalist why Israel used a middle-man for certain items, Israeli embassy spokesman Yossi Gal stated tersely, "Because Israel prefers sometimes to use the services of middlemen." What the *Washington Post* reporter failed to grasp was that Israel's procurements through US foreign aid were a matter of public record. Using middlemen made it harder for outside observers to follow exactly what Israel was purchasing, since the sales were made not to the Israeli government, but to another entity, sometimes even multiple entities. In fact, this is a common counterintelligence practice. The fact that commissions were extracted along the way and funneled into secret accounts controlled by Milchan to finance Israel's covert activities was only the icing on the cake.

The US administration was largely aware of these activities, and maintained a don't ask, don't tell policy of tacit, unofficial approval. However, that message was not and could not be sent to those responsible for enforcing the law at lower levels.

Milco board member and nuclear scientist Robert Mainhardt described on CBS's *60 Minutes* in 1990 how he'd started to feel uncomfortable about Milco after two incidents involving Milchan. The first occurred when Milchan asked Mainhardt for blueprints of an advanced nuclear reactor; the second incident involved Milchan's request for hexachloride, another material useful in the uranium enrichment process. Arthur Biehl

---

1. John Goshko, "LA Man Indicted in Export of Potential Nuclear Bomb Component to Israel," *Washington Post* series, May 14, 15, 17, 1985.

claims that Milchan personally introduced him to an Israeli official who asked him about access to nuclear material "not through the government." Biehl claims that he immediately reported the incident to the FBI and resigned from Milco's board.[2] By 1982, all three of the board members had resigned. Their subsequent statements need to be viewed in the context of men looking to protect their own rear ends after the fact. Milchan claims that his discussion with Robert Mainhardt had nothing to do with a nuclear reactor, and involved developing a new system that would translate musical notes to visual communication, a project that he and his friend actor Richard Dreyfuss were working on at the time. Dreyfuss had starred in Spielberg's *Close Encounters of the Third Kind*, which famously featured such a system to communicate with aliens.

Despite the resignations, Milco worked full speed ahead. During this entire time, Smyth continued to serve on the board of directors of Rockwell International. Even though the position didn't require much work, it allowed Smyth to maintain his top-secret clearance.

* * *

Meanwhile, Milchan's interest in movies was intensifying. He made his first and only real investment in an Israeli film, called *Dizengoff 99*, a 1979 film about a group of young Israelis who, like Milchan, became infected with the movie-making virus and set out to produce a socially conscious film. *Dizengoff 99* made its mark in Israel thanks to a rather lengthy and daring – for its time – sex scene, in which the two lead actresses, Anat Atzmon and Gali Atari, simultaneously make love to the lead actor, Gidi Gov. The film concludes when Gov leaves Israel for the United States after becoming frustrated with the small and difficult Israeli film industry.

Milchan has been asked many times why he hasn't invested in the Israeli film industry since *Dizengoff 99*. The answer in many ways can be found in the script of *Dizengoff 99* itself. Milchan has little interest in the narrow domestic market; he wanted to think and act big: "They make wine in France, they make movies in Hollywood; that's the way it is." He wanted

2.   Ibid.

to produce films for and about the entire world. Being a local film investor in a tiny market fit neither his vast ambition nor his professional needs.

On May 13, 1980, Milchan opened his second Broadway musical, *It's So Nice to Be Civilized*, this time at the Martin Beck Theater in New York. The show had twenty-three runs to sold-out crowds. Then came the harsh review from the *New York Times* theater critic, Frank Rich, and the following night only fourteen tickets were sold.

It was a bitter pill to swallow and put a temporary end to Milchan's short career as a producer of Broadway musicals. Instead he focused his attention on a television spectacular he'd been thinking about. Soon Milchan pitched ABC the idea of a historical miniseries on the ancient Roman siege of Masada. He made his pitch at a time when historical miniseries were still going strong; it had started with *Roots* in 1977 and its sequel *Roots: The Next Generations* in 1979, both on ABC. NBC countered with the successful *Shogun,* narrated by Orson Welles and starring Richard Chamberlain.

Until *Shogun,* ABC had dominated the genre and was now eager to fire back, and Milchan had come up with what they felt was a timely idea. Of course it didn't hurt that he took it upon himself to underwrite the completion bond to fund the entire project, in association with Universal Studios. He was given the green light by ABC executives. The ancient tragedy of Masada represented a good opportunity for Israel to explain its difficult security predicament to the American public and demonstrate why Israel, a small country surrounded by much larger enemies, needed to take extraordinary measures so that "Masada will never fall again."

Milchan was able to secure all imaginable support from the Israeli government, who quickly recognized the public relations opportunity. Moshe Dayan suggested, and Minister of Defense Ezer Weizman authorized, the construction of a ramp leading to the historic mountaintop, created to simulate the ramp built by the Romans to capture the fortress. It was designed by the same engineers who constructed Israel's bridge across the Suez Canal during the Yom Kippur War. Milchan recruited renowned British actor Peter O'Toole, of *Lawrence of Arabia* fame, for the role of Lucius Flavius Silva, the late-first-century Roman general, governor of the province of Judea, who led the Roman army to the fortress mountaintop after a long siege. Peter Straus was also recruited to play the role of Eliezer Ben Yair, leader of the besieged Jews who ultimately committed mass suicide. During the filming, Arnon celebrated the bar mitzvah of his son Yariv at the employees' dining hall at the Weizmann Institute in Rehovot. The waiters and staff were dressed in costumes from the *Masada* set.

Masada was Milchan's first real financial and critical success in show business, and it was nominated for numerous awards – Peter O'Toole was nominated for a best actor Emmy, and actor David Warner, who played Senator Pomponius Falco, won an Emmy for his supporting role. The miniseries was later edited into a two-hour feature film for video and later DVD, distributed by Universal Studios.

Through his first interaction with Universal Studios, Milchan came to know Sidney Sheinberg, president and COO of MCA Inc., Universal's parent company. Unbeknownst to Milchan, during the production of *Masada* Sheinberg took an immediate dislike to him, perceiving Milchan as having negotiated a financial windfall for himself from the production and bonding of the miniseries. In reality, Milchan had shown a business savvy that Sheinberg hadn't expected from the rookie producer. With the help of Milchan's friend and *Masada* coproducer, acclaimed Oscar-winning director Sidney Pollack, the inexperienced Milchan had discovered numerous flaws in the shooting schedule that could have resulted in going significantly over budget. The entire Roman army was to be filmed crossing the desert in half a day; the burning of Jerusalem was to be filmed in one night. When Sidney Pollack pointed out these impossibilities, Milchan returned to Universal and renegotiated the terms, to Sheinberg's annoyance.

Sheinberg was not the kind of man to wear his feelings on his sleeve but he'd later find a way to throw serious obstacles in Milchan's path, which would lead to a legendary and very public Hollywood spat.

Despite this Hollywood animosity, Milchan has admitted more than once that he's a real fan, and even groupie, of a number of actors. It's no coincidence that many like to compare him to Jay Gatsby, the fictional hero of F. Scott Fitzgerald's *The Great Gatsby* – rich and mysterious. His source of wealth is not entirely understood and assumed to be questionable, and he in many ways personifies the distortion of the American dream. Like Gatsby, Milchan felt a "great sensitivity to the promises of life," as described in the Fitzgerald novel. He tends to attract high society, the successful, and the "winners" by his straightforwardness, his sense of humor – and his money.

One of Milchan's closest friends is the Polish director Roman Polanski, who directed such celebrated movies as *Rosemary's Baby* and *Chinatown*. Polanski, a Holocaust survivor, was formerly married to actress Sharon Tate, who was viciously murdered in their home by the Manson family while Polanski was away shooting a film in Europe. Tate was pregnant with Polanski's child at the time. Polanski later fled the United States to France after being charged with having sex with an underage girl.

After fleeing the United States, Polanski had difficulty raising funds for his projects because of his inability to work in Hollywood. Then, one day in Paris in 1978, he met one of his biggest fans: Milchan. Shortly thereafter, the two began to collaborate on a new project called *Pirates*, a dark comedy that mocked old Hollywood pirate movies.

They agreed on a $20 million budget, and Milchan convinced Polanski to produce the movie in Israel. He recruited his friend Ezer Weizman, who had just left the post of minister of defense, to be the movie's line producer, primarily responsible for building a gigantic pirate ship in the shipyards at the port of Haifa. Everything was going along fine until Polanski took a vacation to Bali, where he proceeded to rewrite the script, resulting in a budget increase of $18 million. "Polanski can be like a little boy sometimes, and he stubbornly insisted on a budget that I was unwilling to increase. He took his marbles and left the project. We didn't speak for two years after that," Milchan said. "Fortunately for me, I was able to sell the pirate ship to the Israeli power company, who used it to ship coal to its power plants."[3]

Two years later, in 1981, Milchan received a call out of the blue from Polanski about a play written by British playwright Peter Shaffer, called *Amadeus*. Polanski wanted to stage the play in his home country of Poland,

---

3. Polanski ended up producing *Pirates*, starring Walter Matthau, with Tarak Ben Ammar, the nephew of former president of Tunisia Habib Bourguiba.

during the height of the Solidarity movement and massive political tur-moil, as a statement of support.

Although Milchan didn't consider the profit potential to be worth the risk from a business perspective, he funded the project as an ideological expression, and an act of subversion against the Communist regime. He was also curious about the country from which his own grandfather had escaped years earlier.

Arnon's grandfather, Chaim Eliezer Milchan, who would come to greatly influence Arnon's life, was born on a cold December day in 1879 on the edge of a beautiful little man-made lake, the product of a small dam built by Arnon's ancestors just outside the little town of Goniądz in the Bialystok region in the northwest corner of present-day Poland.

At the age of fourteen, Chaim traveled the long distance south to Odessa on the Black Sea, alone, where he boarded a ship to Ottoman Palestine and arrived off the coast of Jaffa, the oldest continuously popu-lated town in the world, in early spring of 1894.

For eight years he worked as a farm laborer, and eventually, in 1902, purchased land in the new community of Rehovot, where he became an important founding member of that community and established one of the larger vineyards in the region. Within months he had married Arnon's grandmother, Esther Shlank, of Jerusalem, and seven children followed, including their second son Dov, Arnon's father.

For his part, Polanski, a Polish citizen, was able to secure the logistics for *Amadeus*, and the production moved forward under difficult circum-stances. It was a powerful statement in a country that for years had not been exposed to such an artistic production. The main purpose was to lift the spirits of the Poles, who had faced decades of totalitarianism and its accompanying cultural restrictions.[4] Arnon decided to contribute all of the project's proceeds to the Solidarity movement for the purchase of anything that they needed to support the revolution at its most critical moment.

Amadeus ran for thirteen performances to standing-room-only crowds. Long lines formed outside the theater at every performance on the off chance

---

4. Nina Darnton, "Polanski on Polish Stage Amid Political Upheaval," *New York Times*, July 21, 1981.

that some tickets would become available. One of Poland's leading actors and directors, Tadeusz Lomnicki, described the performances as a cultural game-changer: "Maybe *Amadeus* will be the golden nail in our coffin," he said, referring to the hated regime. Arnon was unable to travel to Poland, so Polanski acted as his eyes and ears, some might even say as his agent.

Within months, Solidarity leader Lech Walesa was imprisoned, and it took eight more years for the Communist regime to collapse. When, nine years later, in December 1990, Walesa was elected president of the country, one of his first acts was to invite Arnon to Poland to honor his contributions to Solidarity during the height of the struggle.

Milchan, accompanied by Robert De Niro, Roman Polanski, and his friend Meir Teper, traveled to Warsaw, and later to the shipyard in Gdansk where the revolution began, and met with the former Solidarity leader, and now president, Lech Walesa.

"When we arrived, we were stunned by the chaos, the poverty, and the long lines in front of bakeries for a loaf of bread. There was no food to be had, and we even went to a supermarket but the shelves were empty," Meir Teper told us. "We then flew in a wreck of an airplane to Gdansk, where we met with Walesa, who asked Milchan for help bringing Western banks to Poland. Let's just say that Milchan was more than eager to help," Teper continued.

Emboldened with their Warsaw success, Milchan and Polanski decided to open *Amadeus* at the Marignan Theater on the Champs-Elysées in Paris, with Polanski in the lead role as Mozart. There too, "It was a smashing success that could have run for years," Polanski told writer Ann Louise Bardach in a 2000 *LA Magazine* interview, "but I couldn't do it forever." It ran for a full year.

Polanski describes Milchan as a hard-nosed businessman who keeps his word and is disciplined. The director is understandably loyal to Milchan, who stood by him at a time when it looked like his career would not recover, and since *Amadeus* the two have remained close friends.

Milchan was offered the idea of making the play *Amadeus* into a full-length motion picture. He considered it for not more than a few minutes before turning it down. "It will not translate well into film," he confidently and mistakenly asserted. He even tried to persuade director Milos Forman to avoid the screen version, which ultimately brought Forman an Academy Award for best director in 1984. It would not be the last time that Milchan would turn down an idea that would later materialize as a blockbuster of earth-shattering consequences in the entertainment industry.

Polanski continues to consult with Milchan about the distribution of his films, and one film was actually inspired by a sensitive matter involving his close friend. In 1988, Polanski wrote and directed the movie *Frantic*, starring Harrison Ford. Ford plays Dr. Richard Walker, an American surgeon visiting Paris with his wife for a medical conference. At their hotel room, his wife discovers that she may have picked up the wrong suitcase at the airport.

While Walker is taking a shower, his wife disappears from the hotel room. He assumes she's only gone down to the front desk to deal with the suitcase matter. When she fails to return, he becomes concerned and begins searching for her throughout the hotel. The plot escalates as he enlists the help of polite but mostly indifferent hotel staff, with no success. He then wanders outside to the street looking for her.

A person on the street overhears him in a café and tells Walker he saw his wife being forced into a car. Walker is skeptical until he finds his wife's ID bracelet on the cobblestone sidewalk. He quickly contacts the US embassy and the Paris police but their responses are bureaucratic, and there is little hope anyone will look for her.

It turns out that in the suitcase, hidden within a small replica of the Statue of Liberty, was a single krytron, that same small switch capable of detonating nuclear devices that Milchan had been working so hard to obtain.

The film ends with a confrontation where Arab terrorists release Walker's wife. However, a firefight ensues between the terrorists and an Israeli Mossad unit that had been tracking them. Angry and upset, Walker throws the krytron into the river, rendering it useless.

The 1988 film portrays, in graphic terms, the extreme measures taken for a single krytron. In real life, Milchan had already obtained hundreds of

them. Indeed, Polanski would never have known about the importance –
or even the existence – of krytrons without his friend Arnon.

* * *

In 1981, Benjamin Blumberg finally met his match in Ariel "the Bulldozer"
Sharon, who was appointed Israel's new minister of defense. Sharon decided to replace Blumberg with his close friend of many years and former
head of the Mossad, Rafi Eitan. He viewed the role of LAKAM chief as
one of the most crucial positions in Israel's vast defense machinery. The
infighting continued for a few months, but eventually the transition took
place. The fifty-five-year-old Rafi Eitan was a short man with thick glasses
and a long career in the Mossad behind him. It was Eitan who personally
commanded the squad that captured Adolf Eichmann in Argentina. He
was well acquainted with Milchan, and was well aware of his activities on
behalf of LAKAM.

Within days of taking command of LAKAM he invited Milchan into
his office for a conversation. There was no need for formalities. Following
the meeting it was business as usual. Milchan's assistant Dvora would work
on a daily basis with the new LAKAM chief. Shortly thereafter, Richard
Kelly Smyth received his fourteenth order of krytrons from Heli Trading
Ltd. and he proceeded to fill the order by what was now the usual method,
a standard Department of Commerce export statement. Milco's accounting department documented a total of 810 krytrons purchased at a total
price of $60,750.

But the fourteenth shipment of krytrons was different. This time when
the items arrived at Milco from the Massachusetts manufacturer EG&G,
there was a clear statement on the box: "WARNING: The Export of This
Product Requires a Munitions Export License."

The label was part of a larger campaign in the United States to clamp
down on dual-use exports with nuclear applications. Smyth felt a cold
chill pass through his body. He remembered facing that obstacle before,
but was confident that he'd found a convenient loophole. This time he
checked the thick munitions export licensing manual and was not happy

to see that krytrons were indeed listed, right there under the nuclear weapons applications category.

But he again decided to ignore the munitions license requirement and sent the fourteenth shipment of krytrons using his usual method. He prayed that the shipment, like all the others, would simply go unnoticed.

13 ‖ Once upon a Time in America

You kind of buy yourself into it to be humiliated,
into becoming the next sucker in the business.

Arnon Milchan, *Los Angeles Magazine*, April 2000

New Year's Day, 1983, a few days before the release of his recent production, *The King of Comedy*, Arnon Milchan was in New York, consumed with the debut of one of the most important films of his career.

A world away, Richard Kelly Smyth and his wife Emilie arrived at the Milco offices in Huntington Beach to work on a few orders. The office building was empty, quiet, and the two hoped to get in some productive work. It was not unusual for them, because they had trouble concentrating with seven employees running around and the phone ringing off the hook. Weekends and holidays were a good time to clear their desks.

Upon entering the building, each went to their own office. At first they didn't notice anything was wrong – that is until Emilie needed to type something. She walked over to the reception area and noticed that the typewriter was missing. She then looked around and noticed that a number of computers were missing. "Richard!" she cried out for her husband, who was startled and came running.

They quickly checked every office, every room, and every storage area, including the warehouse out back. Electrical devices and a radio scram-

147

bler, a highly sensitive device that was rejected for export to Israel by the State Department, were all gone.

They knew that the missing computers contained secret information. The first thing that came to their minds was espionage. A deep sense of violation, paranoia, and fear set in. Richard understood that with his security clearance, he was obligated to report the break-in to the FBI. What kind of Pandora's box would that open? He knew that the first question he would be asked is "Who, in your opinion, did this?"

He remembered his last phone call with Milchan. He'd told him that more stringent standards were forced on him, and that he couldn't continue to send the krytrons the same way.

"Why didn't you send them as before?" Milchan asked.[1] Smyth explained that he could no longer do that, and Milchan eventually hung up the phone, frustrated. That was the last that Smyth would ever hear from him. Indeed, that turned out to be the very last direct conversation the two ever had.

Smyth called the Huntington Beach Police Department and the FBI to report the break-in. The police showed up in minutes and filled out a crime report. They quickly determined that the burglar had entered the building through a skylight while lowering himself with a rope. "It doesn't look like a professional job," the detective determined. He then asked Smyth to give him a list of all current and former employees. According to the police report, Smyth reported the missing equipment to be worth approximately $50,000, which included $12,000 in electronic equipment for NASA.

The next day, an FBI agent showed up to interview Smyth, mostly to gather details of the break-in, to determine the sensitivity level of the missing items, and to hear from Smyth if he had any idea who might be behind it all.

Smyth described his last conversation with Milchan. By now he was extremely worried about his multiple shipments of krytrons to Israel without a munitions license, and felt that instead of waiting for the shipments to be discovered by the FBI, his best strategy would be to innocently and

1.   Schiller, *Irrational Indictment and Imprisonment*, 1–3.

openly mention the shipments, and express his "concern" about having made a mistake in shipment procedures. The FBI agent listened quietly and took notes. Smyth was asked to list every possible suspect. On that list, he wrote the name Arnon Milchan.

Matters were moving quickly and Smyth didn't yet grasp the implications of what was happening. Would he now lose his business after saying no to the man who provided him with the bulk of his income? How would his interview with the FBI be interpreted? Frightened, he was determined to act openly, an instinct that would not necessarily serve him well.

Following the FBI interview, Smyth called Milchan multiple times but was only able to reach his assistant. Dvora was instructed by the new LAKAM chief, Rafi Eitan, to maintain a positive relationship with Smyth so that Israel could continue getting updates and strategize accordingly, without the need to bug his phone. Eitan then asked that Milchan avoid all further contact with Smyth and Milco, whom he described as the weakest link in Milchan's chain. Smyth, Eitan said, was "burned."

In essence, that was the end of Milco's thirteen-year run as a productive LAKAM operation. It was time to close the file and move on to other challenges. Eitan told Milchan that they could not afford to be sentimental about such matters.

The FBI and the Huntington Beach Police Department moved unusually quickly and with determination on the Milco case, using every investigative tool at their disposal, and indeed within two months had arrested a suspect, a minor, who had worked temporarily in Milco's warehouse. When the police raided his parents' home, they found a garage packed with stolen goods, including the missing items from Milco.

The young man admitted to the burglary, as well as other break-ins in the area. Strangely, the FBI signed an agreement with the thief, releasing him to the custody of his parents. He would not be prosecuted if he agreed to fully cooperate in the return of every item that he stole from Milco.

Smyth felt a great deal of relief, and Emilie was asked to come to the Huntington Beach police warehouse to collect the stolen items. Upon arrival, Emilie was approached by a man in a dark suit. "Is this your equipment here?" he asked. When she confirmed that it was, he pulled out a badge identifying himself as a US customs agent, and asked to speak with the president of the company. A sense of dread suddenly engulfed her as she fumbled through her purse to give him her husband's business card, saying the agent could call him directly.

In the following weeks, the US customs agent visited the Milco office multiple times, sometimes unannounced, to talk with Richard Smyth. Other times he'd phone in his questions, but barely a day would go by without some form of contact with this agent. Initially Smyth showed eagerness to cooperate, and the discussions were gentle and mildly inquisitive, including innocent questions about company shipping and filing procedures. Slowly, as the days went by, the friendly questions turned more and more forceful, until they began to resemble an interrogation.

The days, weeks, and months following the Milco break-in proved to be very difficult. Orders and even communications from Israel had suddenly stopped, and a federal agent was snooping around on a daily basis. Within a few months it was clear that major cutbacks were in order. Smyth desperately worked to secure contracts from NASA, NATO, and the Pentagon but he was only able to sign a few consulting contracts in the tens of thousands of dollars, hardly enough to maintain Milco at its current level.

The cash flow plummeted. Smyth feared that his security clearance would be downgraded and that the questions from the customs agent breathing down his neck would only intensify. He decided to cut back substantially by closing Milco offices on the East Coast and maintaining only his wife, his children, and himself on the payroll as part-time employees. Yet even with those cutbacks, Milco barely kept its head above water, and it was about to get worse.

As Milco's troubles gradually mounted, Milchan was busy with the premiere of his new film, *The King of Comedy*, a daring production. Robert De Niro played the highly uncharacteristic role of Rupert Pupkin, a stage-door autograph hound and an aspiring stand-up comic with obsessive ambitions far in excess of any actual talent. A chance meeting with Jerry Langford (played by Jerry Lewis), a famous comedian and talk show host, leads Pupkin to believe that his big break has finally arrived. He is mistaken. In a desperate attempt to get on the show anyway, he kidnaps Langford and negotiates an appearance on the show, hosted by a fill-in played by Tony Randall. Pupkin's performance is an unexpected success, but he gets arrested after the show. The final scene shows Pupkin taking the stage for an apparent TV special with a live audience and an announcer enthusiastically introducing and praising him. Through irony, the film ridicules the idea that success is the product of talent rather than luck.

The movie didn't enjoy much success at the box office, although it's easy to understand why Milchan found the script so appealing. Over time, *The King of Comedy* was appreciated for its artistic and somewhat cynical portrayal of American show business.

During *The King of Comedy* Milchan and De Niro forged the strong bond that would last for decades. Milchan introduced De Niro to Moshe Dayan and envisioned him playing Dayan's character in a full-length motion picture based on his life, but he could never pin De Niro down, and the film, which Milchan still wants to produce, has not yet materialized.

Milchan went out of his way to cultivate his relationship with the notoriously shy De Niro, including employing the services of his own assistant Ety Kanner to arrange female companionship for the movie star. Kanner described to us how she received a call from Milchan one day, asking her to identify a beautiful African American woman on the cover of the French fashion magazine *Elle*: "It was a global operation. First I called the magazine's office in Paris to identify the model. I was informed that she was on a photo shoot in Los Angeles. I located her in LA and convinced her to get on the earliest flight to New York for a 'meeting' with Robert De Niro." With visions of stardom in her mind, the model arrived in New York at Milchan's expense, for a night on the town with De Niro.

Shortly after the premiere of *The King of Comedy*, while the Los Angeles district attorney was secretly building a case against Milco, Arnon was busy with a serious personal matter. During production in the United States, he received an urgent phone call from his teenage son Yariv.

That evening, Yariv had gone out and failed to return until well past his curfew. When he arrived home he was shocked to find that his mother,

Brigitte, had packed a suitcase with his belongings, and ordered him to leave.

Arnon learned of the situation while traveling in Los Angeles; it was a painful and life-changing moment. He promptly instructed his Portuguese assistant, Jose Olivera, who managed the chateau, to pick up Yariv and bring him to Montfort-l'Amaury. When Alexandra and Elinor understood what was happening to their brother, they refused to stay without him. Within days Brigitte promptly packed their bags as well, and kicked them all out of the house.

From that day forward, Arnon became the children's primary caretaker and the chateau became their home again. They all attended preparatory boarding schools and spent holidays with their father around the world, and summers in Israel. "My children are the closest people to me, and are my greatest joy," Arnon explained.

On a subsequent visit to Israel, Brigitte stayed at the penthouse. When she discovered a number of photographs of Arnon in the company of various women, including Ulla and Ulrika, she proceeded to tear the apartment apart, ripping up photos, destroying expensive art and furniture. It was rock bottom, and the final break in what had been, for a while, a cordial relationship following their divorce.

* * *

Milchan was a big fan of Sergio Leone, who introduced the world to spaghetti westerns like *A Fistful of Dollars*, *The Good, the Bad and the Ugly*, and *Once upon a Time in the West*, and is credited with discovering Clint Eastwood.

Leone turned down an opportunity from Paramount Pictures to direct *The Godfather*, one of the most important films ever made, and spent the next ten years contemplating his own mobster masterpiece, *Once upon a Time in America*. No one wanted to touch it. That is, until – by chance – Leone met Milchan:

> It happened at the Cannes Film Festival. I was trying to sell another movie there, similar to *Gone with the Wind*. Suddenly I see this guy sitting on the large balcony of the Carlton Hotel overlooking

the beach, somebody who looks like Buddha, or Orson Welles, or Sergio Leone. I wasn't sure. I got closer and I noticed that he wasn't Buddha and he wasn't Orson Wells, so it must be Sergio Leone. I introduced myself in French and told him what a big fan I am of his spaghetti westerns.

I told him that it was a big honor for me to meet him and asked what he was presently working on. "There is this movie that I have been working on for ten years now, and no one wants it," Leone responded. "It's a big American saga; do you want to hear about it?"[2]

Milchan was surprised and honored as he took a seat next to the legendary director and listened intently. It was about three or four in the afternoon as Leone began to describe the movie, scene after scene, frame after frame. "Now the camera will rise, a car will approach, the camera zooms in…" And it went on like that for over four hours as the sun slowly set over the Mediterranean. When Leone was done, Milchan told him that he wanted to make that movie. Leone was surprised, and asked if he had the financial ability. Milchan first answered in the affirmative, and only then inquired about the budget. The answer was $22 million; Milchan didn't flinch. But of course, that was not the end of it. It never is.

One night, well past the time for visitors, Leone snuck into Milchan's room in New York. Milchan suddenly heard a soft voice with a strong Italian accent: "Arnon, Arnon, I need more money."

Startled and stunned, he awoke to a gigantic figure sitting on a chair right next to him. "Jesus, is that you, Sergio? Are you crazy?"

"Arnon, I can't sleep. I need another $2 million, I need to rent the Orient Express."

Milchan had trouble understanding the logic. "Why do you need to rent the Orient Express? Can't we just rent a regular train and present it as the Orient Express?"

2. Caspit, "The Flying Producer."

Leone would have none of it. "Because the audience will be able to smell that it is not the Orient Express," was Leone's reply. He refused to leave the room until Milchan guaranteed to increase the film's budget.

In the end, the film cost $28 million and is considered to this day to be one of the most unique and strange productions in movie history. It's widely viewed as the best film that the gifted director ever made. It's Milchan's favorite film and, in his opinion, the best film that he's ever produced. There was something about the criminal underground and the grim reality it portrayed that was magnetic to Milchan.

Once upon a Time in America is an epic, episodic tale of the lives of a small group of New York City Jewish gangsters spanning over forty years, told mostly in flashbacks and flash-forwards. The movie centers on small-time hood David "Noodles" Aaronson and his lifelong partners in crime, Max, Cockeye, and their friends. The film follows them as they grow up in the rough Jewish neighborhood of New York's Lower East Side in the 1920s through the late 1960s, when the elderly Noodles returns to New York after many years in hiding to rediscover his past.

Milchan was still relatively inexperienced, and when Leone gave him a copy of the script, he was stunned to see that it was 317 pages, to this day the longest script that Milchan has ever read.

Leone warned Milchan from the beginning, "Bambino, you must be patient."

Milchan replied that he didn't know the movie was that long.

"I don't mean the length of the movie, my friend, I mean in our dealings with actors," Leone replied.

As Leone began casting, Milchan rented an apartment in New York, on 48th Street between 2nd and 3rd, right next door to legendary actress Katharine Hepburn. They considered hundreds of actors for the film's various parts, which was a long and difficult process in itself. Early in 1981, Brooke Shields was offered the role of Deborah Gelly after Sergio Leone had seen *The Blue Lagoon*, claiming that she had the potential to play a mature character. However, a writers' strike delayed the project, and Shields withdrew before auditions began.

There had been more than three hundred applicants for the lead female role, including Kim Basinger, Glenn Close, Jamie Lee Curtis, Geena Davis, Jodie Foster, Carrie Fisher, Daryl Hannah, Liza Minnelli, Michelle Pfeiffer, Meg Ryan, Susan Sarandon, Meryl Streep, and Debra Winger – a virtual who's who of America's leading ladies.

As word spread of the production in the works, Leone personally received numerous phone calls from top talents, such as Warren Beatty.

Like he did with most of the others, Leone turned him down cold. "He's a hairdresser, for Christ's sake," Leone said to Milchan.

"But he only played the role of a hairdresser in *Shampoo*," Milchan said, in hopes of changing Leone's mind.

"No, no, he is a hairdresser," Leone insisted.

A few days later he received a call from Clint Eastwood. "No, no, I have already cast him in three movies. I need something fresh."[3]

If there was one person Sergio Leone wanted for the film, it was Robert De Niro, who had played the lead in Milchan's *The King of Comedy*. According to Milchan, it was not easy to convince De Niro to read the long script, but finally the actor claimed that he'd read through the entire manuscript and agreed to meet with Leone.

The meeting was scheduled at the Mayflower Hotel in New York City. Leone, obese at the time, was dressed in a gigantic robe as they convened in a top-floor suite that Milchan had reserved for the meeting. Leone and De Niro were to talk one-on-one as Milchan waited for a call in a separate room.

When the phone finally rang, it was De Niro whispering on the other end. "Arnon, I need to talk with you."

Milchan rushed over to De Niro's room and knocked on the door. De Niro said, "I can't do the movie."

Milchan was stunned. "Why not?"

De Niro led Milchan to the bathroom and pointed at the toilet.

Milchan was puzzled.

"Can't you see that he pissed all over my toilet seat?" he asked in that tone that only Robert De Niro can do.

---

3. Ibid.

The seat was indeed soiled. "Come on, Robert, he didn't do that on purpose. He's fat, he didn't see."

"No way, Arnon, he did this on purpose." De Niro implied that it was a power game, a marking of territory of sorts, showing who's the boss.[4]

Milchan calmed him down, and ultimately De Niro was cast in the lead role as the Jewish gangster David Aaronson.

The highly sought-after lead female role was not filled until shortly before filming began. Milchan had his heart set on Elizabeth McGovern, who, while studying at Juilliard at the age of twenty, had been offered a part in her first movie, *Ordinary People*, in the role of the girlfriend of a troubled teenager played by Timothy Hutton. It was Robert Redford's first film as a director, and it won four Oscars. The next year McGovern earned an Academy Award nomination for best supporting actress for her portrayal of the early-twentieth-century actress Evelyn Nesbit in the movie *Ragtime*, in which she had a controversial and very lengthy nude scene. Out of the long list of star actresses who sought the role, Elizabeth McGovern got it. She was seventeen years Arnon's junior – and his lover.

Robert De Niro, still unaware of the nature of Milchan's relationship with McGovern, resisted giving her the role. Leone and De Niro butted heads over the matter. De Niro complained incessantly as Leone stood quietly and looked at his watch. As De Niro ran out of breath, Leone asked, "Are you done?" De Niro was confused as Leone continued. "It usually takes twenty minutes for an actor to stop complaining. It only took you twelve. Now, you need to remember that this is not your film, it is my film with you participating in it,"[5] Leone snapped. Once again, Milchan stepped in and spoke privately with De Niro. Whatever was said, De Niro relented on the matter.

As Milchan remembered:

> There was a scene in the movie where De Niro was supposed to rape Elizabeth McGovern in the back seat of a limousine, after she informs him that she's leaving and moving to Hollywood to realize

---

4. Ibid.
5. Personal interview with Milchan, November 2009.

her dream. A real complicated scene. De Niro suddenly suggested that I should play the role of the limousine driver. I reacted with skepticism. After all, I'm not an actor. There were four pages of text in that scene; it was not inconsequential. In any event, the idea caught on, and Sergio conducted a formal audition for me. After that my skepticism suddenly disappeared and I found myself wanting to play the role more than anything in my life. It was like catching a bug. It became my lifetime ambition. Sergio, on the other hand, was not impressed and rejected my participation. I, the producer and financier of the entire project, was rejected! I was boiling. I was sure that everyone would come to me on their hands and knees but I was treated like the lowest extra on the set. They continued to do auditions for the part right in front of me and I was completely frustrated.

Then I received a call: "We are ready to film the scene, come on down." But I was in Paris and the scene was to be filmed that same night in Canada. "No problem," they tell me on the phone. "Tickets are waiting for you at the airport. There are three other candidates for the role that are also being called in." I was genuinely hurt by now, but I arrived at the airport nonetheless. I couldn't find my name listed in first class and not in business class. Where did they put me? In coach, all the way at the back next to the toilets!

I finally arrived in Canada and I went straight to the set. It was like magic. Everything was lit up, and there they were, God and his deputy, Leone and De Niro. Two personal friends who in this case were both paid by me. I reached out to them warmly: "Sergio, Robert, here I am!" They gave me a look as if I was the guy delivering the sandwiches, an actor-wannabe, a rank amateur. They were focused like lasers on their tasks. I was looking for direction. "You know this is my first role," I mentioned to Leone, who ignored me. De Niro turned to me and said, "Look, this movie is not about you and it's not about the limousine driver. It's about my character. Remember that."

It took thirteen takes to get the scene down. Leone literally

showed De Niro how to rape Elizabeth McGovern and asked
De Niro to physically repeat his instructions before filming
commenced, and I couldn't remember even once how to open
the limousine door. On take two I forgot to stop the limousine
where I was supposed to. In the meantime, De Niro was repeatedly
"raping" my girlfriend in the back seat, for thirteen takes! And you
know Robert De Niro, a real actor; every take was from the heart!
He was totally committed to the realism of the scene. And I was
supposed to stop the limousine and ask Elizabeth, "Are you all
right?" as I exited the limousine, opened the door, and removed
my hat. That's it.

In the end, they cut the scene down so much that I was only left
with that one line, "Are you all right?" And even after that, Leone
did not like the sound of my voice so he hired another actor to do
a voiceover. It was a completely humiliating experience, but it was
exhilarating at the same time.[6]

It's interesting that De Niro originally opposed McGovern in the female
role and later suggested that Arnon play the role of the limousine driver in
the rape scene. Years later, Milchan would surely recognize himself as the
Hugh Fennyman character in the movie *Shakespeare in Love*, the money
man who was "generously" given a small role in his own play if only he
promised to behave himself and not interfere.

At the end of filming, Leone had about eight to ten hours worth of
footage. With his editor, Nino Baragli, he trimmed it down to almost
six hours, which he wanted to release as two separate movies, three hours
each. Warner Brothers refused (partly due to the commercial and critical
failure of Bertolucci's two-part *Novecento*) and Leone was forced to further
shorten the length of his film, resulting in a 229-minute movie.

The shorter version was screened at the Cannes Film Festival and was
received with great enthusiasm. At the end of the screening, the audience
rose in a standing ovation that lasted an unprecedented fifteen minutes.

6. Arnon Milchan in an interview with journalist Ben Caspit, *Ma'ariv* (Israel), October
    12, 2005.

Throughout Europe, the film was received enthusiastically by audiences and critics alike and was a strong commercial success, grossing over $100 million.

In the United States, however, Warner Brothers was still unhappy with the length of the film after it was test-marketed in Boston in front of an impatient audience who booed from the outset when they heard that the film was over three hours long. Warner Brothers exercised their rights under contract, and butchered it down to 139 minutes, which was what they perceived as a commercially viable length. As a result, it flopped in the US box office, grossing only $8 million.

Over the years, the film made a strong comeback in the US video and DVD market with the release of the longer version. The uncut version of the film is universally considered superior to the severely edited version originally shown in America.

James Woods, who considers *Once upon a Time in America* Leone's finest work, mentions in the DVD documentary that one critic dubbed the film the worst of 1984, only to see the original cut years later and call it the best of the 1980s. Roger Ebert called the original uncut version of *Once upon a Time in America* "the best film depicting the Prohibition era." When *Sight and Sound* asked several UK critics what their favorite films of the last twenty-five years were in 2002, *Once upon a Time in America* came in tenth place.

The film instantly propelled Milchan into the ranks of Hollywood's cutting-edge producers, earning him a reputation as a bold risk taker. Unfortunately, *Once upon a Time in America* took a substantial toll on Sergio Leone's health. It was to be his last film, and on April 30, 1989, he died of heart failure.

But shortly before his death, Leone gave his friend Arnon a gift that to this day sits next to the swimming pool at his chateau at Montfort-l'Amaury. It's a life-sized sculpture depicting a man sitting in front of a table, and a plate full of money. The name of the sculpture is *The Last Supper of a Greedy Man*. There is no hidden message, only a reminder that life is short, and what we do with our limited time is what matters most.

Arnon's friendship with the reclusive De Niro has remained close to this day. As with Leone, it is expressed in art. A symbol of that friendship hangs prominently in Arnon's Malibu home: an abstract painting by Robert De Niro Sr. given to him as gift.

Another close friend whom Arnon acquired during this period was Canadian prime minister Pierre Trudeau. Trudeau was a huge fan of Sergio Leone, and when he heard that Leone was working on a large production, he arranged for a meeting with him in Rome in an attempt to persuade him to shoot at least part of the film in Canada.

Leone introduced Trudeau to Milchan and the chemistry between them was quickly apparent. It didn't take much to persuade Arnon to agree to film in Canada, and the three enjoyed a long evening of Italian cuisine and fine wine.

A week later, Arnon was staying at a boutique hotel in East Hampton, New York, when he was summoned to the only telephone in the hotel.

"Hello, Arnon? This is Pierre, remember me?"

"Pierre? Pierre who?"

"You know, Pierre Trudeau. We met in Rome."

Arnon was stunned.

"Oh, yes, Pierre, how did you find me?"

"Canadian intelligence isn't completely useless. Listen, Arnon, why don't you come up to Ottawa for the weekend? I want to talk. I'll send my plane over to pick you up."

"It sounds interesting, but take my advice and don't send a public plane to pick me up. I'll make it there on my own."

Milchan and Trudeau found that they had much in common. Both were divorced single parents, and the primary caretakers of three children, and both were flamboyant playboys. Between Trudeau's high-profile position as Canada's prime minister, and Milchan's emergence as a big-time movie producer, it didn't take long before the good times began to roll. Extravagant parties, celebrities, wine, women, and rock and roll.

"The level of trust between us was extraordinary," Arnon confirmed. "I even advised him during the 1983 G7 Summit in Williamsburg, Virginia. At one point, Trudeau left me with a stack of confidential documents describing Canada's entire strategy for the G7." Their close friendship lasted until Trudeau's death on September 28, 2000.

* * *

As the sights of the United States Customs Service and the FBI were focused on Milco in Huntington Beach, Milchan was making a movie and executing another large transaction involving the B80 Queen Air light transportation aircraft and the King Air electronic intelligence-gathering aircraft, both from Beechcraft. It was business as usual.

But for Milco, it was anything but. While Richard and Emilie Smyth flew off to Europe for a NATO conference, US Customs agents, armed with a federal search warrant, raided Milco's offices in Huntington Beach in an effort to confiscate all files related to shipments to Israel. They proceeded to tear the place apart, but left frustrated and empty-handed. The files had been moved. They also left the Smyths' children, who were holding down the fort, scared and confused.

Then on Christmas Eve in 1984, Richard Kelly Smyth was going through his daily stack of mail at Milco. Buried deep in the middle of the stack was an official-looking letter from the office of the federal district attorney of the District of Central California. Smyth felt that sudden sinking feeling in the pit of his stomach that told him nothing good was going to emerge from inside that envelope. He had no alternative but to open it, and with hands shaking, that's what he did:

> Dear Mr. Richard Kelly Smyth,
>
> You are hereby ordered to appear at the Federal Prosecutor's office in Los Angeles to answer questions about exporting krytrons without a license, and to discuss possible high crimes and misdemeanors that have been committed by you....[7]

---

7. Schiller, *Irrational Indictment and Imprisonment*, 7.

A deep chill went through Smyth's body. He called a close associate and a Milco shareholder, Brian Carter, who was a past corporate attorney at Rockwell International. The attorney was stunned. He immediately understood the implications for his longtime friend. "Richard, you are about to meet a part of the US government that is very different from the people you have dealt with up until now."[8]

He explained that the job of the federal district attorney was essentially to put as many people into federal prison as he or she could. In fact, the more people the federal district attorney succeeded in putting in federal prison, the more raises, bonuses, and promotions he or she would receive. It was an ugly truth.

The attorney recommended that Smyth immediately hire the best lawyer he could find and gave him a recommendation. Smyth's next phone call was to Milchan. Once again, he was unable to get past Dvora, Milchan's firewall.

8. Ibid., 8–9.

14 ‖ Falling Down

The unbelievable stupid krytron story.... At the end of the day, you can't be expected to read scripts, go to marketing meetings, and still worry about everything else.

Arnon Milchan, *Los Angeles Times*, February 28, 1992

The second most horrifying day in Richard Kelly Smyth's life was also the day that one of Israel's important networks in the United States, established by Milchan, collapsed.

During the first week of January 1985, Smyth walked into the Los Angeles Federal Courthouse for his scheduled appointment with the ambitious federal district attorney. The meeting did not go well. In Smyth's opinion, the prosecutor, William F. Fahey, was antagonistic and accusatory.

According to Smyth, Fahey considered anything coming out of his mouth to be untruthful. He made it clear that he believed Smyth had committed horrible crimes and insinuated that he was in possession of stacks of sensitive information far exceeding the nuclear triggers issue. As far as Fahey was concerned, krytrons were just the tip of the iceberg. When Smyth failed to come clean immediately, he accused him of refusing to cooperate. When Smyth denied that he was not cooperating, Fahey slammed

163

a waiver of statute of limitations[1] document on the table right in front of him and insisted that he sign it: "Really? Prove it!"

The document affirmed that anything that happened more than ten years before could be used in his case. Wanting to appear cooperative, and with the approval of his attorney, Smyth signed it.

He then proceeded to tell Fahey about his illustrious career, and the substantial contributions that he had made to the defense of the United States. He pointed to important science and technology commissions that he served on for the Pentagon, NASA, and NATO, and about his civilian rank as the military equivalent of a three-star general. He also stated that he had no idea what krytrons were actually used for.

"Is this your signature, Mr. Smyth?" Fahey abruptly interrupted him while whipping out another document. It certainly looked like his signature, and it was on a 1975 State Department munitions export license application for krytrons. Smyth confirmed that it was.

Fahey pointed out that the document represented a smoking gun in the form of evidence that Smyth knew he needed a munitions export license for krytrons because he had applied for one in the past and been rejected. He then asked Smyth point-blank why he would ship nuclear triggers without the munitions export license.

By now Smyth was totally confused and literally shaking with fear: "I don't remember that application."[2]

Fahey's tone turned deeply cynical. With all that expertise that Smyth had just described, he pointed out that any jury would have a hard time believing that he didn't know what krytrons were used for and didn't remember his first attempted shipment in 1975.

Now that Fahey had Smyth exactly where he wanted him, he turned his attention to the bigger fish, Arnon Milchan. "Tell us about this Israeli movie producer."

At this critical moment, Smyth had little reason to defend Milchan, but stated that he did not know of anything illegal that Milchan had done,

---

1. Schiller, *Irrational Indictment and Imprisonment*, 9.
2. Ibid.

and that if an error was made, it had been innocent. Fahey pressed harder, implying that he might go easier on him if he cooperated.

Smyth could think of nothing, which only served to exacerbate Fahey's aggressiveness and his sense that Smyth was hiding something.

Smyth learned later that the US Attorneys' Office would have had a much tougher time proving their case against him if they hadn't been able to use the 1975 munitions control export license that Smyth had applied for in his original order of krytrons for Israel. The statute of limitations had expired on that. In essence, he had unknowingly signed on to crucial evidence against himself, with his lawyer nodding in agreement. It was a bad day all around.

Fahey informed Smyth that he'd ordered the interrogation of his children, ages seventeen and twenty, who had worked at Milco. They were to appear before a grand jury that he intended to convene in order to secure an indictment against him. The idea was to scare his children into believing they might be accused of a crime, and to put the fear of God into Smyth.

The investigation into Milco was only a small part of a much larger project known as Operation Exodus, a special US Customs action that the Reagan administration designed and initiated to cut off spying and smuggling of military-related technology and goods in general. The public purpose of the operation was to crack down on the dual-use market.

It was funded with $30 million from the Department of Defense budget, which was transferred to US Customs in 1981. After a few years of operation, pressure mounted to show real results. A total of 2,330 shipments worth $148.8 million and determined to be illegal were seized and 221 indictments were brought down, but in the end only twenty-eight people were actually convicted as a result of Operation Exodus.

That pace was not good enough for the administration. They wanted arrests, they wanted headlines, and they wanted blood. They needed a few heavy sentences to act as a strong deterrent, and to demonstrate that there was a new sheriff in town. The result was what became known in 1985 as the Year of the Spy.

If things were bad at Milco before Smyth's visit to the prosecutor's office, they were verging on absolute disaster now. In April 1985 Smyth's lawyer James Riddet called to inform him that he'd be indicted for smuggling nuclear triggers to Israel. He wasn't sure what charges would actually be leveled and would only know for sure when the indictment was announced the following month. He also warned him there might be some media interest in the matter and that he should prepare himself. Smyth was horrified by the prospect.

Smyth informed his attorney that the indictment was set to come down precisely at the time when he and his entire family had planned to go on a long-scheduled vacation to Israel to visit Jerusalem and other holy sites, with a stopover in Europe on the way back. The prosecutor reluctantly complied with the court's approval of the trip on the condition that Smyth post a $1 million bond guaranteeing his return.

Smyth re-mortgaged his waterfront home in Huntington Beach to get the $100,000 cash needed for the bond. He then purchased nine tickets for his family, which included two of his children and a number of in-laws. On May 12, 1985, the Smyth family took off on a TWA flight from Los Angeles that was scheduled for a quick layover in Paris on the way to Tel Aviv.

At Charles De Gaulle Airport the plane was stocked with the latest edition of the *International Herald Tribune* and Smyth thanked the flight attendant for handing him a copy. He casually opened the paper and was stunned to read the headline "Businessman Indicted for Smuggling Nuclear Triggers to Israel." The article was riddled with his name throughout. He couldn't help but notice other passengers reading the same article and feeling embarrassed, as if they were looking at a wanted poster of him. But what really shocked Smyth was that he learned deep inside the article, for the first time, that he could expect up to 105 years in prison and a $1.5 million fine.

Simply put, he couldn't believe his eyes; it was as if they were talking about somebody else. After all, it was just a question of failing to fill out the proper paperwork on a $75 item. How could that possibly mean 105 years in prison?

Smyth was also shocked to a lesser degree by the fact that prosecutors had revealed publicly for the first time that krytrons were used for the purpose of detonating nuclear bombs. That was not public knowledge until the prosecutors released the sensitive information in their quest for publicity about the case. Normally the release of such information might itself be considered an indictable offense, or at the very least irresponsible. The cat was out of the bag. Now every person on earth with a krytron also knew that they were in possession of a nuclear trigger.

The Smyths arrived in Israel as tourists. There would be no special treatment at the airport this time; they stood in the long lines like everyone else. After going through passport control and customs, they took taxis to the Tel Aviv Hilton.

Smyth was not the only one panicking over the sudden publicity. Similar articles appeared in newspapers throughout the United States, Europe, and around the world, receiving the full attention of Milchan, the Israeli Ministry of Defense, the Ministry of Foreign Affairs, and Prime Minister Peres himself. A rapid series of phone calls and meetings took place between LAKAM, the Mossad, Minister of Defense Yitzhak Rabin, Shimon Peres, and Milchan. Then Milchan asked Peres to call Reagan for help.

In short order, Israel's response was formulated, and the telephone rang at the US embassy in Tel Aviv. Within hours of the worldwide publication of the Milco-krytron episode on May 13, 1985, three well-briefed representatives from Israel's Ministry of Defense and Ministry of Foreign Affairs arranged for a high-level meeting with their American counterparts in Tel Aviv. The Israelis offered the Americans a document stating that the krytrons imported by Heli Trading Ltd. were put to the following uses: remote range finders, radar laser detectors, and fire control systems. The Israelis offered to return the krytrons that had not been used. They stated that exactly one hundred of the krytrons had been "destroyed" during tests.

Negotiations between the two countries lasted for days. Ironically, during the time that Smyth and his family were actually in Israel, staying at the Hilton up the road from the US embassy on HaYarkon Street,

710 krytrons were returned to the US embassy and immediately shipped to the US by diplomatic pouch to serve, among other things, as evidence against Smyth. As for the 100 "destroyed" krytrons, the Israeli Ministry of Defense issued a formal declaration that Israel didn't use them for any nuclear purposes, and that none were transferred to any other country.

It is not known at what level Milchan's name came up in these negotiations, or whether there were any direct phone calls from Peres to the White House as Milchan had requested. But what we do know, from Shimon Peres, is that at the same time, in May 1985, the Israeli prime minister received a top-secret visitor, Michael Ledeen, who was on a mission from Robert McFarlane, President Reagan's national security advisor. Ledeen asked Peres for help in seeking ways to influence Iran with regard to US hostages being held in Lebanon. Israel, of course, was more than happy to assist. The understanding reached between Ledeen and Peres was, among other things, the beginning of Israel's involvement in the notorious Iran-Contra affair.[3]

What Israel received in return is a matter for speculation. "All I know is that after my private meeting with Peres, he called the US ambassador in Israel, Sam Lewis," said Ledeen. It's interesting, to say the least, that shortly after the return of the krytrons, the secret Peres-Ledeen discussion, and the Peres-Lewis phone call, the deputy State Department spokesman and special assistant to Reagan, Edward Djerejian, made a point of publicly stating that he could "only note that the indictment does not mention any Israeli citizen" in regards to Milco. Djerejian added that the United States "has expressed its serious concern to the Israeli government about this alleged violation of US law," and had been assured that Israel would cooperate with the continuing US investigation "to the full extent permitted under Israeli law."[4]

It's almost unheard of for an assistant to the president of the United States to go out of his way to make special public note of who was "not mentioned" in an ongoing indictment procedure. Whatever quid pro quo did or did not take place, Milchan was suddenly in the clear.

---

3. Peres, *Battling for Peace*, 213.
4. Goshko, *Washington Post*, May 14–17, 1985.

Meanwhile, as his family toured the region's historic sites, Smyth didn't join them. Unaware of the negotiations going on at the US embassy, and the top-secret meetings between Ledeen and Peres, Smyth frantically searched for Milchan. He went to Milchan's office; he called every number that he knew; he went to restaurants that they had frequented; he reached out to LAKAM and other high-level officials and politicians with whom he had come in contact over the years through Milchan. Every door was shut. Most insisted that Milchan was at the Cannes Film Festival, which takes place annually in May. Secretaries were nice and polite, but clearly, after days of seeking assistance or even just a sympathetic ear, Smyth began to realize that he was up against a brick wall and that he wasn't going to find a solution to his precarious situation in Israel. There would be no secret asylum there, because Israel had no intention of jeopardizing its special relationship with the United States over a foreign operative, as sympathetic as they may have been. On previous visits he'd been treated like a semi-celebrity, hobnobbing with the who's who of Israel's security and intelligence establishment. Now he couldn't get past their secretaries, not on the phone and not in person. Suddenly he was a nobody. It seemed he would have to face the entire matter on his own.

And then he received a call from Milchan's assistant, Dvora. They met and discussed his situation at length. Smyth was asked what information he'd divulged to the prosecutor about shipments to Israel and about Milchan specifically. Smyth insisted that he'd said nothing incriminating or even embarrassing. Then the conversation turned to his predicament. Obviously, if the prosecutor pressed forward with an indictment involving the possibility of life in prison, then dangled a plea bargain, for the sake of his family and his life he'd be hard put not to take it.

Some suggested that Milchan should delay travel to the United States, at least until the entire matter blew over. But following the understanding with the US, he received the green light for travel. Milchan was in the midst of another dramatic episode related to one of his films, and had no intention of missing a previously scheduled meeting in Hollywood. As his flight approached Los Angeles International Airport, there was no absolute certainty of what awaited him, or whether word of the agreement had trickled down to the lowly customs and immigration officer behind the desk. He approached the immigration counter as he had done a hundred times before. The immigration officer inspected his passport carefully, looked up at Milchan, handed him the passport and said, "Welcome back."

Around the same time, Smyth returned with his family to the United States. Upon arriving home, he was immediately instructed to surrender his passport, and the million-dollar bond was lifted.

The trial was scheduled for mid-August. If business was horrible before, following the devastating publicity of his indictment it was now nonexistent. His reputation as a dedicated patriot with a lifetime of work for the defense of his country was completely destroyed. He couldn't sleep. A long list of people whom he'd considered professional and personal friends, even lifelong friends, were now avoiding him like the plague. He'd become radioactive.

There was no money coming in, and bill collectors were hounding him. He tried to keep up appearances and continued to go to the office. He kept the books in order, like someone straightening the deck chairs on the *Titanic*. Something had to give. His wife Emilie had been strong and supportive. During moments of weakness, Smyth was tempted to call his attorney and instruct him to just throw him at the mercy of the prosecutor. It was his wife Emilie who refused to allow him to do it. She'd even hide the phone in fear that he'd give such instructions when she wasn't present.

But then Emilie had her own breakdown. One day she could take it no longer. Rushing out of the Milco office, sobbing, she drove directly home and promptly drank an entire bottle of vodka, all at once. Their daughter found her unconscious on the floor. She tried to revive her but couldn't. Emilie was rushed to the hospital where she slowly recovered. It was a close call.

Finally August rolled around. Only days before his trial, Smyth received a call from his attorney's assistant informing him that it was the firm's professional opinion that there was a very good chance he'd face prison, and they were urging a plea bargain.

"How can I go to prison? I haven't done anything wrong!" Smyth insisted.

The paralegal thought that was funny. "Don't you know that prisons are full of people who didn't do anything wrong? I've known that since I was nine years old."[5]

Smyth was shocked and not amused by the cavalier attitude, as it was his life on the line. By then he had paid his attorneys $60,000, only to learn from a paralegal that they felt their case was weak. He immediately lost all confidence in his attorney and his ability to defend himself.

At that moment Smyth and his wife made their fateful and final decision to follow the preset plan that would change their lives forever. Since his last meeting in Tel Aviv, he'd been thinking about it and preparing for it. Just days before the trial, they informed their children that they were going to Catalina Island for rest and relaxation before the stressful trial was to begin. "We didn't want them to be accused of helping us," Smyth confirmed. They'd leave all of the real estate and other illiquid assets in the US for their children to take care of. They took Milco's $15,000 emergency cash reserve, and Richard dyed his gray hair completely black.

They packed lightly, and nervously departed from the parking garage. They were in a state of deep fear and paranoia that they might be followed. They drove randomly for about twenty minutes, changing lanes, making quick U-turns and detours to shake potential followers. Once satisfied that they were not being tailed, they merged with the 405 freeway heading north and exited at Century Boulevard toward Los Angeles International Airport.

They left their car in the parking structure in front of the new Bradley International Terminal, left the keys in the ignition, and arrived at the ticket counter about forty minutes before the flight. They checked in and paid for the tickets in cash.

"We were both nervous and kept scanning the waiting area for anyone who might be following us. We were relieved when the announcement came over the loudspeakers and hurried to board the aircraft twenty minutes before engine fire-up. We would fly nonstop to our destination,

5. Schiller, *Irrational Indictment and Imprisonment*, 19.

arriving at just after five p.m. All that we were carrying after our thirty-four years of marriage were the two under-the-seat luggage pieces," Smyth recalled.[6]

The flight was comfortable in coach; they had an empty seat between them but barely spoke the entire flight. They were in a state of shock and disbelief at what they had just done and the implications for the rest of their lives.

When Richard Kelly Smyth failed to show up for his own trial it was big news. Chaos erupted in the courtroom as Federal Prosecutor William Fahey luodly demanded an arrest warrant. The presiding judge in the case, Pamela Ann Rymer, immediately granted the warrant and also ordered that Interpol be notified that Smyth was a fugitive from justice and should be arrested and extradited back to the United States immediately.

Incredibly, upon exiting the courtroom, surrounded by reporters, Smyth's lawyer James Riddet acknowledged that Mr. Smyth had shipped the nuclear triggers without a license.[7] The prosecutor made a note of Riddet's comments and vowed to call Riddet as a witness against Smyth if he was ever brought back to trial, attorney-client privilege be damned.

As all of that was happening, Richard and Emilie Smyth were safely out of the country. Over the years, many journalists and pundits speculated that the Smyths had fled to Israel and were hiding in the upscale town of Herzliya Pituach, north of Tel Aviv, where Milchan maintains a home. Others theorized that as an expert sailor, he escaped by sailboat to Mexico and on to Europe from there. Yet other rumors suggested that he was eliminated by the Mossad.

He was indeed seen in Herzliya Pituach looking for Milchan during his trip to Israel, just as his indictment became public a few months earlier in May 1985, but he returned to the US before the trial in August. That timeline may have been the source of the confusion and rumors of sightings in Herzliya.

Upon arriving in Frankfurt, Germany, and clearing the aircraft, they nervously arrived at their first hurdle: German passport control. The agent

---

6.   Ibid., 21.

7.   "Engineer Pleads Not Guilty to Bomb Component Exports," *New York Times*, November 27, 2001.

slowly opened the passport of a Dr. Jon Schiller. He looked at the photograph and the detailed information. Everything was a spot-on match. He stamped the passport, said, "Welcome to Germany," and handed it back. Smyth had passed the first of many tests to come.

After staying in Frankfurt for the night, the Smyths rented a car and began the long drive through the beautiful countryside to their initial destination, where they planned to lay low and contemplate how to live out the rest of their lives.

15 ‖ Fight Club

Anti-Semitism is anti-Semitism, even when it comes from an assimilated Beverly Hills Jew.

Arnon Milchan, in Jack Mathews' *The Battle of Brazil*

The year 1985 was the worst of times and the best of times for Milchan. Incredibly, as his Milco operation collapsed all around him and his name was splashed all over the international press in association with the only nuclear-triggers smuggling scandal ever recorded, Milchan was producing two high-profile and highly problematic films, and was simultaneously conducting what became notoriously known in Hollywood as the battle of *Brazil*, a monumental struggle involving Milchan and one of Hollywood's most powerful executives that would set a historic precedent and propel Milchan to legendary status in the movie industry. The term "the battle of *Brazil*" was coined by retired journalist Jack Mathews, who covered the entire episode for the *Los Angeles Times* in the mid-80s. In 1987 he wrote a detailed book by the same name with the cooperation of Milchan and director Terry Gilliam, itself worthy of a Hollywood movie.[1]

It all began when the temperamental Gilliam, of Monty Python fame, met Milchan on a cold evening in March 1982 at the Elysée Matignon restaurant in Paris, which served as Milchan's informal office. The meeting

---

1. Arnon Milchan confirmed the details of the production of the movie *Brazil* to the authors.

was arranged by Robert De Niro's agent, Harry Ufland. Gilliam, like many directors who consider themselves artists above all, had a strong distrust of the Hollywood system, and Milchan was already gaining a reputation as a maverick producer willing to take on risky projects that institutional Hollywood would not touch. There were also rumors, and perhaps even a certain allure, about the source of his funding, which only enhanced his emerging status as a Hollywood rebel with deep pockets. "Everybody I talked to said, 'Stay away from this guy. He's an arms dealer making movies. He's too slippery. He can't be pinned down.' It was a matter of the pots calling the kettles black and he sounded better all the time. I figured if everybody in Hollywood is badmouthing him, if everyone's against him, he must be OK."[2]

In reality, Milchan was uncomfortable with his growing reputation as the unconventional producer of unconventional films. He ultimately wanted to find his way into Hollywood's establishment, but he felt he first had to pay his dues and make his mark, and that inevitably would involve risky and attention-getting projects.

His choice of the Elysée Matignon restaurant as his "office" was no accident. It was down the street from his apartment, and walking distance to the stage production of *Amadeus*, starring Polanski, who would often join him for dinner after the show, usually high on adrenaline.[3] The dinners would often turn into wine-fueled, raucous social events, with friends and guests getting sloshed and arguing about everything from modern art to geopolitics. After small talk and more than a few drinks, Gilliam and Milchan hit it off, and Gilliam proceeded to tell Milchan about a project that he'd been working on called *Brazil*, adding that Paramount Pictures had already signed on.

Milchan was mesmerized as Gilliam painted a colorful picture of *Brazil*, scene by scene, frame by frame, his hands flying excitedly in all directions and strange sounds coming out of his mouth. Milchan had trouble following the structure of the storyline – but as a visual learner, he could clearly

---

2. Cited in Mathews, *The Battle of Brazil*, 30.
3. Ibid.

see the images in his mind and was moved by the emotional foundations
of this abstract and surreal story.

Imagine a strange world somewhere in the twentieth century, a gritty,
urban hellhole patched over with cosmetic surgery. Automation pervades
every facet of life, and paperwork, bureaucracy, inefficiency, and mechanical
failures are the rule of the age. *Brazil* begins with Sam Lowry, a low-level bureaucrat whose primary interests in life are his vivid fantasies about a woman,
to the tune of the 1940s big-band hit "Brazil," hence the name. Lowry inad-
vertently gets involved with a terrorist intrigue when his dream girl turns up
as the neighbor of a man arrested for terrorist activity on account of a typo-
graphical error. The real terrorist is actually a renegade heating technician.

A mysterious wave of terrorist bombings is met by an increasingly
powerful Ministry of Information, whose jackbooted thugs would never
admit to arresting and torturing the wrong man. Lowry's simultaneous
pursuit of the truth and the girl draws him into the higher echelons of the
Ministry of Information despite mounting warning signs that his quest
will inevitably endanger him, subject him to "friendly torture," and, ultimately, drive him to insanity.

As an independent spirit, Milchan could identify with Lowry's character and couldn't help but think of another Ministry of Information that he
was keenly aware of in his own life through South Africa's former secretary
of information, Eschel Rhoodie.

Along with the wine, he could feel Gilliam's powerful vision sinking
in. It was a strange story that took Gilliam about an hour to tell. Just as
he was winding down, Polanski arrived from his show and that's when the
fine wine really began to flow. In the midst of the relaxed conversation,
Milchan turned to Gilliam and casually mentioned that Brazil was the
kind of project that he'd like to have his name on.

"Are you serious?" Gilliam asked.

"Sure, I wish I could," Milchan answered.[4]

The very next morning, Gilliam called his attorney in Los Angeles and
instructed him to cancel the deal with Paramount. Gilliam then called
Milchan to give him the news.

---

4. Ibid., 29.

Milchan had casually discussed envisioning his name on Gilliam's strange fantasy over a few glasses of wine, and the next thing he knew, he had committed to putting up millions of dollars.

He hadn't read the script; he had no idea what the budget was; he had no idea who was going to be in the movie; he had no idea what Terry Gilliam's director's fee might be.[5]

He only knew that he instinctively liked Gilliam and the vision that had been presented to him the previous evening.

Milchan called his attorney Kenneth Kleinberg in Los Angeles and told him to draw up the papers. Kleinberg strongly suggested that Milchan had lost his mind. Nonetheless, the project was a go as far as Milchan was concerned. Gilliam extracted from Milchan total creative control and final cut rights.

It was a little over a year later, at the Cannes Film Festival in 1983, when things started to get interesting for the *Brazil* project. Everybody was talking about *Once upon a Time in America* going into production and *The King of Comedy*, which had opened in the United States. Milchan arrived in Cannes with his entourage of Robert De Niro, Jerry Lewis, and director Martin Scorsese. The studio suits took notice.

Gilliam was also an attraction that year with the release of Monty Python's *The Meaning of Life*. Milchan and Gilliam decided to allocate a portion of their time to selling *Brazil*, and calculated a rough budget of $12 million.

Sean Daniel, Universal's president of production and a Monty Python fan, set up the meeting with Milchan and Gilliam at the Carlton Hotel, the same hotel where a year earlier Milchan had connected with Sergio Leone.

In the room were Bob Rehme, the new head of Universal Pictures, Ian Lewis, Universal's international production chief, and Sean Daniel himself. Gilliam pitched the story with his typical animated enthusiasm on steroids. Unfortunately, without the wine, there only seemed to be a modest level of interest and no firm commitment. The appetite for an art-house film was limited.

---

5. Ibid., 30.

On the way out of the hotel, Milchan and Gilliam ran into Joe Wizan, the new head of Twentieth Century Fox. Milchan immediately pumped up the meeting they had just had with Universal, exaggerating the level of excitement in the room and suggesting that Wizan should strike while he still could.

Wizan mentioned that he might have an interest in the international rights, which would amount to about one-third of the budget, on the condition that they have a firm commitment from Universal on the domestic rights, which represented the other two-thirds of the budget.

Milchan took Wizan's limited verbal agreement and ran for the end zone. He rushed to a hotel house phone and tried to reach Rehme back in the suite from which they had just come, but he was not answering. Boldly, Milchan went directly back up to Rehme's room and barged in on a meeting that he was conducting with two associates.

"Excuse me, gentlemen, but I need just two minutes," Milchan insisted.[6] Rehme waved Milchan over to the next room to speak with him privately.

"Bob, I have to know right now what you want to do. Joe Wizan is waiting." A blatant exaggeration.

"How much is this movie going to cost?"

"Fifteen million."

"Can we have the world?"

"No, I've already promised foreign to Fox. You can have domestic for two-thirds."

"I cannot do that, Arnon. I can't go ten million. The most we could go is nine."

"That's fine, nine it is, I'll put up the rest," Milchan said.

Thus the deal was sealed with Universal in less than a few moments. Milchan then rushed back to Wizan with the confirmation from Universal and got him to commit to the $6 million based on Universal's commitment. Within a blink of an eye, Milchan had upped the *Brazil* production budget by $3 million. Gilliam, frantically running behind Milchan

---

6. Ibid., 39.

through the corridors of the hotel, marveled at his maneuvering. Within weeks, the contracts were drawn up.

Unfortunately, both Wizan's and Rehme's days at Fox and Universal were limited, and when the personnel change at the studios occurred, Milchan and Gilliam strongly suspected that *Brazil* would be on the chopping block, especially at Universal, where Frank Price moved over from Columbia Pictures to become chairman of the motion picture group. Milchan and Gilliam quickly rushed *Brazil* into production to place Universal in a position where they would be in serious and expensive contractual violation should they pull the plug. Price, who was indeed in the process of pulling the plug on *Brazil*, now had to live with it.

The script approved in the contract between Universal and Milchan was 161 pages long. Both parties knew enough about their industry to know that a single page of script, generally speaking, translates into one minute of film, so the film would obviously come in at around two hours and forty minutes – and that's exactly how long it was a year later when it was presented to the studio suits at Universal and Fox.

The executives from the two companies walked away from the original screening with two vastly different perspectives. Fox's Larry Gordon, who had taken over from Joe Wizan, was comfortable with what he saw; as far as Fox was concerned, the movie was ready for distribution internationally. But the executives from Universal, though complementary, were adamant about the film being too long and too bleak. They were concerned about how such a surreal movie could be marketed. It was viewed as a provocative art-house film, a polite term in Hollywood to describe films perceived as commercially unviable.

Following the original screening, months went by without Gilliam or Milchan hearing from Universal regarding domestic distribution. Then one day Milchan received a call from Universal's lawyer Melvin Sattler pointing out that the provision in his contract with Universal regarding the length of the film had been mistakenly left blank. He explained that it was a simple clerical error and requested that Milchan and Gilliam sign an amendment confirming the length issue.

Sattler framed the issue as a routine matter, and asked Milchan to sign the amendment as a personal favor, if only for the sake of covering the lawyer's rear end. Milchan did not think much of it, but Gilliam was immediately suspicious and urged him not to sign it. He sensed that Universal intended to use the time-limit clause to force creative control.

At this stage, Milchan was far less paranoid than Gilliam and more interested in maintaining a positive relationship with Universal. On October 10, 1983, he faxed in the signed amendment, which read, "Running time: not less than 95 minutes and not more than 125 minutes."

By now Gilliam had sent in his final cut, and thirty or so senior Universal executives convened in the Alfred Hitchcock Theater on the Universal lot in Los Angeles to assess the project. Gilliam watched as they filed out of the theater and noticed that the younger executives seemed genuinely excited, but the higher-ups and the older executives seemed tense and concerned.

Frank Price quickly disappeared. Sattler, the lawyer who had asked for the running-time amendment, thought that it was "too long." The senior person in the room was Sidney Sheinberg, the president of MCA, the parent company of Universal. Sheinberg thought that the film was too long and depressing, and not commercially viable. He said, "We're going to have to sell this as the film of the decade," a Hollywood euphemism for "I don't know how the hell we are going to sell this piece of crap."

Milchan, with his limited grasp of American culture, didn't comprehend the euphemism and took Sheinberg to mean that it was a great movie, but Gilliam immediately understood that they were in for a rough ride with Universal and prepared himself for a fight. Milchan didn't yet share that view.

A subsequent marketing meeting did not go well, as Universal executives decided that perhaps it was best to treat *Brazil* as a specialty film with a careful and selective release to artsy film festivals first, such as the New York Film Festival in September. Gilliam, meanwhile, insisted on a full-scale release. Things deteriorated quickly from there. Milchan, ever the peacemaker, tried to arrange a phone call between Gilliam and Sheinberg.

Gilliam was to call Sheinberg at a specific time but when he called, he was told that Sheinberg was currently "unavailable." Gilliam was insulted and told the secretary that when he did become available, "Please tell him I think he's very rude." Sheinberg took offense, and when he and Gilliam did connect, he told him so.

Sheinberg, one of the most powerful studio executives in Hollywood, had been through his share of battles and knew how to play the game. He called up his boss Lew Wasserman, the legendary chairman of the board at MCA, and asked that he view the film as a favor. Wasserman was from the old school and *Brazil* was completely incomprehensible to him; his verdict was, predictably, "This picture is unreleasable." Sheinberg had his license to go to war.

Following a film test conducted with UCLA students, which showed that fifty percent of the audience liked the film and fifty percent did not, Milchan and Gilliam met with Sheinberg in his office in the Black Tower on the Universal lot. After a few quick positive comments about how interesting and creative elements of the movie were, he got down to business: The movie needed to be cut back, with a different ending, and some scenes needed to be changed. As Milchan sat silently, Gilliam was steaming.

He rejected every suggestion Sheinberg made, claiming, "This is the movie that we all agreed to make." But Sheinberg stood his ground, insisting that the movie was not going to be released by Universal without the changes. Gilliam rose from his seat and loudly declared, "Before that happens, I will burn the negative and the Black Tower."[7]

Needless to say, this was developing into more than a slight misunderstanding.

The only thing in the contract that Universal had working in its favor was the amended running-time clause. Gilliam could have cut the picture down by a few minutes and Universal would have had nothing to hang their hat on legally. But Gilliam refused to do it. By now, Universal owed Milchan $4.5 million for *Brazil*, and was refusing to pay until it conformed exactly to their contract, which at this point was only an issue of

---

7. Ibid., 74. The "Black Tower" is the executive building of Universal Studios.

length. Sheinberg held the money over Milchan's head, and Milchan was beginning to resent it.

Although angry, Gilliam was also entertained by the irony of the whole situation: Universal was coming to represent in his mind the exact kind of institutional bureaucracy that *Brazil* mocked. It was a case of life imitating art. Gilliam was concerned, however, that Milchan was being torn between his loyalty to his vision of the film and the money Universal was holding back. But as Milchan explained to him, "There is nothing wrong with trying to get back nearly $5 million from an organization that is fucking you."[8]

Out of courtesy to Milchan, Gilliam arranged for the film to be edited down to just 125 minutes and sent it to Universal. The only person to view that version was Sid Sheinberg. He was not happy with it, and had Universal's attorney Melvyn Sattler draft a letter to Gilliam informing him that he intended to proceed with his own editing of *Brazil*, which was their right under contract after "reasonable" attempts at collaboration were rebuffed by the director, a clause that has very rarely been enforced by any studio in Hollywood history.

Universal then sent Gilliam an official request for all of the film and sound tracks so that they could begin their own editing process. Gilliam responded by sending them a complete pile of scrap; little bits of film and sound tracks that he knew would take them months to make sense of. By that time he should have his final version ready. Sheinberg, who was paying his editors by the hour to go through the mess, was fuming.

In early July, Gilliam sent his second cut to Universal. Again, Sheinberg did not like it, but this time he had no choice but to release Milchan's $4.5 million, as they had met the terms of the contract. He informed Gilliam, through Sattler, that Universal was taking over full editing of the film without his input and would be changing it substantially. As far as Gilliam was concerned, it was a declaration of war. Heated letters shot back and forth, but over time it became clear to Gilliam and Milchan that Universal had no intention of releasing *Brazil* as the film was envisioned.

---

8. Ibid., 78.

Despite everything, Milchan naïvely still believed that he had a positive relationship with Sheinberg and Universal Studios. But Sheinberg viewed Milchan much differently. From their earliest encounters it seemed that he had looked down on Arnon as a Middle Eastern rug merchant and an unrefined Jew, obsessed with money – unlike Universal, of course – looking for respectability by using his "questionable" source of wealth to get into the movie business.

It was an interesting outlook, considering the well-documented previous mafia ties of Sheinberg's boss, MCA's longtime chairman Lew Wasserman.[9] It's entirely possible that Sheinberg's attitude would have been different had he known about Milchan's more covert exploits.

It took time for Milchan to realize where Sheinberg was coming from, but eventually he'd be forced to choose between what he perceived as a working relationship with Universal and his commitment to his director's artistic vision. And that day was rapidly approaching.

* * *

By late August 1985, the *Los Angeles Times* and many other publications ran front-page stories on Richard Kelly Smyth's failure to appear for his trial on nuclear-triggers smuggling charges, and Milchan's name appeared in almost all of those articles.

Around the same time, his name also appeared in the *Los Angeles Times'* calendar section in relation to the other explosive conflict that he was involved in. In the article, Milchan described to reporter Jack Mathews a colorful story about an incredible movie that had been delivered on time and under budget but was being nitpicked to death and held hostage by a crusty old studio bureaucrat who had no understanding of the film's artistic vision and wanted to play editor with somebody else's work of art. He told Matthews that he wanted as many film critics as possible to see *Brazil*

---

9.   There are countless documents on this subject. For example, Kathleen Sharp, *Mr. and Mrs. Hollywood: Edie and Lew Wasserman and Their Entertainment Empire* (New York: Carrol and Graff, 2004), 106.

so they could decide for themselves if this studio executive was justified in his actions or even competent enough to judge.

After Milchan hung up the phone with the *Los Angeles Times*, he realized that he had reached the point of no return. He'd crossed the red line and his relationship with Sheinberg (and by extension Universal Studios) would be taking an immediate turn for the worse. Arnon also knew from his earliest days as a child in Israel that if you are in a fight, you must fight to win, and from that moment on the gloves were off. As expected, the newspaper then called Sheinberg to get his side of the story. Needless to say, Sheinberg was not happy.

Within days, the *Los Angeles Times* entertainment section headline read: "*Brazil*: Too Much Movie for America." The article was devastating for Sheinberg. Milchan was portrayed as a producer standing up for the vision of his embattled director against the Hollywood machine and its aloof, suit-wearing executive in the Black Tower. The entire issue was framed as a matter of artistic suppression, censorship, and bureaucratic abuse. Milchan even offered to "pay all expenses for any serious American journalist willing to go outside the United States to see it." He said that he would be renting a theater in Tijuana, Mexico, and busing movie critics down to review *Brazil* and make up their own minds about Sidney Sheinberg's judgment in this matter.

It was devastating stuff. Sheinberg was made out to be obstinate, arrogant, and unreasonable. He was a top Hollywood studio executive, a man accustomed to being respected and even feared. He was used to being sucked up to day and night, answerable to no one but God and Lew Wasserman, and not necessarily in that order. Suddenly, two outlaws were humiliating him in public, making him out to be a bumbling, frustrated filmmaker-wannabe, and he knew that it was probably only the beginning. He was right.

Milchan followed the *Los Angeles Times* story with an appeal to Sheinberg via numerous letters to release his movie in time to qualify for the 1985 Academy Awards. The implication was that Sheinberg didn't even recognize Academy Award material when he saw it. It was the beginning of what Gilliam described as a relentless guerrilla-type war that

Sheinberg, a stationary target, couldn't possibly hope to win in the PR sense. Milchan offered to show *Brazil* at film festivals outside the United States, saying, "Please, come and see what the American studio executive doesn't want you to see."

The international screenings reached the American press and created the kind of relentless buzz that studios usually pay millions for. The most important trade magazine, *Variety*, reported that "Gilliam and producer Milchan declare that they are going to do everything in their power to foil the intention of Universal to trim and re-cut their futuristic black comedy, *Brazil*...."

Milchan and Gilliam then placed a full-page ad in *Variety* that shouted loudly "DEAR SID SHEINBERG: WHEN ARE YOU GOING TO RELEASE MY FILM, *BRAZIL*?" The ad became the conversation piece of the week in the industry, with legendary director Orson Welles publicly taking up the cause. Gilliam decided to show *Brazil* at two film schools in the southern California area and he invited the press. These were not to be official screenings, but for the purpose of "academic discussion." The two schools that he selected for the stunt were USC and CalArts. When Sheinberg got wind of it, he personally called USC's operations manager, Roy Heidicker, and told him that Universal owned the rights to *Brazil* in the United States and that any screening was unauthorized. He did not specifically request that the film be banned on the USC campus, but Sheinberg was a powerful man in town and Heidicker got the message loud and clear.

He canceled the screening just as the theater was packed above capacity, with students hoping to see what all the fuss was about. A tense hostage-like standoff then commenced involving Gilliam, his lawyer Eric Weissmann, and Heidicker. Students waited impatiently as Gilliam would intermittently come on stage to give them updates, but Heidicker refused to allow the projectionist to show the film, to which Gilliam accused him, loudly and on stage, of being "like a Nazi camp guard, turning a blind eye to evil."

Weissmann tried to go over Heidicker's head and called Russell McGregor, head of the USC School of Cinematic Arts, but he couldn't get past his secretary, who said that he was busy. When Gilliam announced that McGregor was "too busy to take our call," about sixty students departed the theater and walked to McGregor's office demanding that he come out to speak with them. McGregor hid in his office and the students began chanting, "Come out! Come out!" It had the potential to get much uglier but Gilliam moved in to calm matters and avoid a full-blown riot. The USC screening was aborted but the point had been made.

The CalArts screening a few hours later was a different experience. The theater was so packed it had become a fire hazard. The film was received with great enthusiasm by the students, who felt like they were involved in something subversive. The students then drafted an emotional letter to Sheinberg demanding the film's release.

Gilliam went on to conduct underground screenings at private homes for LA's leading film critics. Some of the critics were inspired to publish rave reviews in newspapers and magazines, which made Sheinberg seem even more unreasonable. In the press, it seemed everyone loved the film. Sheinberg finally began to realize that he needed to get his side of the story out and he agreed to an interview with Jack Mathews at the *Los Angeles Times*.

Sheinberg then completely trashed *Brazil*, Gilliam, and Milchan in ways that had never been done before or since by a studio executive. He called *Brazil* a rip-off of *1984* with some elements of brilliance but basically unreleasable. He called Gilliam an "unproven filmmaker with a precocious ego." Sheinberg then offered to sell the film back to Milchan.

Milchan jumped at that opportunity and immediately opened discussions with United Artists. He then called Sheinberg offering to buy the film back for $4.5 million. Sheinberg insisted on $5 million plus thirty percent of film rentals and thirty percent of profits from video, paid TV, and syndication. He then went public with his offer, saying to the press, "In Texas, we have a saying, Arnon: 'Put your money where your mouth is.' I'm sure there is a Hebrew equivalent." It was a curious declaration considering that Milchan was taking risks out of his own pocket while Sheinberg was playing with corporate money.[10]

---

10. Personal interview with Milchan, November 2009.

Milchan responded to what he takes to this day as arrogance and an anti-Semitic slur: "Anti-Semitism is anti-Semitism, even when it comes from an assimilated Beverly Hills Jew," was his response in 1985.[11]

Tense and fruitless negotiations continued, but then something happened that even Sid Sheinberg couldn't dismiss, something deeply embarrassing that caused him to surrender. On December 18, 1985, the Los Angeles Film Critics Association met at the Beverly Hills Gun Club to select the winners in the various filmmaking categories for 1985. There was nothing in the bylaws stating that films that had not yet been released could not be nominated. It was decided to place *Brazil* in the pot along with *Prizzi's Honor, Ran, Out of Africa, The Color Purple, Kiss of the Spider Woman, Mask,* and *Back to the Future.* When the votes were tallied, *Brazil* had won best screenplay, best director, and best picture of 1985. Of course the news flash came as a shock to Sheinberg. Milchan received the call while in bed at the Diplomat Hotel in Stockholm, Sweden. When told the news, he jumped out of bed in the dark and smashed his head, nearly knocking himself out cold. The phone went dead.

Gilliam got the news on his answering machine. He broke out in a dance in his kitchen in London as the family looked on in amusement. He knew that by tradition, Universal would be placing an ad in the *Daily Variety* congratulating its winners, and he knew that nothing would make Sheinberg cringe more. "Maybe we'll be pleasantly surprised, and the film will be a hit. I hope audiences love it and that it makes $100 million and I can give Mr. Gilliam and Mr. Milchan credit for making it happen," Sheinberg was quoted as saying.

When the film was finally released, Sheinberg's dismal commercial predictions proved to be correct. For a variety of reasons, including Universal's marketing and distribution failure, *Brazil* went on to be a short-term box office disappointment. However, it has since taken its place among cinematic cult classics, and over time has financially redeemed itself. But few people take note of that today. Primarily, *Brazil* is remembered as the spark for what remains probably the most famous feud in movie-making history. Two underdogs took on one of the industry's most powerful ex-

---

11. Cited in Mathews, *Battle of Brazil,* 114.

ecutives at the largest studio and not only defeated him but humiliated him in the process.

When Sid Sheinberg took on Milchan and Gilliam, he had no idea what he was getting himself into. He assumed that he would squash them like bugs, like anyone else who dared to take on the studio system. People took note, and far from damaging his career, Milchan had made a name for himself at Sheinberg's expense. In an interview a few years later, Sheinberg would claim that he had no recollection of the dispute other than it being about a few contractual issues, implying that it was a small bump in the road for him.

But for some reason he was able to recollect enough about Milchan to state the following: "No one has asserted that Mr. Milchan has any known talent in this business. He has a string of total failures. I think the greatest help he can be to the future of the movie business is to continue his activities in other businesses."[12] He naturally had no idea what Milchan's "other businesses" actually were.

Sid Sheinberg remained at the helm of MCA-Universal until 1995, when he was ousted by the new owners, Matsushita. He received a golden parachute and a studio production deal on his way out the door. He set up a company called The Bubble Factory, which went on to produce the box office flops *Flipper* and *McHale's Navy*. Universal were so unimpressed that they exercised an escape clause in their contract, ending the relationship. Milchan went on to become the largest independent producer in Hollywood with a string of huge blockbusters.

Years later, according to Milchan, on a sunny Sunday on Broad Beach in Malibu, he was strolling along when he encountered a friendly dog and began to play with it. Within moments, the dog's owner suddenly appeared and he was not happy, saying, "Excuse me, that's my dog."

Milchan turned around and saw Sid Sheinberg. "Oh, I guess that means we're neighbors now," he said, surprised.

Sheinberg was neither friendly nor amused. "You're going to reduce the property values around here," he replied. They have never spoken since.

---

12. Ibid.

Following *Brazil*, Milchan's relationship with Terry Gilliam fell apart over a financial conflict. Milchan owned fifty percent of their next film, *The Adventures of Baron Munchausen*. In exchange for relinquishing his interest in the film, Milchan demanded compensation. "We had a signed working relationship, he and I. I had fifty percent of the movie and I didn't have to give it up. Selling fifty percent of a movie for $75,000 isn't being difficult.... I told my attorney to make the deal as painless for Terry as possible."[13]

In the end, Milchan's instinct to walk away from the *Munchausen* project and from Terry Gilliam proved wise from a business perspective. What started off as a $23 million budget ballooned to almost $50 million. The film grossed less than $600,000 on opening weekend, and $8 million in total in the US. It was one of the biggest box-office disasters in Hollywood history. Milchan had dodged another bullet. However, when we asked Milchan to reflect on his early films, he echoed comments that he had made to reporters a few years earlier: they were the best years of his life. "I've made many movies since, but the earliest ones were the most challenging. I have never felt more passionate, in the professional sense, than I did with those early projects." With his unusual ability to compartmentalize, he doesn't take note of the incredible risks, difficulties, and setbacks that his other, more covert enterprise suffered that same year. In 1985 he felt more alive than he ever had, despite the challenges – or rather perhaps because of them.

---

13. Andrew Yule, *Losing the Light: Terry Gilliam and the Munchausen Saga* (New York: Applause Books, 2000), 53.

16 ‖ Mr. and Mrs. Smith

I'm not saying I'm an innocent person, but in
this specific case, I knew nothing about it.

Arnon Milchan, *Premiere* (June 1993)

With a whirlwind of mixed emotions, "Dr. Jon Schiller" and Emilie arrived in their temporary new hometown, Zurich, traveling under their new identities. They knew they'd be in hiding and on the run for the rest of their lives and they planned to make the best of the uncertain situation. They knew that if the Israelis came through, they'd have enough resources to live a modest but comfortable lifestyle. They tried to keep a positive outlook and view the entire matter as early retirement.

Their first order of business was to find the Union Bank of Switzerland in the center of town, where they would open their account. They had a long conversation with their new account executive, who came to recognize their voices and arrange for their ability to bank by phone. They deposited most of the $15,000 that they had brought with them from the Milco emergency fund and immediately began to look for an apartment to rent.

Within a short time they found a small place in the northern part of the city for $400 per month. Emilie rented the unfurnished flat, and went to a nearby department store to purchase minimum necessities: an inflatable mattress, a feather comforter, sheets, towels, and pillows. They also needed to buy a few dishes, pots, pans, and silverware. As soon as they

190

moved their modest new belongings in, they returned the rental car and would rely on Zurich's efficient streetcar system while nervously waiting for instruction.

Both of them were overweight, in their mid-fifties, and they were now both without health insurance. They made a firm decision to shape up and began going on long walks every day toward nearby Uetliberg Mountain, and adopted a rigorous program of early morning exercises. They also became strict vegetarians. Soon they were losing weight and feeling much better. They hoped that their changing physical appearances would help them avoid being easily recognized, as well as put them in good enough shape to increase their chances of escaping on foot if it ever came to that.

They were delighted to discover that Zurich had a first-rate classical opera company that performed in the old opera house almost every night, which they quickly began to take advantage of as a welcome distraction from their ever-present fear and paranoia. Long walks along Lake Zurich and through the campus of the University of Zurich were also helpful distractions. Communication with the locals was manageable; Smyth had learned German as part of the language requirements for his PhD, and they were learning more words every day.

Every week, either Richard or Emilie would visit the UBS branch to inquire about the funds they were expecting so that they could begin to make more permanent arrangements. Beyond their fears of being arrested by the FBI or the CIA, they were terrorized by the thought that the Israelis would fail to deliver, in which case their financial situation would rapidly become desperate.

But with all the fear and the trauma, Richard and Emilie quickly came to love Zurich and their sparsely furnished apartment, which contrasted greatly to the upscale, five-bedroom waterfront lifestyle that they had enjoyed for so many years in Huntington Beach. No more yacht clubs, no more fancy cocktail parties. They rediscovered the joy in simple things and they rediscovered each other.

By early October they sent their first cryptic message to family to inform them that they were alive and OK. The first message arrived anonymously to a friend of Gene Manns, Emilie's mother, living in retirement in Laguna Hills, California. The message was short and simple: "Tell my mother I'm safe."[1] Shortly thereafter, they let their children know where they were, and with great discipline, the family kept the secret from US authorities. From time to time an FBI agent would come by to probe family members about any contact they may have had, but nothing was revealed. Direct letters were never exchanged for fear that the authorities were monitoring the mail; elaborate methods of communication and contact were established over time.

Their youngest son came to Zurich, bringing some of their personal items. He also brought a copy of the *Los Angeles Times* that described the chaotic scene in the courtroom the day Smyth failed to show up for trial: the furious judge, the prosecutor's loud demands for immediate action, the comment from his attorney admitting to his client's guilt, and the fact that the judge had instructed Interpol in London to be notified immediately. That reinforced their need to take every precaution and avoid using any of their old identification, which might be flagged, revealing their location. In Europe, renting cars, staying in hotel rooms, and many other basic activities involved presenting identification, and for foreigners, that meant passports. Their new identities were therefore crucial for basic survival purposes.

And then there was the Smyths' daily paranoia and fear of being caught; sleepless nights were often interspersed with terrible nightmares of being arrested and thoughts about US satellites watching over the world that could read license plates, and wondering whether they were being redirected to search for them. A silly concern in hindsight, but rational thought was not an easy thing to come by under the circumstances.

Smyth describes in his later accounts how one day Emilie had been out shopping and returned earlier than planned, ringing the doorbell to their

---

1. Jane Applegate, "Tell Her 'I'm Safe' – Those Are the Only Words Heard from Wife of Man who Disappeared in Illegal Sales Case," *Los Angeles Times*, October 21, 1985.

apartment. There was no peephole on the door and Smyth was afraid to open it or even respond verbally. He had horrid visions of being arrested and dragged off to jail, extradited back to his tormentors while Emilie would have no idea what happened to him. A panic attack ensued and he couldn't bring himself to answer the door. After a tense few minutes that seemed to last forever, Emilie began to walk around the building hoping Richard would see her outside the window and realize that it was only her. But Richard, a grown man of significant intellect, was squatting in the bathtub behind the shower curtain, too afraid to even peep out the window. Finally, Emilie went back to the front door and did what she was hoping to avoid. She yelled as loud as she could while praying that the neighbors wouldn't hear and report something suspicious; so much for keeping a low profile. Richard heard her yells and with great relief jumped out from behind the curtain and finally let her in. His heart was racing.

Back in Hollywood, in the midst of the battle of *Brazil*, Milchan heard the news that the Smyths had successfully escaped.

While Milchan and Terry Gilliam were advancing both of their reputations in California, Milchan's former operative was now a fugitive living in exile, away from his family, his country, his once solid reputation, and the only life he had ever known. As family members testified, "It was like a death in the family."[2]

By early November 1985, the Smyths were becoming nervous. The first deposit had yet to arrive, the weather was becoming cold and dreary, and their financial resources were rapidly dwindling. Their visits to the bank to check on any deposit that may have been made were becoming more frequent and more desperate. In addition to the fear and paranoia of being discovered and extradited, they became consumed with the terrible idea that they'd been abandoned by the Israelis.

Then on the morning of November 23, 1985, their fears were exacerbated further. Smyth purchased a copy of the *International Herald Tribune* and read news of a naval intelligence analyst by the name of Jonathan Jay Pollard, and his wife Anne, who were arrested on suspicions of espionage after attempting to escape an FBI surveillance team. They couldn't help

---

2. Ibid.

but notice that their personal situations were strikingly similar – husband and wife fleeing for their lives as the husband faces a potential life sentence. They would also later learn that, like the Pollards, they too were handled by a secret organization called LAKAM.

* * *

On the morning of November 21, 1985, Jonathan and Anne Pollard packed their bags, grabbed their wedding album, their cat Dusty, birth certificates, marriage license, and vaccination papers. Just as the Smyths had done only a few months earlier, they were frantically preparing to leave the United States forever. They got into their green 1980 Mustang and, just like the Smyths had done, proceeded to drive in circles, changing lanes, making quick U-turns and detours, desperate to shake any followers. Just like the Smyths, they were frightened and paranoid. Finally, at 10:20 a.m. they arrived at the Israeli embassy gate at 3514 International Drive NW in Washington, DC. They had failed to notice that the FBI had multiple unmarked cars following them.

In close radio communication, when one car dropped off, another would take its position. Pollard never saw a single car following him. Richard and Emilie Smyth had successfully escaped a few months earlier under similar circumstances and the FBI had no intention of allowing it to happen again. This time they had planted an electronic signaling device in the bumper of Pollard's Mustang. Even if he eluded his followers, the electronic signal would reveal the vehicle's location.

According to Pollard, as he had previously arranged with embassy security, the gate at the embassy would be open at precisely 10:20 a.m., and Pollard arrived exactly on time. He drove directly into the embassy compound and the gate closed behind him. "Welcome home," Pollard later recalled one of the guards saying to him as he felt a great sense of relief. Finally, he was safe. But within one minute, the embassy was surrounded by the FBI; a dozen cars, vans, and trucks created a huge commotion on the street outside. FBI agents were spilling out of vehicles and assuming positions around the embassy with high-powered binoculars and communication radios blaring. Embassy security personnel realized what was going on and they quickly huddled. Confused and unsure what to do, they spoke over the phone with a senior officer inside the embassy.

When they returned to Pollard, their entire demeanor had changed. "You must leave," the agent insisted.

"What?"

"You heard me, you must leave."

"Do you know who I am?"

"You must get out."

Pollard couldn't believe his ears. He began to loudly declare that he was a Jew standing on Israeli territory and demanded his rights to citizenship under the Law of Return. It was to no avail. The Israeli agents pushed him back into the car, opened the gate, and ordered him to back out as the small army of FBI agents observed in astonishment from outside the gate. "Drive out now!" Pollard was instructed loudly. He had no alternative, and Anne began crying hysterically in the passenger seat.

Reluctantly, Pollard backed out of the gate, and he and his sobbing wife were immediately handcuffed and placed under arrest by the waiting agents.[3]

Pollard was the last of the eight infamous agents exposed in 1985, widely known as the Year of the Spy. The eight were John Anthony Walker, Sharon W. Scranage, Larry Wu-Tai Chin, Ronald William Pelton, Randy Miles Jeffries, Edward Lee Howard, Jonathan Jay Pollard, and Richard Kelly Smyth.

It was a stunning blow, but it was the abandonment of Pollard to his FBI pursuers in broad daylight that concerned the Smyths most when they read about it. If Pollard could be abandoned like that for the whole world to see, then what was to keep the Israelis from abandoning them as well?

---

3. Wolf Blitzer, *Territory of Lies: The Exclusive Story of Jonathan Jay Pollard: The American Who Spied on His Country for Israel and How He Was Betrayed* (New York: Harpercollins, 1989), 157.

Fortunately for the Smyths, they had misread the events; Israel could ill afford at that moment another high-profile case in the United States. Richard and Emilie Smyth would need to be hidden and well protected as a matter of Israeli national interests. If there were internal dilemmas in Tel Aviv about how to handle their case before the Pollard bombshell, those dilemmas were quickly settled by the new circumstances.

Within days of Pollard's arrest, a substantial deposit was made into the "Schillers'" account. A sense of joy and relief overcame them. They were not alone; the Israelis had come through. But it wasn't just the money; they had also received the message that a more permanent arrangement was awaiting them.

In the wake of Jonathan Pollard's arrest, and his subsequent interrogation, the United States became aware for the first time of an organization called LAKAM. Israel took the official position that the organization was running a rogue operation. In negotiations with the United States, Israel agreed to completely disband LAKAM as part of a wider agreement reconfirming existing understandings that the two nations would refrain from covertly gathering intelligence on each other. Rafi Eitan, Blumberg's successor, was forced to resign, and is banned from travel to the United States to this day. LAKAM, however, continues to operate outside of the United States under a different structure and name.

Despite US righteous indignation of Israeli spying in the United States, the US has continued to spy on Israel. Usually, incidents of US spying in Israel that come to light are handled quietly between the two allies. But as 2010 Wikileaks documents clearly illustrate, US spying on Israel is aggressive, seeking top-secret details about anything from Israeli command, control, and communications systems, to information about current and planned upgrades to communications systems and technologies used by government and military personnel, including cellular phone networks, mobile satellite phones, very small aperture terminals (VSAT), trunked and mobile radios, pagers, prepaid calling cards, firewalls, encryption, international connectivity, use of electronic data interchange, and cable and fiber networks. (See appendix A.)

Oblivious to the political side of the situation, and with their clarified finances, new identities, and a renewed sense of confidence, Richard and Emilie Smyth began to prepare for the long drive to their final destination, their place of retirement and hiding, to live out the rest of their lives. The season was closing in hard and they had no intention of hunkering down through a freezing Swiss winter. Over the decades they had become accustomed to California's mild climate and had mentioned their preference for a location with similar weather if exile and hiding was their only option.

So at the end of November 1985, as the battle of *Brazil* raged, Dr. "Jon" and Emilie "Schiller" packed their few belongings and set out early in the morning in a rental car from Zurich to their new destination. In one full day of driving they had reached Barcelona, Spain, before continuing the next day down the coast to beautiful Malaga, on the Costa del Sol, the hometown of Pablo Picasso and Antonio Banderas. Malaga was a place with a reputation as a haven for fugitives, as well as a place to retire. Rules were lax and immigration status was usually overlooked for anyone not causing trouble under the Mediterranean sun.

They handed in their Avis rental and with a thousand-dollar deposit, a small Fiat Seat Panda awaited them for rent from an independent dealer, with no car registration recording their names. It was this car that became their permanent vehicle in exile.

They then drove to the new home that had been arranged for them at 6 Marcos de Obregon Street, apartment C/2, and were delighted by what they found. The apartment was situated in an upscale, wooded area of town well west of the Malaga harbor, only half a block from a beautiful Mediterranean beach and a lovely promenade lined with restaurants and shops that ran along the length of the beach, ideal for their daily walks.

When the landlord, who was expecting them, asked how long they intended to stay in the apartment, the old lady was pleased to hear the word "forever." They then opened a bank account at a nearby branch of Banco Bilbao under the Schiller name and were able to transfer money back and forth to their UBS account in Switzerland.

The Smyths-turned-Schillers quickly adapted to their comfortable new surroundings, and as the days turned into weeks, and weeks turned into months, the extreme fear that had gripped them was gradually beginning to fade. A sense of security and even normalcy began to return. They realized they were not being followed and that spy satellites in space were not being redirected from their regular activity over the Soviet Union. They were important fugitives, but not that important. In fact, it was convenient for the United States to look the other way; as long as they kept a low profile, no real resources would be allocated to track them down.

Smyth later described how their life in Malaga evolved into a pleasant Mediterranean dream world. The apartment was furnished with everything they needed, including a table for twelve, wonderful carpets, and large original oil paintings throughout. There were fully grown trees in the area providing plenty of shade and a gentle Mediterranean breeze to keep them cool. For additional companionship they purchased two cute Siamese kittens and called them Malaga and Mobettah.

Eventually, they began to make new friends. They discovered that Malaga had a large English-speaking community that had formed a club that met every Monday night at a local beachfront restaurant about a mile from their apartment. After attending their first meeting and enjoying the people they encountered, they joined the club and over time became very active members.

Emilie became the secretary of the club responsible for issuing the monthly newsletter and "Jon Schiller" became the club's vice president. Both "Jon" and Emilie had been relatively proficient in Spanish but within months were almost fluent. Eventually they became quite the social butterflies and well known among the large expatriate community in town.

They discovered the classical music scene in Malaga; the musical university in town offered free recitals each year performed by graduating students, and the university orchestra gave free concerts every month. Malaga even had a 100-member city orchestra, made up of truly talented musicians from all over Europe who were only too happy to live in the Mediterranean sunshine for a modest wage. The concert tickets were very inexpensive, less than a hundred dollars for a season ticket.

Over time, they almost forgot that they were high-profile fugitives, wanted in a notorious and internationally known case. They even participated in the Malaga census and voted in the Malaga municipal elections.

According to the Smyths, Milchan's assistant Dvora Ben Yitzhak maintained regular communication with them by phone and by a fax machine that they purchased for their home office. Eventually, as the age of the Internet dawned, the Smyths purchased a computer and began to communicate via email from the address jonsch@vnet.co.es.

The relationship with Dvora remained close and warm and they updated each other on their activities.

As the Smyths followed Milchan's growing wealth and fame from their relatively modest exile, they also began to wonder why Milchan was not sharing at least a tiny portion of his wealth with them. After all, what would a million or two really mean to a person whose wealth was rapidly being measured in the billions?

The funding that the Smyths received from Israel was enough for all of their basic needs, but not more than that. This was the way to verify that a harbored fugitive would keep a low profile and avoid raising the kinds of suspicions that may accompany a more ostentatious lifestyle. But the Smyths were accustomed to a higher standard of living, and actively sought ways to achieve it. It would be their downfall.

17 ∥ Pretty Woman

No doubt about it, if Arnon didn't exist, fewer films would be made.

Director Sydney Pollack, *Los Angeles Times*, February 28, 1992

While Richard Kelly Smyth was safely tucked away in Spain, far from the grasp of federal prosecutors, Milchan was free to pursue his grand Hollywood dreams. His businesses in Iran had come to an abrupt end following the Islamic revolution; the South African information war had deteriorated into an international scandal; LAKAM had been dismantled, at least officially; and even Taiwan was winding down as Israel established a working relationship with mainland China, which led to full diplomatic relations between the two countries by 1992. All that was left was his bulging bank account, his agrochemical fertilizer business, and the routine defense transactions between the Israeli government and a few elite US defense contractors. Lucrative stuff to be sure, but hardly enough to keep a person like Arnon stimulated.

By then, Ulrika was gone, and a new beauty, Ase Thastrom, took up residence at the chateau in Montfort-l'Amaury. Incredibly, Ase was also from the Swedish town of Gothenburg; Arnon's third companion, after Ulla and Ulrika, was from the same neighborhood of the same city in the same country. Ase accompanied Arnon on many professional and social occasions. "He's a fantastic person, and I have nothing but the highest regard for him," she insisted in our conversation.

200

It was time for some serious soul searching. According to Milchan, "I could have spent the rest of my life sailing around on a yacht but that is not me."[1] And so he began to execute his assault on Hollywood.

Despite his deep desire to become part of Hollywood's ruling elite, he had a long way to go. Even though he loved to work with high-powered, megalomaniacal directors, he was not entirely happy with his reputation as a producer of art-house films. He'd earned wide respect from the artistic community, but felt that the time had come to put his personal tastes and his attraction to prestigious but complicated projects aside, and to focus on commercial success – the kind of films that the big studios stand in line for.

People come to Hollywood to reinvent themselves all the time; it's a land of opportunity that embraces its new players and easily forgets their pasts. Milchan's mysterious background didn't hurt his prospects, and his run-in with Universal's top executive Sidney Sheinberg had only served to enhance his image. Hollywood loves a bad boy.

Rumors of weapons dealings, and the references to his name in a nuclear smuggling case, only served to brighten the halo of mystery and intrigue that hovered over his head. By Hollywood standards, it doesn't matter so much what kind of publicity you get; the matter of concern is whether they spelled your name right. A movie-making "arms dealer" was guaranteed to be an attraction at a cocktail party even if Milchan was certainly not an "arms dealer" in the conventional sense of the term. But in Hollywood people didn't know the difference, and rumors have a way of sinking in.

When Milchan arrived on the scene he was an authentic anomaly from the outset, as he explained to us:

> I was very quickly perceived as a different creature. I didn't easily fit in, and I operated outside the standard practices of the time. Most Israelis that people in Hollywood have met were folks like Menahem Golan and Yoram Globus, in the good case.[2] Or more likely, taxi drivers, street venders, and wheeler-dealers. Suddenly, they met a person who not only understands the financial aspects of

---

1. Caspit, "The Flying Producer."
2. The producers of *Runaway Train*, *Hanoi Hilton*, and *Delta Force*, among many others.

the business, but wants input on the artistic side. It was difficult for others to digest. In Hollywood, there are two parallel tracks – the business side, and the artistic side, and never shall the two meet.

People were skeptical; their attitude amounted to "What do you understand about art? Stick to the money thing and if you want to play with the arts, organize a fundraiser instead of actually doing it." This whole mixing of art and finance was looked down upon. That led to suspicion of my motives. They asked "What is he in it for? Fame? Women? Money?" They kept looking for a hidden agenda that was not there. I just wanted to play in both sandboxes.

The seemingly humble, unpretentious, wealthy producer showed up to important meetings in jeans and a T-shirt, carrying a bag that he presented as his "office." He charmed his way through the system and knew how to impress the right people with a winning mixture of enthusiasm and a shy, humble disposition, even using his status as a foreigner to take advantage of others' natural instinct to be of assistance.

His low profile started a buzz; the man would not attend movie premieres, not even for his own films. He understood that Hollywood throws money at those who have money, so from time to time he would flaunt it, but only with a larger strategic purpose in mind. Metaphorically speaking, the trick was to use the million dollars in the bank to project an image of thirty million. It was his modus operandi since day one. Alan Hirschfield, the past president of Twentieth Century Fox, explained three elements that he perceived as the key to Milchan's success in Hollywood: "He has a lot of money and is willing to risk it. His word is his bond, and he is one of the brightest people that I have ever met."[3]

His ability to hyper-focus on details and his legendary memory were also factors. Others, like director Sergio Leone, describe the key to Milchan's success in simpler terms: "It is his personal charm and the simple fact that he is fun to be around." Milchan has his own explanation:

---

3.   Shanken, "An Interview with Arnon Milchan."

People see in me qualities that in all honesty, I don't see in myself. I am not nearly as refined, humble, or clever as others seem to think I am for some strange reason. Most of my success was built on mistakes. In hindsight, I have no idea how I succeeded. I am without fear and I take risks; perhaps that is the secret. I have never had a master plan for my life, not a business plan and not a personal plan. I am very instinctive, I throw myself into situations and then ask "How in the hell am I going to get myself out of this?" or "How am I going to get this going?" I fall in love with something and then I invest all of my energy so that it will work and succeed.[4]

There are many fitting quotes that in their totality reflect on Milchan's formula; one of them comes from Woody Allen, who famously said in the film *Play It Again, Sam* that "eighty percent of life is just showing up." Milchan showed up.

After a few mediocre films, Milchan hit a modest success with *The War of the Roses*, the ultimate divorce movie, starring Michael Douglas, Kathleen Turner, and Danny DeVito. Shimon Peres recommended the Warren Adler novel to Milchan, and he ran with it. But it was the following year, in 1990, that Milchan's greatest breakthrough occurred with a genuine commercial blockbuster, *Pretty Woman*, the cultural phenomenon and the film that to this day is most often associated with his name.

Pretty Woman is a romantic comedy centering on a down-on-her-luck prostitute, Vivian Ward, who is hired for a week by a wealthy businessman and corporate raider, Edward Lewis, to be his escort for several business functions in Los Angeles high society. The plot focuses on their developing relationship, which materializes into a modern version of Cinderella.

The script, written by J.F. Lawton, circulated around Hollywood for years under the name *Three Thousand*, which was the amount that Lewis pays Ward for her escort services. It was owned by a defunct production company called Vestron. Milchan sent a representative to go through the company's library to see if there was any gem in the pile of scripts during their going-out-of-business sale. The representative phoned Milchan from

4.   Bardach, "The Last Tycoon."

the Vestron library to inform him that he had found an interesting little story involving a prostitute and a businessman. Instinctively, Milchan instructed his representative to offer no more than $3,000, the same price offered to the prostitute. He ended up buying the full rights for a measly $2,500.

Milchan read the script and was unhappy with the unhappy ending: Edward drives Vivian back to Hollywood Boulevard, gives her a mink coat, and drops her off at the exact spot where he had picked her up a week earlier. The following day, Vivian boards a bus to Disneyland to fulfill her pathetic life's dream. The end.

Milchan envisioned a much happier ending in which, after the hotel driver dropped her off, he returns with Edward the same day on a white horse – actually a white limousine – to ask for her hand, if not in marriage, then at least in an exclusive relationship. When Milchan described his vision for the ending, in his conference room, his staff was baffled. His chief operating officer, Steve Reuther, cynically said, "It sounds like a Disney flick."

Milchan reacted with a sudden burst of enthusiasm. "You know what? That's a great idea, get me Jeffrey Katzenberg on the phone." Katzenberg headed Disney Studios at the time and in a few moments he and Milchan were in deep conversation.

"You know, I have a great Disney movie in my hand right here, with a fantastic happy ending."

"What's it about?" Katzenberg asked.

"I'll give you the kosher version. It's about a hooker and a businessman," said Milchan.

"We would not do that in a million years," countered Katzenberg.[5]

But somehow Milchan convinced him to at least read the script. He decided right then and there that if Disney went for it, he'd produce it; if they didn't, he'd drop the script altogether.

A few days later, Milchan received the call back from Katzenberg. He informed Milchan that he had a director, Garry Marshall, who had just done *Beaches* for Disney, and that he had a commitment to do an-

---

5. Shanken, "An Interview with Arnon Milchan."

other movie. Disney had nothing suitable in the pipeline for him, and Katzenberg suggested that Marshall would be an ideal candidate to direct this film.

Katzenberg also expressed his approval of Milchan's idea of a happy ending, and had a long list of additional changes to make it more compatible with the Disney brand. Vivian needed to be new to prostitution, in her first week having fallen into it in order to pay for her college education. In the original script, Ward was addicted to cocaine. That was a nonstarter and quickly nixed. Additionally, Disney insisted that she be "clean," and multiple scenes involving personal hygiene were inserted, including bubble baths and dental floss.

Katzenberg suggested Sean Connery and Michelle Pfeiffer for the lead roles, and Milchan loved the combination.

The first obstacle occurred when he received a letter from Sean Connery declining the role because he felt that he was "too old" for the part. When Milchan informed Katzenberg, he came up with Al Pacino as a replacement.

Three weeks before filming was to commence, disaster struck. First it was a call from Pacino who informed Milchan, "I don't know how to play a businessman, I've never been a businessman. I mean, really, Arnon, it's not for me. I can't do it."[6]

When Michelle Pfeiffer realized that both Connery and Pacino had backed out, she notified Milchan that she was dropping out as well. To this, Milchan responded with one word in Yiddish: "*Farkakta*."[7]

Over the next few days, emergency auditions were conducted. Kim Basinger, Sharon Stone, Madonna, Bridget Fonda, Emma Thompson, and others were considered, but none captured the essence of the role. Wynona Rider and Drew Barrymore seemed too young, and some, like Daryl Hannah and Molly Ringwald, dropped out, considering the role to be demeaning to women.

That evening, Milchan went home depressed and decided to watch a movie to take his mind off of things. The movie he chose was the 1988

---

6.   Five years later, Milchan cast Pacino along with De Niro in his movie *Heat*.

7.   "Messed up."

romantic comedy *Mystic Pizza*. During the film, he noticed a young actress in a supporting role, and instinctively felt she had the appeal and the appearance that he wanted for Vivian Ward. He didn't know or recognize her, and she was largely unknown at the time. He waited for the credits to get her name.

The next morning, he called her agent and asked her in for an emergency audition. She passed the test with flying colors, with an ability to cry and expose deep emotions on a whim. Her name was Julia Roberts.

When Katzenberg was informed of Milchan and Marshall's decision, he expressed his discomfort: "But can she play a hooker, Arnon?"

"Jeffrey, what's wrong with you, any woman can play a hooker. I mean, if she can cry, and be emotional, I'm not worried about her being a hooker."[8]

Katzenberg reluctantly went along.

Now Milchan needed a businessman. John Travolta, Albert Brooks, Sylvester Stallone, and others were considered; all said no.

Then out of the blue, Milchan received a call from Richard Gere, who was on a horrible losing streak at the time with such flops as *King David* and *Power*. "God knows, he couldn't get arrested," Milchan stated.

The budget for the film was lowered to a modest $17 million, along with overall expectations. Milchan instructed COO Steve Reuther not to waste time going to the set. "This thing's not going to make money. Let's concentrate on more commercial opportunities."

When the film was at the rough-cut stage, the mayor of Jerusalem at the time, Ehud Olmert,[9] was visiting Los Angeles. Milchan invited him to a screening of *Three Thousand* on the Warner Brothers lot. In the small theater with Milchan and Olmert were Disney chairman Michael Eisner, Jeffrey Katzenberg, and director Garry Marshall.

During the screening, a number of songs were tested for the soundtrack. One of the songs was Roy Orbison's "Pretty Woman." Olmert turned to Milchan and suggested excitedly that *Pretty Woman* should be

---

8. Shanken, "An Interview with Arnon Milchan."

9. In 2006, Ehud Olmert became prime minister of Israel.

the name of the film. With typical Israeli tact, Milchan replied, "What the hell do you know? How can you call a movie *Pretty Woman?*"

Everyone agreed with Milchan, but Olmert continued to insist. "Do me a favor, try it."

Milchan teased his guest, "What do you know about movie titles?"

In any event, Olmert's suggestion was thrown in, along with a long list of potential titles, to be tested by a focus group. When the results came back, Milchan and everyone else were surprised that *Pretty Woman* received the highest score. Milchan secured the song rights, and *Three Thousand* became *Pretty Woman.*

The movie opened in the US to a modest $12 million at the box office on the first weekend. But momentum built from there and continued to grow in the coming weeks. By the time it faded from the theaters, box-office numbers were about $180 million domestically and $300 million internationally. Not bad for a movie that cost only $17 million to produce, at a time when the average price of a movie ticket was $4.22.[10]

Milchan continues to earn royalties from *Pretty Woman* to this day. Ehud Olmert is satisfied with his modest artistic contribution to the naming of the film, while PLO chairman Yasser Arafat once declared that it was his favorite movie; he kept a copy in his bedroom, and had seen it twenty times, according to Milchan.[11]

The one person who benefited far less than he should have was the screenwriter, J.F. Lawton, who wrote the script for *Pretty Woman* while in his twenties. Lawton, the son of novelist Harry Lawton, overcame severe dyslexia and attention deficit hyperactivity disorder (ADHD) to become an accomplished writer in his own right. Milchan was sensitive to the inequity and promised to purchase Lawton's next script for a million dollars.

* * *

From their distant exile, Richard and Emilie Smyth followed Milchan's Hollywood career and were frequent customers at the local movie theater

---

10. National Association of Theater Owners.
11. Bardach, "The Last Tycoon."

in Malaga where they saw films like *Man on Fire*, *The War of the Roses*, and *Pretty Woman*.

As comfortable as their situation may have been, they couldn't help but feel a mixture of amazement and a little resentment reading Milchan's name at the top of the credits for the whole world to see, literally, while they were forced to hide.

In 1994, only a short flight up the Iberian Peninsula from Richard and Emilie Smyth, in the Hôtel de Crillon in Paris, Arnon's Swedish girlfriend Ase Thastrom arranged for an extravagant surprise party in celebration of his fiftieth birthday.

Sixty Hollywood stars, friends, and family flew in for the grand occasion from all over the world: in attendance were Robert De Niro, Oliver Stone, Roman Polanski, Christopher Lambert, Terry Semel of Warner Brothers, and Rob Friedman of Paramount, among others. Arnon's mother, his sister, and his children were all there. The champagne flowed freely, and Milchan recalls, "It was like the United Nations of the movie business." The highlight of the evening was a twenty-minute film produced by Thastrom as a tribute to her lover, called *Natural Born Seducer*.

18 ‖ Entrapment

*You should write negative things about me;
I was stupid.*

Richard Kelly Smyth, to the authors on August 20, 2009

The Smyths felt comfortable enough to travel throughout Europe, repeatedly rendezvousing with family members at coordinated locations. On one occasion they traveled to the new Euro Disney outside Paris to spend time with their grandchildren. On another occasion they traveled to the south of France to witness their eldest son Randy race catamarans.

Randy Smyth is a renowned sailor, gracing the covers of the world's most important sailing magazines. He skippered for Kevin Costner in the movie *Waterworld*, and for Pierce Brosnan in *The Thomas Crown Affair* (he flipped that large catamaran off of Manhattan as Rene Russo looked on in awe). He also won two Olympic medals and the America's Cup in 1988.

After nine years of living in Spain, Smyth reached the age of sixty-five. In what was a mind-boggling risk, he decided to apply for his US Social Security benefits, betting that no low-level bureaucrat at the Social Security Administration would make the connection. He called up the US embassy in Madrid, gave them his real name and social security number, and made the request to have his monthly payments sent to their account at Banco Billbao in Malaga.

Apparently, Smyth bet correctly, and the lower echelons of the United States government didn't make the connection to a wanted fugitive; they proceeded to make payments of $1,600 every month to that account. It was a brazen – and irresponsible – risk, which seemed to have paid off. A year later, Emilie turned sixty-five and was entitled to a spouse's payment of $400 a month. She was approved for her payments as well. The regular Social Security deposits brought in an additional monthly income and boosted the Smyths' lifestyle to what Emilie described as "idyllic."

Over the years, they stopped looking over their shoulders altogether. They celebrated their freedom again at midnight on December 31, 1999, by watching the fireworks over Malaga as the new millennium was ushered in. For fifteen years the Smyths had eluded authorities while living in their own little paradise.

In June 2001, the manager of Banco Billbao in Malaga asked "Jon Schiller" to stop by the bank for a short meeting. The manager apologized and informed Smyth that in order for him to continue to use the account, he would have to obtain a non-resident permit. He handed Smyth a copy of the form that he would need to fill out and take to the Malaga police station to get stamped. He described it as nothing more than a routine bureaucratic procedure. Smyth complained that he had been able to use the account for years without a problem, so why the hassle now? The bank manager shrugged his shoulders as if to express that he too thought it was ridiculous, but that he had to follow procedure.

From the bank, the Smyths drove to the Malaga police station, parked the car, and briskly walked up the front stairs to the officer sitting at the entrance behind a desk. They showed him the form they had filled out and told him that they needed it stamped. The clerk took the form, looked it over, and extended a return appointment slip while explaining that they should come back on July 9 to pick up their permit. Things moved slowly in Malaga.

As instructed, the Smyths returned on Monday, July 9, 2001, expecting the matter to take no more than five minutes. Upon arriving at the station, they were instructed to go to the back office area and wait. After about fifteen minutes passed and nobody came, Smyth turned to Emilie and asked, "What's taking so long? We're going to be late for our walk along the beach." Five minutes later a tall, blond, blue-eyed officer dressed in a dark blue uniform entered the room, walked over to a fax machine in the corner, and pulled out a paper that had just arrived. He then walked over to them, handed Smyth the fax without saying a word, and watched for his reaction. Smyth looked at the paper and was shocked to see a black-and-white photo of himself appearing to be about twenty years younger than his current seventy-two years of age.

He noticed the word "Interpol" at the top of the page. A sudden sense of dread overcame him and a massive knot tightened in the pit of his stomach. After sixteen years he'd virtually forgotten about his fugitive status. By applying for Social Security benefits, he'd pointed the finger directly to his location. By applying for the non-resident permit he'd fallen into a well-laid trap, walked right into a police station, and given himself up. For a highly intelligent man, it was unimaginably stupid.

After a moment that must have seemed like an eternity, the officer asked, "Is this you?"

Smyth was stunned but confirmed that it indeed appeared to be him.

The officer turned to Emilie and said, "OK, you may leave now. I am placing this man under arrest."

Emilie was speechless and immediately turned pale as the officer began to put handcuffs on her husband. Smyth explained that he needed to give Emilie the car keys so she could drive home. He extended his hand with the car keys and Emilie grabbed the keys and his hand. The officer pulled his hand away, maneuvered it firmly behind his back and firmly placed the handcuffs on his wrists. No hugs, no kisses. Emilie stood in the center of the room in complete shock as her husband of almost fifty years was swiftly escorted out of sight. They didn't realize it at the moment, but that would be the last time that Smyth would see her as a free man for years to come.

Smyth was shoved into a concrete, windowless cell with a raised cement area to serve as a bed, with two filthy blankets. The toilet was down the hall and was a simple hole in the floor. There was no toilet paper. Food was served in small plastic containers. There were no guards available at night, so when the seventy-two-year-old prisoner had to urinate because of an enlarged prostate, he did so on the floor of his cell.

That first night was hell. He went through the process that led to his capture over and over in his mind and began to realize how clueless he'd been. He'd missed all of the obvious signals that were right in front him. He realized that he'd had multiple opportunities to avoid this outcome once the ball had begun rolling. He could have avoided applying for Social Security; he could have avoided the police station – twice. He could have walked right out of the police station once there. He could have denied that the man in the picture was him.

His mind then drifted back eighteen years. He could have refrained from telling the FBI agent about his "mistaken" krytron shipments after the break-in; he could have refrained from signing the statute of limitations waiver; he could have refrained from sending the last krytron shipment after having read the warning; and he could have stayed at Rockwell and avoided the whole thing altogether, though that would have meant no yacht clubs or beachfront properties. The list in his mind went on and on.

Emilie got back to their apartment dazed and confused. Within a single moment their entire world had crumbled for the second time. When higher-ups in Washington learned of the arrest, they were not happy. Better to let sleeping dogs lie. But the Smyths, by their actions, had practically begged to be caught and Interpol had little alternative but to follow minimal procedures.

When Milchan heard the news of Smyth's arrest he knew, like everyone else who read the paper that day, that it would be a big deal. His name would be mentioned yet again in connection to what he called "the unbelievable stupid krytron story."[1] A range of emotions swept over him. On the one hand he was furious at the mind-boggling carelessness of it all; on the other hand, he felt sorry for them. Smyth was only one of numerous Milchan recruits, and he was not the most consequential. He was, however, the most problematic. The following day, Smyth was brought before a judge who ordered that he be held at the Alhaurin de la Torre prison, about twenty minutes west of Malaga, until extradition arrangements could be made. The judge mentioned that he might be transferred later to Madrid to appear at the international court for extradition.

---

1.   Dutka and Citron, "A Mogul's Bankroll – and Past."

The Alhaurin de la Torre prison was a nightmare. Smyth, an educated and cultured gentleman, suddenly found himself in close quarters with every imaginable criminal.

> Each cell had a primitive metal toilet with no seat cover and a small metal wash basin where he could wash his dirty underwear, socks, eating utensils, and food tray. The worst thing was that two times a day there was no water for the toilet to flush. He had to fill the washing bucket and then dump that in the toilet to suppress the horrible stench. There were so many prisoners with AIDS, that the prison laundry would not accept underwear or socks. These had to be washed by hand in the small metal wash basin. There was no laundry soap. Almost everyone smoked and it was impossible to escape the smoke even in the sleeping cells.[2]

Days turned into weeks.

Emilie was allowed to visit Smyth once a week. They would talk through a thick glass pane fitted with a small loudspeaker, *Midnight Express* style. As Smyth said:

> One of the nice aspects of the Spanish prison system was the conjugal visits. I filled out an *estancia* form requesting a private visit in a bedroom complete with a double bed, clean linen, and a bathroom with a shower. The private encounters were allowed twice per month for a one-hour-long visit.
>
> I was unbelievably happy when I received notice that permission was granted to have a private visit with my wife of fifty years after twenty long, tortuous days of separation. We became completely relaxed during these love-in visits, a most humane custom of Spanish prisons![3]

---

2. Schiller, *Irrational Indictment and Imprisonment*, 52.
3. Ibid., 55–56.

During one of those conjugal visits, Richard and Emilie celebrated their fiftieth wedding anniversary.

The difficult prison conditions took their toll on Smyth, and in his imagination he began to compare his situation to that of his former friend, Milchan. He became consumed with the idea that if only he had never met Milchan, everything would be different. If only he had stayed at Rockwell and forgotten about being a big shot with his own company. One day in despair, he wrote a letter that he gave to Emilie asking that she fax to it Milchan.[4]

Date: 22 August 2001

To: Arnon Milchan, Big Time Movie Producer

From: Richard Kelly Smyth,
Prisoner in Alhaurin de la Torre Prison, Malaga, Spain

CC: Dvora Ben Yitzhak

My Dear Arnon,

I really wish you could learn what it's like to be in prison. I can tell you, it's not very pleasurable. The worst part is that I'm separated from my wife, Emilie, on our 50th wedding anniversary, which is 30 August 2001.

I realize you believe you have never done anything wrong, but as a matter of fact, you have. You are the reason I'm in prison because I sent your company, Milchan Bros. in Tel Aviv, some electronic tubes called krytrons. Remember? I thought you might. I used Commerce Department Licenses instead of Munitions Licenses so the US government thought I should go to prison for one hundred and five years. I read in the newspaper that you sold four hundred and fifty million dollars worth of movies to Channel

Plus, the TV Channel for 'coded' movies. I hope you put most of that money in your Union Bank of Zurich secret bank account like the sixty percent profit on each of the things, including krytrons that I shipped to Heli Trading. I expect that nobody in the Israeli Government is interested in the fact that you skimmed off sixty percent of all the profit on things that Milco International, Inc. sent to Milchan Bros. After all, Netanyahu, the Prime Minister of Israel before Sharon, worked for Milchan Bros. Could it be that part of the sixty percent you "skimmed" was for Israeli Government Officials?

I also saw the movie, "Pretty Woman" that you produced. Congratulations! It was an excellent movie.

What's it like to have so much money? I've often wondered what it would be like to have the one and a half billion dollars that you are reputed to have. I couldn't eat any more, my car wouldn't go any faster on the freeway, my bed wouldn't be any more comfortable, no woman could make love as well as my wife of fifty years, my computer wouldn't be any faster. What do you do with the money? Is it the satisfaction of feeling powerful? You're not as well educated as I am – I have a Ph.D. so I'm mentally more powerful than you. I believe brainpower is more important than money-power. But to each his own.

Arnon, let me tell you a little bit about what it's like to be in prison: first, neither your education nor your money means anything to the prison guards – you're just another prisoner, like the drug addicts, the armed robbers, the murderers, the people who committed fraud against banks and the government. You get to eat what the prison serves at meal time – no choice. You follow the prison routine: go to bed when they say, go to the walk areas when permitted. In other words, you do what the prison wants – not what you want. How would you like to trade your current lifestyle for the prison lifestyle? I can tell you now you wouldn't like it!!

So, Arnon, thanks for the business I did with Milchan Bros. I'm learning what prison life is like. I never thought it would happen to me. Perhaps having a billion and a half dollars is enough to buy your way out of any situation no matter how criminal it is.

Well, Arnon, if I'm extradited to the US and stand trial for shipping krytrons to your company, Milchan Bros., the world is going to know all the shady dealings you were involved in – I'm sure.

I did not appreciate that you never lifted a finger to help me after I was indicted or after I fled to Spain. I know you knew where I was in Spain. Dvora was going to visit me until her visit was cancelled. Did Netanyahu advise you not to help me? Or was it your own idea? I presume you ordered Dvora not to visit me in Spain once she reported to you where I was. I remain in awe of your one and a half billion dollars, but remain repulsed by you personally.

Your former friend,

Richard Kelly Smyth

As Emilie read the letter, she immediately recognized that her husband had taken leave of his senses. She never sent it on, and Milchan had never seen it until the day we presented it to him. Milchan responded forcefully by telling us, "The letter reflects a great deal of misperception on the part of Smyth, who never knew that my supposed percentage was, in fact, not mine at all. This lack of knowledge led Smyth to make wild accusations in a time of distress."[5]

He went on to say, "I didn't know, and had no relationship with, Bibi Netanyahu until the 1990s, well after Smyth's indictment in 1985. I didn't know of Smyth's location until he was caught in Malaga because of LAKAM and the Mossad's request that I distance myself completely from the matter by letting them handle it."

Smyth's threat, "If I'm extradited…the world is going to know all the shady dealings you were involved in," has proven over time to be com-

---

5.   Personal interview, November 17, 2009, in Malibu, California.

pletely empty, and no charges or accusations against Milchan have ever been filed.[6]

The United States knew of Smyth's condition in the Malaga prison because they had sent an embassy representative to visit with him, yet they took their sweet time during the extradition process. They knew that he was surrounded by the absolute worst of society: violent murderers, AIDS-infected addicts, drug dealers, and armed bank robbers. Fights were constantly breaking out around him. He felt his life to be in danger and he lived in a permanent state of fear. He contemplated suicide, but the thought of the emotional impact his death would have on Emilie and his children kept him from doing it. Every day was a nightmare. During his darkest personal hour in the prison infirmary he watched the second airliner crash into the Twin Towers in New York, and yet another into the Pentagon. He recalled walking down those very same Pentagon halls as a respected member of the Scientific Advisory Board; he couldn't help but compare those glorious days to his current predicament.

By late September 2001, he decided to give up on the idea of fighting extradition or somehow salvaging his idyllic life in Malaga, and Emilie started preparing to ship their most meaningful belongings back to the United States.

Finally, on November 15, 2001, more than sixteen years after his frantic escape on that Lufthansa flight to Frankfurt, Germany, Richard Kelly Smyth was extradited back to the United States. He was led out of prison without handcuffs into a waiting black Volvo sedan, accompanied by two Spanish Ministry of Justice officials for the five-hour drive from Malaga to Madrid, where he spent his last night in Spain in a reasonably comfortable jail cell. The next morning at 10:00 a.m. he was checked out of the Madrid prison and met by two large US marshals.

On Friday, November 16, 2001, he departed on a Delta flight for Los Angeles, via Atlanta, never to return to Spain again. He arrived at LAX around 8:45 p.m. and was immediately taken to the federal Metropolitan

---

6. In an article published on October 24, 2003, on MSNBC.com, US officials were quoted as saying that "Milchan has no exposure to any smuggling charge, as the statute of limitations on conduct dating from before 1982 has expired."

Detention Center in downtown Los Angeles, where he was checked into a two-man cell. Compared to prison in Malaga, it was the Grand Hyatt, though without the conjugal visits. Within days he was interviewed repeatedly by the FBI.

A little over one month after Smyth's return to the United States, the US Attorneys' Office was having second thoughts about their case. By now, krytrons no longer required a munitions export license at all. Most of the krytrons shipped by Smyth to Heli Trading had been returned to the United States under an agreement between the two governments.

With the benefit of hindsight, the idea that an old man, a married grandfather, could spend 105 years in prison for what was essentially a clerical error while shipping an item to what was, after all, the US's principle ally in the Middle East, was beginning to look more and more like a hysterical overreaction amounting to cruel and unusual punishment, especially given what had already transpired. The strong assumptions in 1985 that the krytrons were just the tip of Milco's iceberg, correct as they may have been at the time, no longer seemed as urgent sixteen and a half years later. And then there was the concern that no jury would send an old man off to prison for the rest of his life as his wife, children, and grandchildren sat in the courtroom in anguish.

On December 20, 2001, the United States government blinked. They offered a drastically reduced plea bargain, and after a few days of negotiations, it was agreed that Smyth would plead guilty to a single count of violating the US Arms Export Control Act, and one count of lying about the contents of a krytron shipment. A sentencing date was set for April 29, 2002, and Smyth would remain in jail at least until that time.

To prepare for the sentencing, Emilie reached out to every person she could muster to write letters testifying to the good character of her husband. This would be the truest test of who his real friends were – those who would be willing to stand up and connect their names to the legal troubles of another, when the easiest thing would be to remain silent.

Many people they hoped and assumed would come forward simply ignored their requests, but a good number of people, some of whom they hadn't expected, stepped forward: former classmates, a former girlfriend from his college days, a number of professional colleagues, many family members, a few yachting friends, numerous friends from his English-speaking club and the American Club of Malaga – and then there was the letter from the administrator of Milchan Bros. Ltd.:

To whom it may concern,

I am an ex business collaborator of Dr. Richard Kelly Smyth. I was employed by Heli Trading Ltd. (an affiliate company of Milchan Bros. Ltd.) and by Milchan Bros. Ltd., since 1966 and retired in 2000. On behalf of my company I had very close business contacts with Dr. Richard Kelly Smyth since 1973 and until he was arrested.

On top of our business connections, Dr. Smyth, and his wife and his children, have become good friends of my husband and myself. We met many times in Israel and also in Los Angeles when we came over for the wedding of his daughter. From many years of close acquaintance, I feel that I know Dr. Smyth well. He is a wonderful person, honest, sincere, a proud family man and a proud American. There is no doubt in my mind that he is a law-abiding citizen and would never do anything willingly to break the law. He always guided me and instructed me on the US legal procedures and on what could or could not be done. I am absolutely convinced that if he did anything wrong, it was done in good faith and without intent of malice. I am convinced that, should he resume his business life, he will be extremely cautious in the future and his conduct in violating the law will not reoccur.

Dr. Smyth is not a young man. To my knowledge he is seventy-two years old and not in good health. He already paid a very high price for the mistake he made. For many years, he gave up everyday contact with his family that he cherishes and adores, he lived away from his country, and lost all he had worked for his entire life. I hope you will take all of these factors into consideration and will find it in your heart to be merciful and compassionate when you come to pronounce his sentence.[7]

Dvora Ben Yitzhak

On April 29, 2002, Richard Kelly Smyth entered the courtroom with high spirits even though at age seventy-two he was still forced to wear his orange prison clothing and his ankles were shackled, with chains around his waist connected to handcuffs, Guantanamo Bay style. The probation officers recommended that the old man be released for time served, which would have amounted to ten months since his arrest in Malaga. He had been assured by his lawyer and by fellow prisoners that judges usually go by the recommendations of the probation officers. The courtroom was filled with supportive family and friends, his children, wife, classmates from his college days, friends from his days at Rockwell, and members of the press. Finally, his moment of truth had arrived.

Judge Pamela Ann Rymer, the same judge who was in the courtroom when Smyth failed to appear for his trial in August 1985, had since been promoted to the Federal Court of Appeals. Rymer took the extraordinary action of stepping down from her position in order to sit in judgment of the man whom she felt had humiliated her and the judicial system almost seventeen years earlier. From experience, she knew that the courtroom would be packed with reporters.

Taking her position on the bench, she proceeded with an introductory speech, proclaiming that Smyth had spent all those sixteen years in an "idyllic" setting in subtropical Spain. She didn't believe that he had forgotten the 1975 application for a munitions license for the krytron order that had been cancelled.

She gave him little credit for his many contributions to the defense of the United States over a period of many years during the height of the Cold War. Neither did she credit him for the long ordeal, including prison time, that he had endured in Spain. She took no note of the fact that most of the krytrons had been returned and that by now, munitions

---

7.   Schiller, *Irrational Indictment and Imprisonment*, 219.

licenses were not required for krytrons. She disregarded the fact that all of this involved shipments to one of the US's closest allies in the world, not to an enemy state.

Judge Rymer then handed down a prison sentence of forty months with two years of probation and a $20,000 fine. Friends and family in the courtroom were shocked, disgusted, and appalled. Smyth sat in the courtroom unable to move or think. If it wasn't real, it could have been a scene right out of one of Milchan's movies.

He was led shackled out of the courtroom and back to his prison cell as his family looked on in horror. He was later transferred to the Federal Correctional Complex in Lompoc, north of Santa Barbara, where he was confined until he was transferred to a prison camp in Taft, California, in April 2004.

In September 2004 he was transferred to a halfway house in Taft. In January 2005 he was finally released on probation and allowed to live in a modest mobile home in Lompoc, California. He finally reunited with his beloved Emilie, who had courageously stuck with him throughout the entire decades-long ordeal. If nothing else, it was an extraordinary love story.

On the fifteenth of December, 2005, at the age of seventy-five, Smyth was summoned for an interview at the FBI offices on Wilshire Boulevard in Los Angeles. During the three-hour interrogation involving a rapid fire of questions, he was asked to break down his entire relationship with Milchan from the moment he met him in the late 1960s to his last communication with him in 1983.

In May 2006, Smyth finished his probation period, and for the first time since 1985 was neither a prisoner of the system nor a fugitive from it. With his release, the Milco saga finally came to an end. Milchan had dodged the bullet again.

* * *

Following the ordeal, the Smyths sat down to document their story in a self-published nonfiction manuscript titled *Irrational Indictment and Imprisonment; or, Exporting Krytrons to Israel.* Once again, Richard used his longtime alias of Dr. Jon Schiller and gave all of the main players pseudonyms. For his own character, he used the name Dr. Ernst Kelly. His wife Emilie is called Annie and Milchan is called Dani Roto.

In an e-mail to us, Smyth confirmed that "all the information you need" can be found in his writings. It's safe to say that few have ever made the connection between a Dr. Jon Schiller and the famous fugitive from the 1980s until now. They are indeed the same person.

Given everything that happened, Smyth found it impossible to reconcile Milchan's reality with his own, living in a mobile home right next to the railroad tracks, as he imagined his former friend jetting between his numerous estates around the world – a bitter pill to swallow for a man who was once in the elite company of America's leading aerospace engineers.

Certainly, Milchan sees it much differently. It would not be a stretch to presume that Milchan sees the State of Israel as actually having saved Smyth from a far worse fate, and believes that Smyth himself, who botched it on numerous occasions, is responsible for his own predicament. His actions jeopardized Milchan and embarrassed Israel and even the United States in every possible way.

There is more than one way to look at it, but what is perfectly clear is that during the 1990s, as all of this was going on, Milchan executed one of the most successful runs in Hollywood history, and he did so on his own merits. Between the summers of 1985 and 2001, Milchan produced a total of sixty-six films, impacting our popular culture with some of the biggest blockbusters of the era.

19 ‖ The Negotiator

I saw in Arnon a highly intelligent person with
a unique talent for the business. I had, and still
have, almost no knowledge of his world beyond
Hollywood.

Terry Semel, former chairman and CEO
of Warner Brothers, to the authors

Following *Pretty Woman*, Milchan quickly became one of the hottest commodities in Hollywood, and by 1991 had made a commitment, in partnership with Warner Brothers, to market and distribute forty full-length motion pictures. But his relationship with the studio got off to a rocky start.

"I was the one to originally approach Arnon about doing multiple movies at Warner, rather than one movie at time," said Terry Semel, former president and CEO of Warner Brothers, who would become a personal friend.[1]

Their first project together was *Under Siege*, an action thriller starring Steven Seagal. The story involves the hijacking of the USS *Missouri* by a disgruntled group of ex-special forces led by Tommy Lee Jones as Bad Billy. Seagal plays the ship's cook, a former Navy Seal, who through an arduous ordeal retakes the ship. The script was written by J.F. Lawton.

---

1. In a phone interview with the authors, December 2009.

Lawton, who'd written *Pretty Woman*, received $1 million for his follow-up script as Milchan had promised. When Terry Semel, chairman of Warner Brothers, heard of Milchan's million-dollar payment to Lawton, he was not happy.

Warner Brothers was convinced that they had a standard contract with Milchan as they had with every other independent producer, which stipulated that the studio had final say on every major budget decision. But Milchan had a different understanding.

He wanted Warner Brothers to distribute films that he would decide on, and which he would have the sole authority to green-light, including all aspects of the budget. When he grasped that there seemed to be a misunderstanding, he called Terry Semel from Paris and asked to cancel the contract. Semel was stunned, exclaiming, "But we just signed the contract two weeks ago!"

Milchan asked if he had read the contract, and Semel admitted that he hadn't, and had assumed it to be standard. "All I am asking for is the right to spend my own money on projects that I believe in," Milchan said. He was in fact asking for complete freedom.

This sort of tail-wagging-the-dog arrangement was not the kind of contract that Warner Brothers had with independent producers. Semel was completely within his rights to tear up the contract and forget about Milchan altogether. But Milchan was in demand, and Semel admired and liked him. He was so determined to keep Milchan in the flock that he quickly boarded a jet to Paris to personally explain to him how things worked in Hollywood.

As soon as he entered his room at the Ritz Hotel, Semel picked up the phone to continue the conversation with Milchan. "But what if tomorrow morning you wake up and decide to stop making movies in English? You expect me to distribute those films? I represent a public company, Arnon," Semel warned.

"I won't work otherwise," Milchan replied.[2]

Then Semel came up with an idea of how to give Milchan the opportunity to climb down from the high tree that he was negotiating from. He

---

2.   Shanken, "An Interview with Arnon Milchan."

explained to Milchan that if he wanted complete freedom, he would have to start a separate partnership backed by a billion dollars, so the studio would be at minimal risk. Let's see how he reacts to that, Semel thought to himself.

"OK," Milchan surprised him. "How much are you guys ready to put in?"

"We can do three hundred million," Semel replied, assuming in his mind that there was simply no chance that Milchan could ever cover the $700 million balance. In a worst-case scenario, if Milchan could do the impossible, Warner would still own close to a third of the company.

"If I come up with the balance, you assure me that I will have carte blanche?" Milchan inquired.

"Yes," Semel mumbled, calling his bluff.

"And you just take distribution fees?"

"Yes," Semel replied again.

"OK, so I will call you in your room at 7:00 p.m. with an answer."

Semel hung up the phone, not sure what to make of it, but he was still confident that he could talk Milchan down from his high perch.

Senior executives at Canal Plus, France's largest TV pay-per-view company, were surprised when Milchan called to inform them that a major American studio intended to invest $300 million in his independent production company. They promised Milchan to invest dollar per dollar, matching the studio's investment.

For Canal Plus, it represented a unique opportunity to partner with a major US studio. They were already paying an exorbitant amount of money for distribution rights in French-speaking countries. This was their chance to get at least partial payback on their content expenses.

At exactly 7:00 p.m., the phone rang in Terry Semel's suite and Milchan asked him to join him at the hotel bar downstairs.

When Semel arrived, three people were awaiting him, Milchan and two principles of Canal Plus. Without delay, Milchan got down to business: "Terry, did you say that you would put in three hundred million?"

"Ah...yes, I did say that."

Milchan turned to the Canal Plus executives and asked in French: "Did you guys say that you would be willing to put up three hundred million if I get the studio?"

The Canal Plus executives confirmed, "Oui, oui."

"OK, I'll put up three hundred million. So we have nine hundred million to finance movies that I decide on."

In the following days, the entourage flew to New York and rendezvoused with Time Warner CEO Steve Ross and corporate attorneys to draw up the papers. The meeting lasted well past two in the morning. When the attorneys asked what they should call the new entity, Milchan asked in return, "What's the name of this hotel?" When told it was the Regency, he asked the attorney to call the company New Regency.[3] It was a name that would become instantly recognizable to every moviegoing enthusiast on the planet.

The additional $100 million Semel required was raised by Milchan from the German TV and film studio Scriba & Deyhle, and from his friend Silvio Berlusconi, an Italian media tycoon and future prime minister of Italy. That is how Milchan established himself in the heart of Hollywood under the name New Regency Films.

Lawton's *Under Siege*, which had sparked the matter to begin with, was produced for $35 million and grossed $157 million in worldwide box office receipts. In the coming years, other tycoons partnered with New Regency, including Leo Kirch and the South Korean electronics giant Samsung.

Milchan had established the largest international media partnership of the time. Since then there have been many such deals, large and small, but Milchan's was the first of its kind. It was also a transaction that created a

---

3. Milchan already owned a company called Regency Enterprises in partnership with Joseph P. Grace, formed in 1982 as Embassy International Pictures (he had changed the name to avoid confusion with Norman Lear's Embassy Pictures).

new type of system in Hollywood called "rent-a-studio" or "studio within a studio," meaning that filmmakers could pay the studio to distribute their products without the studio controlling the content.

* * *

One of the last known defense systems deals brokered by Milchan was the purchase of sixteen electronic-warfare aircraft by Beechcraft, King Air RC-12Ds and RC-12Ks, in an $80 million transaction with the State of Israel in the mid-1990s.

In January 1991, the first Gulf War broke out, and Saddam Hussein threatened to fire Scud missiles into the heart of Israel if US forces dared to attack him. The only answer to these missiles at the time was perceived to be the new Patriot made by Raytheon.

Israel's primary concern was that Iraq would fire chemical or biological warheads into its major population centers. Milchan proudly put on his arms-dealer hat once again, and brokered multiple batteries of Patriot missiles that were sent to Israel and manned initially by US forces until Israeli crews were sufficiently trained on the system.

Once again, Israel acted as a testing ground for a sophisticated US weapons system. This time, it was discovered that the Patriot was not up to the task of knocking out incoming missiles, and ended up creating more physical damage on the ground than the Iraqi Scuds themselves. Despite that, Israel decided to purchase the Patriot system at $170 million per battery, then upgrade the system substantially, making them integral to Israel's overall antimissile strategy to this day.

* * *

In Hollywood, Warner Brothers learned to use Milchan's inclination for risk taking to their benefit, and offered his new operation at New Regency some of their more hazardous material. One project that ended up on

his desk was a controversial conspiracy epic, examining the events leading up to the assassination of John F. Kennedy and an alleged subsequent
cover-up through the eyes of former New Orleans district attorney Jim
Garrison.

Warner Brothers viewed the script as a sharp pebble in their shoe for a
number of reasons. It was a political hot potato with an uncompromising,
big-ego director, Oliver Stone, and a never-ending script. They passed it
on to Milchan for his consideration. "I read it, looked at all the conspiracy
theories, but there was one thing that intrigued me. Somebody shot the
president of the United States, two days later his assassin is shot by Jack
Ruby, and until today we cannot open the files on Lee Harvey Oswald.
And the reason is 'national security.' And I, scratching my head, said what
is it in this 'national security' that can't bring them to open the files?"
Milchan said, describing his attitude toward the script. "That was good
enough for me to absorb bullshit theories, or maybe not, but there was
one thing that was real, that we would inspire people to demand that the
files be opened."[4]

Despite the controversy surrounding the movie's conspiracy theories,
JFK, starring Kevin Costner, was a commercial and critical success. It was
produced by Milchan for $52 million and raked in over $200 million at
the box office. It was nominated for eight Academy Awards and many
other accolades. And it raised Milchan's reputation as a man with solid
instincts for winners.

Milchan continued his friendship with the controversial Oliver Stone,
producing two more films with him, *Heaven and Earth* in 1993 and
Natural Born Killers in 1994. Stone sought to continue the relationship
with another politically controversial figure, Nixon, but Milchan balked.
This led to one of Hollywood's more notorious disputes, as explained by
Milchan:

> In the beginning, Oliver wanted to do the film for eighteen million
> with Tom Hanks, which we said yes to. Then Oliver changed his
> mind and wanted Tommy Lee Jones, and it was more expensive.

4. Shanken, "An Interview with Arnon Milchan."

Then it was Dustin Hoffman, then it was Warren Beatty…and the budget kept going up. Then at Christmas he changed his mind again. He wanted to do it with Robin Williams. Robin Williams playing Nixon?! I started to get nervous. And then he came with Anthony Hopkins. And the budget kept going up, and up, and up. Finally, Terry Semel and I said no. Terry got very upset, the budget ended up at sixty-five million. We divorced.[5]

Oliver Stone didn't take this very well. He had a contract for another movie with Milchan. He briefly considered the outrageous idea of a film from a script that had been circulating in Hollywood more as a joke than anything else. The working title was *Uzi Falafel*, and it told the story of an obnoxious Israeli arms dealer who made a lot of money and parlayed it into a new career producing movies.[6]

Milchan did not find it amusing. A bitter Oliver Stone found other opportunities to lash out at his former friend. "A top Hollywood executive once warned me to stay clear of Milchan," Stone said in an interview. "He told me that Arnon was a Middle Eastern rug dealer. Beware. I should have listened to him, he was right. He is as cheap as they come. He is sick about money, obsessed with losing it. I learned a very hard lesson, and it cost me a lot of my personal money. I don't want to get into a pissing contest, but Arnon can be very nasty."[7]

Milchan responded in typical fashion: "I like Oliver, I'm very fond of him, truly."[8] Milchan continues to invite Stone to various functions hosted at his home. And, occasionally, Stone actually attends. That's the way it is in Hollywood. Love and hate.

As Ase Thastrom, Arnon's lover, held down the fort at the chateau in France, Arnon set his sights on a new love interest on the other side of the world, his new personal assistant, Shauna Beal, who had moved over from

---

5. Ibid.
6. Eric Hamburg, *JFK, Nixon, Oliver Stone and Me: An Idealist's Journey from Capitol Hill to Hollywood Hell* (New York: Public Affairs, 2002), 214.
7. Bardach, "The Last Tycoon," 128.
8. Shanken, "An Interview with Arnon Milchan."

TriStar Pictures to join Milchan and New Regency. Another double life ensued, although this time it didn't involve a marriage certificate.

Milchan was not satisfied with only producing films and continuously worked to enlarge his empire. He purchased a recording company, Restless Records, and began to distribute sound tracks through that outlet, backed by the largest music distribution company in the world at the time, BMG. He didn't hide his ambitions of eventually joining the Big Six studios as an equal. As he said, "I have never liked the word *mini*; either you are in or you are out."

The same held true in play as in work. Milchan established a winter vacation tradition involving some of Hollywood's top talent, such as Christopher Lambert, Joe Pesci, and Robert De Niro, sailing a yacht to Necker, a tiny, exclusive private island owned by Sir Richard Branson in the British Virgin Islands, where they would lounge around without worrying about paparazzi.

While Milchan orchestrated such excursions, New Regency worked efficiently with a relatively small staff of about thirty, out of two adjoining bungalows on the Warner Brothers lot in Burbank. Milchan was content to work out of a small office. Only the expensive artwork on the wall indicated his status in the company, as well as his expensive taste.

In contrast to its humble new offices, New Regency worked with the best of Hollywood's talent at the top of the industry's food chain, producing movie after movie in rapid succession, and often simultaneously. Beginning with the suspense thriller *Q&A*, starring Nick Nolte and Timothy Hutton and directed by Sidney Lumet, the studio within a studio quickly delivered an eclectic variety of genres, such as the McCarthy-era drama *Guilty by Suspicion*, starring Robert De Niro and Annette Bening in 1992; the romantic comedy *Memoirs of an Invisible Man*, starring Chevy Chase and Daryl Hannah; and the action movie *Under Siege 2*.

Among many other projects, New Regency was also quick to purchase the rights to John Grisham's best-selling novels, and produced *The Client* in 1994 and *A Time to Kill* in 1996. Milchan also focused on family films like the *Free Willy* series, message movies like *Six Degrees of Separation*, horror flicks like *Copycat*, and teenage popcorn movies like *Carpool*, starring Tom Arnold.

To keep up with ongoing demand, with multiple projects in the pipeline, Milchan had been forced on occasion to compromise. "There are some movies – and I don't want to degrade my own company – but sometimes I say, guys, this is so stupid. And they would say, Arnon, there is an audience for this. And I would say OK, let's have a 'stupid division' and make these dumb movies… and please don't tell me the story… so we have done a few spoofs like *Epic Movie* and *Date Movie, Meet the Spartans*."[9] Perhaps lucrative, but clearly Milchan is not proud of it.

Robert De Niro, who starred in five of Milchan's films, including *Heat* in 1995, explained why so many of Hollywood's top talents are eager to work with him: "Compared to some of the people out there, who have nothing on them but an Armani suit, Arnon is the real thing. He has paid his dues, he's got good taste, works very hard and he's totally committed. He spins circles around those other guys."[10]

Over time, Milchan developed his own philosophy and formula for success in the movie business, a far more complex outlook than in his earlier years when he was operating on pure instinct and passion. "Let me compare it to a guy who builds a building," Milchan said. "The producer is like a real estate developer who is constantly looking for a good location. In our case, the best location is the script. A script to a movie is what location is in real estate. It's location, location, location."

Indeed, screenwriters working with Milchan report that he is extremely demanding.

As Milchan described in an interview with *Cigar Aficionado* magazine in October 2008: "If I don't have a great story to tell, why would I take a great cast to tell a stupid story? A great script can be told by few actors, but there is more than one cast that could tell a great story."

In terms of importance, after the script comes the director. He compares the director to the architect in a real estate project:

---

9. Ibid.
10. Bardach, "The Last Tycoon," 79.

If you want to control him, you won't get the best product. You have to be able to say, OK, let's agree up front, here are the keys, you carry our common vision. Very often we also have in mind a movie star or an actor for the lead role, or maybe we have a list of three names, so the guy could be Kevin Costner or Brad Pitt or Danny DeVito. And then, we talk about who you can match them with: Jennifer Aniston or Cameron Diaz or whoever. You have a lot of conversations about chemistry.

Take the film *Sommersby*, produced by Milchan in 1993, as an example. The movie, a romantic drama adapted from the screenplay of the French novel *Le Retour de Martin Guerre* (*The Return of Martin Guerre*), tells the story of a young married woman in the post–Civil War South who is barely able to maintain her farm without her husband, who has gone missing in action. Suddenly, her husband returns after a seven-year absence, a completely changed man – for the better. Over time, she and others suspect that he's not her real husband but an imposter.

Milchan wanted Richard Gere in the role of the returning husband, and others suggested Julia Roberts for the female role, in a repeat of the *Pretty Woman* combination. Milchan insisted on Jody Foster instead. He stated that if a man left a Roberts-like character, she'd certainly have found another man after seven years. Foster's persona, on the other hand, radiates principled loyalty. She'd remain steadfast, and when he does return, all handsome and nice, she'd make the decision to live with him, even if deep down in her heart she suspected it to be a lie. Foster got the role.

With the script, the director, and the cast in place, Milchan then decides on a budget. His formula is to divide the target audience into four categories: males above or below age twenty-five, and females above or below age twenty-five. If the film is a comedy suspense, like *Mr. and Mrs. Smith*, a movie for both males and females above age twenty-five, and high-caliber stars like Brad Pitt and Angelina Jolie agree to participate, Milchan will budget it up to $110 million. If the film is a heavy drama, like *Bee Season*, a movie he also produced in 2005, whose primary target audience is only females over twenty-five, Milchan won't invest more than $14 million, even if its stars are Richard Gere and Juliette Binoche.

Only after all of these elements are in place – script, director, cast, and budget, in that order – will Milchan then hire an executive producer. In real estate terms, the executive producer is the general contractor. Like many real estate developers, Milchan offers his executive producer a basic fee, plus a percentage and an additional bonus if the project comes in below budget. If the film is profitable, they'll receive even more bonuses. A lot of performance incentives are built into the contract.

When New Regency joined Hollywood's major league, it started to receive a steady flow of unsolicited scripts, which eventually formed into a tidal wave. Before, Milchan was on a constant and vigilant search for that one great story; now scripts were pouring into his offices at a rate of more than 2,500 per year. Under such conditions, a full-time staff became necessary to filter the material; out of the thousands of scripts coming into his office, only eight to ten will ever go into production.

Statistically, he can only hope that two or three will become the hits that will carry the company financially. If he's lucky, three or four of the films will break even, or make a little money; two will likely lose money; and two will likely be total disasters. "It's a horrible business," Milchan said.

One of the problems with becoming a major player inundated with material is that occasionally, in hindsight, a once-in-a-lifetime, earth-shattering blockbuster is overlooked. Milchan was the first producer to be offered the exclusive rights to the very first Harry Potter book, and for the entire forthcoming series of books yet to be written. He was offered the rights for the ridiculously low price of $35,000. But he had trouble connecting with the story and turned it down, believing that it would probably go nowhere. After that first Harry Potter book became the wildly successful *Harry Potter* movie, Milchan said that he didn't know what to do first, throw up or commit suicide.

It wouldn't be the last time. Milchan had a fifty percent interest in what became the billion-dollar animated series *Ice Age*. When *Ice Age*'s original budget jumped modestly from $57 million to $61 million, he backed out, refusing to believe that the animated feature would break even.

On the other hand, if Milchan truly believes in something, he's capable of producing it twice if the first production doesn't live up to his expectations. That was the case with *Man on Fire* starring Scott Glenn, which he produced in 1987. Milchan deeply believed in the script but the production proved to be a huge box office disappointment. In 2004, he decided to try it again, changing the location, dumping the film noir, and casting Denzel Washington in the lead role of an ex-CIA operative and assassin-turned-bodyguard who takes revenge on a Mexican gang that kidnapped the child he was hired to protect in Mexico City.[11]

Seventeen years earlier, the film had lost him a substantial amount of money, but Milchan doubled down and invested another $70 million in the second production, which brought in more than $130 million dollars, more than enough to cover his previous losses from the 1987 disaster.

The fact that principle is important to Milchan is also illustrated in another incident in which he was willing to take a $17 million loss rather than give in to something he felt to be unjust. In 1993, on the eve of the release of *The Nutcracker*, starring Macaulay Culkin, who was eleven years old at the time, his father, a well-known stage parent who was acting as his manager, gave Milchan a list of demands involving major changes to the final cut. His demands were accompanied with threats that if Milchan failed to make the changes, he'd prevent his child from participating in the promotion of the film.

Milchan was taken aback by the display of chutzpah, but swallowed his pride and went along. And then the father gave even more ultimatums. At that point Milchan informed him that he could go to hell. Culkin's father prevented him from promoting the film even after his $8 million fee was paid. It was a $17 million financial boondoggle for Milchan, but it was also a disaster for Culkin and his reputation – through no fault of his own.[12]

---

11. Gregg Kilday, "Milchan Kept His Heart on Fire for Twenty Years," *Entertainment News Wire*, April 30, 2004.
12. Bernard Weinraub, "The Top of Hollywood," *New York Times*, November 1, 1993.

Despite Milchan appearing to be a hands-on decision maker involved in every detail at New Regency, most of his time is spent well away from Hollywood as he moves frequently between his bases of operation around the world. His reputation for being hands-on is the product of him burning up phone lines from his far-flung locations with his managers in Burbank. It's not unusual for him to call in ten times a day to get updates and give instructions at virtually every hour of the day, including weekends and holidays.

Milchan maintains seven homes in seven countries, and had no permanent residence anywhere until he recently took advantage of an Israeli government offer to officially reside in Israel without being taxed on income earned outside the country for the next ten years. "I follow the sun," he explained with a smile.

Given Milchan's jet-setting lifestyle, it was not surprising to find him at the Australian Open finals in 1994. In what Milchan described as a bizarre set of coincidences, he met media tycoon and world-renowned gambler Kerry Packer, the richest man in Australia, while about to board a helicopter to depart after the match. Packer, an abrasive and hard-charging man, approached Milchan, un-introduced, and informed him, "You and I are going to be partners."

Milchan laughed and said, "Are you sure? Because I don't have any shares for sale."

Packer retorted, "You'll see."

In the coming days, Packer sent an army of lawyers and accountants to Milchan's office in Burbank sporting blank checks but getting nowhere. Eventually, within a few weeks, Packer had managed to purchase twenty-five percent of New Regency from Milchan's other partners and through the issuance of additional New Regency stock. Packer viewed Milchan as his ticket into Hollywood, and his vehicle for competing with his arch rival, Rupert Murdoch, in the movie business. Packer's partnership with Milchan indeed caught Murdoch's attention and would lead to interesting business maneuvers down the road.

* * *

With his high-profile involvement in the film industry, people might easily have gotten the mistaken impression that New Regency was Milchan's sole pursuit.

In 1996, Milchan attempted to take control of MGM Studios, one of the Big Six film studios in Hollywood, but was outbid by billionaire Kirk Kerkorian, who broke the bank with his $1.3 billion offer. Milchan's attitude was "sometimes you win by losing." Around the same time that his MGM bid failed, Milchan wrapped up his fortieth movie with Warner Brothers, completing the terms of the initial contract between them. As a condition of extending the agreement, Milchan demanded that Warner Brothers increase their investment in New Regency and sign a longer-term contract. The studio refused, and his friend Terry Semel warned Milchan that if he failed to sign on Warner Brothers' terms, he'd personally see to it that Milchan would never work in this town again – a famous and almost humorous cliché. Milchan didn't take kindly to Semel's dictates, and in 1997 he executed the next big move in his career by going shopping for a new home for New Regency. He informed Semel that no matter what, he was leaving.

First Milchan called Edgar Bronfman Jr. at Universal, but as Semel promised, Bronfman didn't return his phone call. His next stop was Paramount, where his good friend Sumner Redstone was happy to make him an offer that he *could* refuse; it was well short of what he was already getting over at Warner Brothers. He was becoming concerned, but he had one more card to play.

Milchan will not forget that first dinner with the person who became one of his best friends and business partner, Rupert Murdoch, the owner of News Corporation, the parent company of Twentieth Century Fox. The meeting took place at Spago in Beverly Hills. "I had a bag with Puma shoes and *Free Willy* merchandise, and I got so excited that the first thing I did was spill a bottle of Coca-Cola on him," Milchan said.

The dinner was awkward, and many things were lost in translation, but at one point Murdoch turned to his chief operating officer Peter Chernin, who was also at the dinner, and said, "I don't understand half the things he is saying, but I do like him."

Milchan was surprised by Murdoch's soft persona, which contrasted sharply with his image as a tough media tycoon. But Milchan immediately understood that as soft spoken as he was, Murdoch was not the kind of person to be trifled with.

The deal with Murdoch was quickly sewn together, but there was an obstacle that had yet to raise its ugly head: Milchan's partner in New Regency was Kerry Packer, and Packer and Murdoch were the Hatfields and McCoys (or Montagues and Capulets) of the Australian business world. Their hatred for each other was legendary, going back to their earliest days as competitors in the Australian media market. Furthermore, Packer's primary motivation for partnering with Milchan had much to do with his ambition to compete with Murdoch's existing Hollywood operations.

When Milchan and Murdoch met to finalize their deal, Murdoch presented Milchan with rapid-fire questions:

"Did you ever risk your own money?"

"What do you mean? New Regency owes me $50 million."

"If I put a few hundred million dollars in your company, do you plan on taking my money out to pay yourself?"

Milchan answered honestly, "Yes."

Murdoch then suggested to Milchan that he reinvest his own money on the same terms that he was offering Murdoch.

Milchan immediately replied in the affirmative.

At that stage, Murdoch became more relaxed. "Are you healthy?" he asked.

"Yes," Milchan replied.

"Will you run the company?"

"Why not?" replied Milchan.

"Do you have some money on the side?"

"Why?" Milchan asked.

"I don't like to work with desperados."

Milchan said, "Yes, I do."

"OK, now to a little thing that concerns me. How are we going to handle Kerry?"

"Let me try and convince him."

"Where do you think we can find him?"

"Probably in a casino somewhere," Milchan replied.

Milchan then started making phone calls from Murdoch's office to familiar places where he thought he might find Packer. Eventually he tracked him down at the Aspinalls Casino in London and asked to have him summoned to the phone.

"Kerry, I'm sitting here with Rupert Murdoch and we are about to make a deal that can change my working life. I need you to say yes."

"No fucking way!"

"Kerry, this is my life."

"Oh, yeah, this is my life too."

"Come on, Kerry, this is not your life."

Murdoch, sitting on the other side of the table, was amused by the exchange and by watching Milchan squirm. He was unable to hear Packer on the other end.

"Oh, great! I'm glad you love him. He loves you too," Milchan shouted sarcastically into the phone.

Murdoch rolled his eyes.

"Hey, why don't you say hello to Rupert?" Milchan then reached across the table and placed the phone in the startled Murdoch's hand. Murdoch was baffled but had no real alternative but to speak to his longtime rival.

Milchan listened in nervously as Murdoch mumbled on the phone: "Hello…yeah. Yeah, this Israeli guy, yeah…we better gang up on him." Slowly a smile formed on Murdoch's face.

It suddenly dawned on Milchan that New Regency was the vehicle for bringing peace to two of the most notorious business rivals in history.

In a few moments, Murdoch hung up the phone, turned to Milchan, and said, "You are a miracle worker."

Milchan then asked Murdoch for a favor. He didn't want to consummate the deal without the blessing of his friend Gerald Levin, president and CEO of Time Warner. Murdoch agreed to call him and Milchan left the room to give him privacy. When he returned, Murdoch said that there were two possibilities: "Either he can't wait to get rid of you, or he really likes you."

"Why?"

"Because he said that you need wings to fly, and with me you will fly higher." After a short pause, Murdoch indicated his agreement to move forward with a nod.

"Rupert, you just gave me a few hundred million. Why?"

"I don't analyze the past, I analyze the future," Murdoch replied.

"How do you make these kinds of decisions?"

"It's very simple, I look behind you and see no dead bodies. I know your partner and he seems happy. And by the way, I didn't give you a penny."

"What do you mean?"

"I put money in our company."

"Help me out, I'm not sure I get it."

"OK, let's say you are playing baccarat, and you are a great player but you don't have enough chips. So I come and say, 'This guy seems to know what he's doing,' and I give you a bunch of chips. The minute I leave the casino, you rush to the cashier and ask to cash in your chips. But the cashier is going to ask you, 'Are you Mr. Milchan? I have a note from Mr. Murdoch here. He says that you cannot cash the chips for another fifteen years.' So you find a table, you put the chips on the table and wait.

"Then a guy with a suit and tie from the casino comes by and asks, 'Are you Mr. Milchan? We have a note from Mr. Murdoch that says you can't just sit around like that; you are supposed to play baccarat every five minutes.' That's it. Whatever is left after fifteen years is yours."[13]

Fifty-five percent of New Regency remained in Milchan's hands. Kerry Packer kept his twenty-five percent, and Murdoch picked up twenty percent for about $200 million. Milchan brought in a $600 million line of credit from a combination of banks that included Chase Manhattan, Bank of America, and Banque Nationale de Paris, among others.[14]

---

13. Shanken, "An Interview with Arnon Milchan."

14. "Milchan Lines Up $600,000,000 for Production, Music," *Hollywood Reporter*, June 15, 1998.

Part of the deal between Fox and New Regency was the establishment of a new TV division. Milchan brought in a good friend, ambitious Israeli TV personality Yair Lapid, to head up the new department. The first project to emerge was *Malcolm in the Middle*, a wildly successful children's comedy series.

One of the last and most important films that Milchan produced at Warner Brothers before establishing his new partnership with Murdoch and Twentieth Century Fox was *L.A. Confidential* in 1997. The plot involves three Los Angeles police detectives with vastly different personalities and motivations who establish an alliance of convenience in order to clean the department of systemic corruption. The director, Curtis Hanson, asked to pitch the film to Milchan directly, before he actually read it. Milchan was impressed by his chutzpah and agreed. When they met, Hanson insisted that Milchan watch a few clips of old footage from the 1950s to get him in the proper state of mind. Milchan played along. Hanson then pitched the film in a dramatic fashion that reminded Milchan of his first meeting with Terry Gilliam in Paris when Gilliam described *Brazil*. "His body language convinced me that he was talking in a different cinematic language," Milchan remembered.[15]

After Milchan approved the script, Hanson had another unusual request. He wanted a guarantee that two little-known Australian actors would be cast for two specific characters that he had in mind. The two actors were Russell Crowe and Guy Pearce. At first Milchan balked but later relented. After meeting Russell Crowe, all of his doubts disappeared. The next concern he had was whether Kim Basinger would agree to play the prostitute. He had nothing to worry about, because as soon as Basinger had read the script, she immediately called Milchan back and with great excitement said, "This part was written for me!"[16] Basinger went on to win an Academy Award for best supporting actress, one of seventy-one awards the film won.

15. Martin Grove, "Hanson Put Milchan in the Mood for Confidential," *Hollywood Reporter*, September 3, 1997.
16. Martin Grove, "Quickly, Bassinger Got Hooked on Confidential," *Hollywood Reporter*, September 5, 1997.

The partnership between Milchan and Rupert Murdoch has since yielded an avalanche of over fifty-five full-length motion pictures, among them *Fight Club*, *Daredevil*, *Mr. and Mrs. Smith*, and *Knight and Day*. It was the best deal that Murdoch has made since arriving in Hollywood, generating more than $5.3 billion in box office sales by the end of 2010.[17]

---

17. Rachel Abrams, "Fox, New Regency Renew Distribution Pact," *Daily Variety*, January 17, 2011.

20 ‖ City of Angels

*When I heard that Brad left home and was
looking for a hotel, I offered that he stay at my
house in Malibu.*

Arnon Milchan

Milchan adopted a business model that cross-promoted movies and sports.
Rather than purchase a sports team, as did his partner Rupert Murdoch
with the Los Angeles Dodgers, or spend twenty years building his own
sportswear company, Milchan found a shortcut: buy a sportswear company. His first target was Adidas, which he tried to buy in partnership
with actor and friend Richard Dreyfuss, but that didn't pan out. His fallback plan was to take control of the sluggish German sportswear company
Puma, a deal in which he invested an initial $250 million, and to simulta-
neously purchase the broadcasting rights for the lagging Women's Tennis
Association (WTA).

The idea was to use Hollywood stars to promote the WTA, and to use
the WTA and his movies to promote Puma. Within a short time, Puma
began to appear more widely on the uniforms of leading sports franchises
around the world, from FC Barcelona to the national Israeli soccer team.
In the year 2000, both teams competing at the Super Bowl, the Saint Louis
Rams and the Tennessee Titans, were wearing Milchan's Puma logo.

In 2001, Milchan arrived at the French Open in a private jet accompanied by Arnold Schwarzenegger and supermodel Naomi Campbell. He

arrived at Wimbledon with Sean Connery and Kevin Spacey. Earlier that year, at the Cannes Film Festival, he rented a three-hundred-foot yacht and hosted a party mixed with WTA superstars and many of Hollywood's elite. "If I'm paying a star $18 million to appear in one of my films, I don't think that it's too much to ask that they show up to a few WTA tennis matches."

Through his connections with Murdoch, Milchan successfully secured live broadcasting contracts worldwide for the WTA. His command of the WTA radically changed women's tennis and upped its profile immeasurably.[1] Young tennis stars such as Martina Hingis, Anna Kournikova, and the Williams sisters were invited to appear on the covers of magazines across the globe, posing as the new sex symbols of the era. The results were that more often than not, the female players of the WTA outperformed their male counterparts in the international TV ratings race.

Milchan related to women's tennis in the same way that he related to his movie productions. His focus was on the "script" and his cast of characters. The glamorous players were suited in top-of-the-line designs, with outfits meant to radiate a certain level of sex appeal, and the cameras covering the matches would frequently cut to the celebrity spectators in the crowd, like Leonardo DiCaprio and Brad Pitt, cheering on their favorite players. The entire spectacle was meant to convey the glamour and excitement of women's tennis. And it worked. Women's tennis is a worldwide success story thanks in large part to Milchan.

But his relationship with a long list of Hollywood's A-listers went well beyond invitations to his tennis tournaments, and in many cases became far more personal. Back in 1983, he hosted Barbra Streisand in Israel for the opening of her movie *Yentl*. Milchan denies it, but it has circulated for years in a small circle of Hollywood insiders, and has even been confirmed for us by Ety Kanner, Milchan's personal assistant of thirty years, that he and Streisand were more than just friends. He introduced her to Shimon Peres, who extracted from her a $25,000 donation to the Labor Party, and he introduced her to the prime minister at the time, Yitzhak Shamir, who had no idea who she was. When Milchan told him that Streisand was in

---

1.   Brad Wolverton, "Volley of the Dolls," *BusinessWeek,* August 17, 1998.

the singing and acting business, Shamir's response was one of amusement: "And with this she can make a living?" Thirteen years later, Milchan and Streisand coproduced the movie *The Mirror Has Two Faces.*

In addition to being well connected himself, Milchan is notable for matchmaking on the sets of his movies. He introduced Whoopi Goldberg and Ted Danson on the set of *Made in America.* They became Hollywood's most famous interracial couple of that time. He also introduced Ben Affleck and Jennifer Garner during the making of the movie *Daredevil.*

He met Angelina Jolie on the movie *Pushing Tin* in 1999, and introduced her to her future husband Billy Bob Thornton. Six years later he cast Jolie in *Mr. and Mrs. Smith* with Brad Pitt, a story about a married couple who are surprised to discover that they're both assassins hired by competing agencies to kill each other.

Initially, Pitt was cast with Nicole Kidman, but there was no chemistry between the two and Pitt dropped out. Milchan then paired Johnny Depp, and later Will Smith, with Catherine Zeta-Jones, but again, the chemistry was wrong. When Pitt heard that Milchan was considering Angelina Jolie, he jumped back on board.

Milchan introduced Pitt to Jolie and immediately sensed that there was a spark between them, and not just in the acting sense. A passionate romance ensued, with one slight problem. Although Jolie was recovering from the recent breakup of her three-year marriage to Billy Bob Thornton, Pitt was married to actress and American sweetheart Jennifer Aniston. Pitt and Jolie initially denied the romance, but when Aniston kicked Pitt out of the house, all hell broke loose and the paparazzi swarmed like a pack of hyenas. As Milchan told us:

> When I heard that Brad left home and was looking for a hotel, I offered that he stay at my house in Malibu. I thought it would give him greater security and privacy. He drove to the set, and everywhere else, on a motorcycle, and he wore a wrap-around helmet with a tinted visor so no one could recognize him. He would pull directly into my garage off of Pacific Coast Highway, using my garage door opener, closing it behind him before removing his helmet. That was how we fooled the paparazzi, and Brad was able to stay sane....

We played a lot of Ping-Pong. He's a great player. Professionally speaking, I would say that Brad Pitt and Will Smith are the easiest actors to get along with, and are fun to work with.[2]

Milchan doesn't have a problem with romance on the set and sees the phenomenon as a PR opportunity. "Let's put it this way," said Milchan. "If it's hot, the guy is sexy and married…and the girl is sexy and kind of married, and they are shooting lots of hot scenes, and they deny it, the paparazzi get curious…so it's free publicity."[3]

Milchan's Malibu home was also where Senator Robert Kennedy stayed the night before he was assassinated at the Ambassador Hotel. Kennedy spent the day swimming, sitting in the sun, talking to friends, and sleeping. He became so relaxed that he considered not attending his own election-night party, suggesting that he and his family and friends watch the primary results on television. He wanted to invite the media to join them, but because the television networks refused to haul their equipment out to Malibu, Kennedy reluctantly agreed to go to the Ambassador Hotel instead, where he was shot by Palestinian immigrant Sirhan Sirhan.

* * *

Over time, Milchan began to manage his crown jewel, New Regency, as a family affair.

One day in 1995, Milchan called David Matalon, his childhood friend and a founder of TriStar Pictures, to bounce an idea off him. Milchan had a meeting scheduled shortly with New Regency CEO Steve Reuther, and almost every time they met Reuther asked for a raise, followed by ultimatums. Milchan had had enough and was resolved to let Reuther go if he did it again. He asked Matalon if he'd step in and replace Reuther if it came to that, assuring Matalon that it would only be for a few months until he found a permanent replacement.

2.   Personal interview with Milchan, November 2009.
3.   Shanken, "An Interview with Arnon Milchan."

Matalon was considering retiring from the movie business and going on an endless vacation but said he'd consider it, depending on what happened with Reuther.

A few days later Reuther met with Milchan, and as expected he rubbed his boss the wrong way with demands. Milchan fired him on the spot, and Matalon stepped in to fill the gap. But Milchan was in no rush, and it was twelve years before Matalon was finally able to return to his vacation.

Gradually, after the year 2000, Arnon began to bring his children into key positions at New Regency. Yariv and his sisters, Alexandra and Elinor, had grown up in boarding schools with a heavy dose of French culture, but as they matured they were exposed to a very wide world thanks to regular international travel with their father. Every year they spent at least one month in Israel and were brought up knowing that they were "members of the tribe," with all of the historical connotations and responsibilities that implied.

"Growing up, I would read that my father was an arms dealer, that he was in the Mossad, that he was a movie producer," Alexandra said. "We wanted to spend more time with him. But as we grew, we came to understand that with Father, it was a question of quality, not quantity. We understood that our comfortable life outside of Paris was the best present that he could possibly have given us. What I love about him is that his feet are firmly grounded and that he is very real," she told Ann Louise Bardach in an interview with *Los Angeles Magazine* in April 2000.

Arnon's son Yariv began his career as the exclusive distributor of Warner Brothers merchandise in Israel, operating out of the MilchanBros. offices. He then became a fashion and celebrity photographer. Among other projects, he delivered a unique, revealing, and provocative series of photographs of Angelina Jolie that raised more than a few eyebrows. He has since joined New Regency in Los Angeles as an executive, while still dabbling in photography.

Alexandra is a daddy's girl and has, among all Milchan's children, the personality widely viewed as most similar to his. She began her involvement in New Regency with the movie *Heat* in 1995 as an assistant art department coordinator. Over the years she became more involved in the day-to-day management of the firm. In 1998 she produced her first film, called *Goodbye Lover*, which was a financial flop but a growing-experience for her. "What I am most proud of is that I have never had a call made for me by my dad. I remember one day Michael Douglas said to me that it's going to be much harder for me than anyone, and he's right. It's not an industry that welcomes the kids."[4] As the son of Kirk Douglas, Michael should know.

Alexandra married Scott Lambert, a former agent with William Morris.

Elinor is an independent spirit. After a short stint at New Regency she became an art photographer and lives in Soho, New York. "My father is my best friend. I inherited his enthusiasm, his goal-oriented approach, and his inclination to follow his instincts. He told me that I will never go wrong with such an outlook and he was right."[5]

In the 1990s Elinor produced a unique documentary called *Todo Cambia* depicting the saga of three generations of a family of artists in Castro's Cuba. Her still photographs adorn walls from the executive offices of Twentieth Century Fox to the gigantic screens in Times Square. In November 2008, she married Oded Barak, an Associate at Goldman Sachs and the son of an Israeli nuclear physicist, in a modest wedding ceremony in Tel Aviv.

In February 2003, Arnon's relationship with his former assistant Shauna Beal took on a new dimension when she gave birth to his fourth child and third daughter, Maayan. "Maayan makes me feel younger," Arnon gushes. "We have had many happy times together." Beal and Maayan live comfortably in a separate house in Malibu, and Arnon maintains a close relationship with his youngest daughter, and a very friendly relationship with her mother.

* * *

From his earliest days, Milchan has had a passion for Israeli politics, and despite his global interests, he has consistently sought to influence the course of historic events in the Middle East from behind the scenes.

---

4. *Daily Variety*, September 2, 2007.
5. Haspel, "My Dad Is My Best Friend."

In 2005, Prime Minister Ariel Sharon walked out of his Likud party, which he'd helped establish in the mid-1970s, and created a new, more centrist political party called Kadima, which he intended to lead in the next elections as its candidate for prime minster.

Shimon Peres, on the other hand, was the senior statesman of the Labor Party, which was the opposition at the time. The right-wing Sharon and the left-wing Peres were ideological rivals for decades and their personal relationship bordered on hostility, but Milchan believed that if he could bring his close friend Peres and Sharon together, the dynamics of Israeli politics would change irreversibly.

Within hours of Sharon's announcement, Milchan was on the phone applying pressure on both Peres and Sharon, the two most dominant political figures in the country, to join forces. "I have no intention of calling him," Peres insisted.

"I'm coming over," Milchan replied.

Shortly thereafter, Milchan was sitting with Peres in his home making the case for a centrist party that would reflect a greater expression of national unity. Peres, who'd lived his entire life in the liberal camp of Israeli politics, simply could not imagine himself married to Sharon, known as the Bulldozer and founder of the modern nationalist camp.

Remembering his moment of truth when faced with a similar situation involving Rupert Murdoch and Kerry Packer, Milchan picked up the phone and dialed Sharon's number at his ranch in southern Israel as Peres looked on, not quite sure what Milchan was actually doing.

When Sharon answered the phone, Milchan said, "Mr. Prime Minister, there is a person here who needs to talk with you." He then extended the phone to his stunned friend.

When Sharon realized that it was Peres on the other end of the line, he immediately softened his voice and uncharacteristically started off by apologizing for his hostile statements about him during recent debates. Peres, the veteran, thick-skinned politician, had taken no offense, and the two warriors settled in for a polite conversation, as Milchan sat on the sidelines listening in satisfaction.

By the end of their conversation, Sharon extended a general invitation for Peres to join the Kadima party and move Israel in a different direction. In the following days, Milchan hosted Peres and Sharon's top political advisor Reuven Adler at his penthouse in Herzliya Pituach overlooking the Mediterranean. During that meeting Peres surprised Adler by informing him that he was not interested in maintaining his seat in the Knesset, and that he wanted to establish a new government agency to promote the peace process and development of the Negev and the Galilee. "We don't need to waste a seat for me in the Knesset."

Before Sharon even expressed his approval, Milchan ordered his attorney to draw up an agreement between the parties.

Milchan and Peres spent the entire week together. They flew to Barcelona in Milchan's private jet to attend a promotional, friendly soccer match between FC Barcelona and a joint Israeli-Palestinian "peace team" in Europe's largest stadium. The entire event was arranged by Milchan, mostly in Peres's honor, and was executed like a giant Hollywood production. Well-known personalities such as soccer star Ronaldinho, actor Sean Connery, and political personalities including Bill Clinton and the king of Spain, Juan Carlos I, were in attendance.

Peres was mesmerized, and Milchan used his influence on various leaders to suggest to Peres that his involvement was indispensible, and that he should stay a key figure in the Middle East arena. It worked. In Barcelona, Peres made his final decision: he would join forces with Ariel Sharon.

Kadima won the elections, Peres was appointed deputy prime minister, and all of his demands were fulfilled. But like his Rafi adventure years earlier, his dream never really materialized. Sharon suffered a series of strokes and became incapacitated. Another close friend of Milchan, the man who named his movie *Pretty Woman*, Ehud Olmert, became prime minister instead.

Then another dramatic turn of events unfolded. Israel's president, the ceremonial head of state Moshe Katsav, became embroiled in an unprecedented sex scandal involving a number of his female employees who complained that he had forced himself upon them. The situation quickly became intolerable. Recognizing that a resignation was in the offing,

Milchan kicked into high gear, maneuvering behind the scenes to replace the president with his longtime friend and mentor, Shimon Peres. By the time Katsav finally resigned, Milchan had already arranged virtual wall-to-wall support for Peres to replace him as the country's president.

Peres's name was placed in nomination. He didn't lobby, he didn't campaign, he didn't purchase media. He did only one thing: he depended on his friend Milchan to make it happen, and shortly thereafter, the votes were counted in the Knesset and Shimon Peres became the ninth president of the State of Israel.

The first official letter written by the new president was to thank his longtime friend Milchan, who had stuck with him through thick and thin, to see him to this day.[6]

While today Milchan spends much of his time at one of his homes in Israel, operating behind the scenes of his country's complicated political system, he's also the de facto Israeli consul general on the West Coast of the United States. When Israeli VIPs arrive in Hollywood, Milchan more often than not hosts them in his home, and, depending on their rank, may organize a high-powered meet-and-greet with the who's who of the entertainment industry.

He also serves as the primary host of Hollywood's elite when they come to Israel, usually at his initiative. An invitation from Milchan to visit Israel is an indication of having arrived in Hollywood. These trips are, for the most part, very low-key in terms of publicity but are powerful and extravagant in the extreme, and are also very effective in terms of Israel's public relations efforts.

In a routine Milchan operation, Richard Gere, Terry Semel, and Barbara Walters arrived in Israel for a lightning three-day visit in 2005, at his invitation. Using helicopters and executive jets, the three VIPs criss-crossed the entire country during the day, visiting every important historic and strategic site in the Holy Land, from Eilat on the Gulf of Aqaba in the south to the Golan Heights in the north, and everything in between.

6.	From articles by Ben Caspit in *Ma'ariv* (Israel), December 2005, and Ronit Vardi in *Globes* (Israel), June 2007.

During breakfast, lunch, and dinner, they were wined, dined, and briefed by military experts and generals, captains of industry, and the top leadership of the country, including then minister of finance Benjamin Netanyahu and then prime minister Sharon. Their trip was not unusual. Like all those before and after them, they walked away with a clear understanding of Israel's strategic situation.

When it comes to women, Arnon is a reformed bad boy. At the age of twenty-nine he was already divorced with three children. After French model Brigitte Genmaire, American actress Elizabeth McGovern, the Swedish mystery women Ulla, Ulrika, and Ase Thastrom, and Shauna Beal, Arnon met his last and only love, South African tennis star Amanda Coetzer. As the owner of the broadcasting rights of the WTA and a huge fan, it's not surprising that Arnon would discover his second wife, twenty-seven years his junior, in the tennis world.

Coetzer, born in 1971, has been dubbed the Mini Mouse of professional tennis because of her tiny measurements, just a hair above five feet tall, weighing in at about 119 pounds. Other nicknames she earned over the years are the Little Assassin and the Little Gladiator for her stunning ability to defeat far larger and physically stronger opponents on the court, such as Steffi Graf and Lindsay Davenport. Between 1992 and 2001, she was ranked annually among the world's top twenty players, and was ranked third in 1997 at her peek. She was the subject of tabloid gossip for her long romance with American baseball star Brady Anderson, who played for the Boston Red Sox, Baltimore Orioles, and Cleveland Indians.

Coetzer began to play tennis at the age of six and dropped out of school at fourteen to begin a successful professional tennis career, during which she raked in over $5.5 million, and millions more from endorsements from Nike, Ferrari, BMW, and others. Being independently wealthy, clearly she did not marry for money. From Milchan's perspective:

> Our friendship developed slowly. We talked about South Africa and apartheid. Our relationship became closer when I invited her for dinner during the Australian Open and we talked about the movie *JFK*, which she had not seen, but showed a lot of interest. The next day I sent her the DVD, and we talked about it on the

phone, a conversation that lasted for months and drifted into many topics. Our next meeting was at the Indian Wells tournament in Palm Springs.… It was a gradual process. Eventually I found myself back at the Australian Open cheering her on loudly, perhaps too loudly. She was annoyed by my boisterous behavior, and I fell in love.[7]

They quietly married in 2004. Arnon was preparing to reinvent himself all over again. In her company, and at age sixty, he promised to finally be a good boy, not the *"sheigetz"* that Shimon Peres jokingly describes him as.[8]

In August 2009, Amanda and Arnon welcomed their new son, Shimon, named after Milchan's longtime mentor, Shimon Peres.

---

7.   Personal interview with Milchan, November 2009.
8.   As with many Yiddish words, there is a mixture of spite and admiration attached to the term *sheigetz*. In its more modern meaning, it is usually used as a lighthearted reference to a naughty boy who has traded in his "Jewish values."

21 ‖ Jumper

Arnon is too smart to waste his life on pessimism.

Israeli president and Nobel Peace Prize laureate Shimon Peres

It's almost impossible to follow every frantic business transaction involving Milchan, activities that literally, like the character David Rice from the movie *Jumper*, span the entire globe. His hand is in everything. Buying and selling, wheeling and dealing with barely a pause, he is never tired – and never completely satisfied. As Milchan explains,

> I have tried to understand why I never reached satisfaction or internal peace. Why I never reached the point of saying, OK, now I have enough. Why I was so devastated by any failure, and why after every big success I felt depression and anxiety.... Why I couldn't fall asleep without the assistance of sleeping pills. I have come to understand that I was trying to stop the passage of time, and that it was impossible.
>
> I understood that I've always tried to be liked, or even loved by all, and that too is impossible. I understood that I invested so much of my energy trying to achieve the impossible, that I found myself missing out on the joys of life.
>
> Because I have always sought perfection, I set myself up for disappointment. Every failure was long and bitter, and every success was short-lived.

The moment that I made peace with my limitations, I internalized that I am simply not capable of being everywhere at the same time, or everything to everybody, and maybe that's a good thing. This has given me peace, an ability to focus on my family, and to work to make those close to me happy.[1]

In business, he still has an uncanny instinct for knowing when to get on board and when to fold; he bought into the struggling sportswear company Puma at its low, for $250 million, passionately promoting it until it was finally successful, and unsentimentally dumped it at its height for a cool $650 million.

Since 2004, he's been steadily rising up the list of *Forbes'* richest men in the world. But the editors of *Forbes* surely know that there's absolutely no possibility of accurately assessing his real net worth. Milchan has assets dispersed around the globe, in dozens of banks, that may far exceed his transparent assets. How can *Forbes* possibly estimate the value of a giant agricultural project in Kazakhstan, one of many Milchan transactions through one of his many foreign subsidiaries? Chances are they're probably not even remotely aware of it.

Since 2000, the *Los Angeles Business Journal* has rated Milchan annually as one of Los Angeles' fifty richest residents. They base their estimate on his Hollywood transactions alone, even though he's not even an official resident of Los Angeles, where he spends only a few months out of the year. The Internet site Box Office Mojo estimates that since his film *The King of Comedy*, which premiered in February 1983, up until *Just My Luck*, which premiered in May 2006, Milchan produced eighty-one films for a total box office take of $2.75 billion in the United States and at least $5.5 billion globally.

Milchan has no intention of retiring, even though he's at an age when most people begin to think about it. Instead, he's reinventing himself again. In 2007 he established a new investment group called the Muse Group, which took control of Meridian, an unknown state-of-the-art audio-video manufacturer from the UK. Within months the Meridian system was sold

1. Personal interview with Milchan, November 2009.

to Steve Wynn and placed in every room of his megaresort and casino, *Wynn*, on the Las Vegas strip. Suddenly, Meridian became a worldwide luxury brand. In Israel, Milchan invested in Arden, a green-energy solutions company well positioned to capitalize on the wave of environmentally friendly energy technology.

On April 25, 2007, Milchan toured the European Organization for Nuclear Research (CERN) facility, where the ATLAS experiments are expected to open up new frontiers in the exploration of matter, energy, space, and time. It's the most ambitious scientific experiment in human history.

One billion high-energy proton collisions will take place every second inside the vast ATLAS detector on the French-Swiss border, housed three hundred feet underground in a cavern ten stories high. More than 2,500 scientists from thirty-seven countries, including from the Weizmann Institute in Israel, will sift through this data in search of tiny signals that could answer some of mankind's biggest questions. If and when new technologies and commercial opportunities emerge from ATLAS, Milchan intends to be at the forefront.

In addition to all these side projects, following the summer 2008 death of his friend and partner in New Regency, Kerry Packer, Milchan bought Packer's shares and became the majority shareholder in absolute terms.

That same year, for the first and only time in his life, Milchan agreed to accept an award, honoring him on the occasion of Israel's sixtieth anniversary. The event didn't take place in Israel, but rather on the Paramount lot in Hollywood. Among the 740 guests in attendance were celebrities such as Annett Bening, Warren Beatty, Kiefer Sutherland, Jason Alexander, Seal, Serena Williams, and Los Angeles mayor Antonio Villaraigosa. It was also attended by Hollywood studio chiefs such as Amy Pascal of Sony, Peter Chernin of Twentieth Century Fox, and Sumner Redstone of Paramount.

His instincts for forward projecting didn't fail him as the current global economic downturn descended. He liquidated real estate assets such as residences in London, Monaco, and New York shortly before the down-

turn. He parlayed money into foreign currencies, betting against the value
of the dollar, and hedged many other assets just in time. Yet he was not
completely immune, and lost more than $18 million in the Ponzi scheme
run by Bernard Madoff.

Today, an older, perhaps wiser Milchan wouldn't dare enter into an
adventure like *Once upon a Time in America*.[2] The insanity, the total commitment, the courage, the blind following of a megalomaniacal genius director, eleven months of filming, more than 150 characters with speaking
parts, renting the Orient Express for a single shot, rushing from Paris to
Venice for a single scene, handpicking every garment – all this work only
to end up witnessing the deep disappointment of the American audience's
reaction. Yet to this day, Milchan is still the first choice for any unconventional screenwriter or director looking for a producer crazy enough to
consider his outside-the-box project.

The massive historical drama *1066* is the biggest Hollywood gamble
currently in the pipeline, scheduled for release in the coming year or two.
It's the kind of project that can easily break any studio, but it's also the
kind of movie that can make the most money if it succeeds. Together with
Murdoch's daughter, Elizabeth Murdoch, Milchan is likely to produce
this historic drama depicting the battle of Hastings, where the Norman
army of William the Conqueror and the English army led by King Harold
Godwinson met on the field of battle, the outcome of which would impact
English history for almost a thousand years.

* * *

The offices of the founding company from which everything began,
Milchan Bros., underwent a facelift in 2005. The gray hallways that led
to characterless office suites were opened up into a large, modern working
space, fashionably decorated with Le Corbusier furniture and fine Italian
wood tables. The walls are adorned with projected, streaming images of
the Mediterranean captured by Elinor Milchan. But the designers decided

---

2. Jill Kipnis, "Once in a Lifetime," *Billboard*, June 14, 2003.

to leave in place the many awards and accolades covering the walls of the giant renovated conference room.

Over time, Milchan lost interest in Milchan Bros., which for years now has been managed by his childhood friend Yossi Geva, a man who served with Arnon in the military many years ago and a person well briefed on the importance of secrecy and confidentiality. Under Geva's stewardship, Milchan Bros. branched out beyond its traditional areas of interest into projects such as printing operations in partnership with a prominent Arab family from the town of Acre, and partnership in the largest motor vehicle importing company in Israel.

In 2008, Milchan sold Milchan Bros. to a former Mossad agent by the name of Yossi Maiman. When signing the sale documents, he thought long and hard about his grandfather Chaim Eliezer, and his father Dov, who laid the foundation through a small fertilizer business for Milchan Bros. and for virtually everything that Milchan has become in his life. Milchan had only one condition for the sale: that the pictures of his grand-father, his father, and himself remain hanging in the lobby forever. Not everything in life is about money.

Milchan's grandfather began his adult life in the little town of Rehovot, the future birthplace of a little boy named Arnon. He sowed the seeds of his vineyard with his own hands, nurtured them with care and passion, and watched them, along with the small town around him, grow and bear fruit. The fruit of his labor was meant for wine that would bring pleasure to others.

With the birth of a new millennium, Milchan purchased a modest vineyard and built a small winery called Jonata, on the other side of the world, near the little town of Santa Ynez, California, about a half-hour drive from Richard Kelly Smyth's mobile home in Lompoc.

Milchan didn't experience the daily physical challenges of creating and maintaining a vineyard as his grandfather had before him almost exactly a century ago. But he learned the patience required before one can taste the fruits of a first harvest. Six years passed before he finally sipped from a cup of his own wine. It was a fine wine: cabernet sauvignon, pinot noir, and his specialty, NV La Miel dessert wine.

Among his many accomplishments, Milchan's movies have received many awards and accolades, but Milchan himself has never received the ultimate award, a best picture Oscar. In 1991 he came about as close as it gets. He could almost touch it. *JFK* was nominated in eight categories, including best picture, but the best picture Oscar went to *Silence of the Lambs* instead. When he understood which way the wind was blowing in the middle of the ceremony, he bolted from the Dorothy Chandler Pavilion for the nearest bar to drown himself in whatever wine they had available.

Six years later, in 1997, he was confident in the chances of his new film *L.A. Confidential* after the film won more critics' awards than any film that season. On his way from Paris to Los Angeles to attend the Academy Awards, in the company of his friend Donald Sutherland, he had difficulty suppressing his growing excitement and began to practice his acceptance speech out loud.

"Just say what you really feel, Arnon," Sutherland insisted.

What did he really feel? Did he feel sadness that his grandfather and father never lived to witness the heights of his achievements? Did he think of Richard Kelly Smyth in hiding and in exile? Did he feel for the thousands who sacrificed for his country?

Milchan held up a bottle, imagining it to be the Oscar that he fully expected to win. He suddenly stood up, in the middle of the first class cabin on his Air France flight, and began to speak with a higher purpose in mind. "Ladies and gentlemen, I would like to dedicate this award to Anwar Sadat and Yitzhak Rabin. Peace, Salaam, Shalom."[3]

---

3. Both Egyptian president Sadat and Israeli prime minister Rabin were assassinated for their roles in the Middle East peace process.

Epilogue

L.A. Confidential narrowly lost to *Titanic* for best picture of 1997, and the Oscar has eluded Milchan ever since.

New Regency continues to flood our culture with motion pictures. In the summer of 2010, *Knight and Day*, starring Tom Cruise and Cameron Diaz, hit the big screen along with *Love and Other Drugs*, directed by Ed Zwick. Other films in the pipeline include *Marmaduke*, directed by Tom Dey; and the biggest gamble of all, *Conquest* (aka *1066*), written and directed by William Nicholson of *Gladiator* fame. *Alvin and the Chipmunks 3* is in the pipeline, and from here on out the furry rodents will appear in 3D.

Alexandra Milchan is currently working on a spy thriller loosely based on the supposed exploits of former Israeli "Mossad agent" Yuval Aviv, who served as the inspiration for Steven Spielberg's *Munich*. Alexandra's own father would be a far more credible source, because, unlike Aviv, his exploits have the added benefit of being true. She describes the project as "*The Bourne Identity* for the next generation," and has cornered *Twilight* star Taylor Lautner for the leading role.[1]

On January 14, 2011, New Regency and Fox signed an agreement to extend their distribution relationship through 2022, while at the same time providing a more active role for New Regency involving Fox releases.

Milchan has officially returned to Israel as a resident, where he continues to oversee a global and diverse empire. He is still pursuing his political

---

1. Jeff Snider, "Taylor Lautner Gets 8 Figures to Star in Untitled Spy Thriller," *The Wrap*, January 11, 2011.

vision with the idea of Middle East peace at the forefront. He remains optimistic: "Warren Beatty once told me that if you stubbornly continue to ask women out, eventually one of them will say yes. And that's my approach to the peace process. We need to just keep going at it until one day, one of our adversaries will say yes."

The women in Arnon's life have each gone on with their lives. Brigitte Genmaire remarried a plastic surgeon in Paris, gave birth to another child, and got divorced again. In the 1990s she took a job in a Paris clothing boutique.

After releasing her horse into the residential streets of a Tel Aviv suburb and departing Israel in a huff, Ulla moved to Greece, and later to Barbados, and then to Australia, where her tracks ran cold. Ulrika found a new love and left the field to her friend Ase Thastrom, who remained in a close relationship with Arnon for over twelve years. Thastrom continues to live at the chateau in Montfort-L'Amaury outside Paris, and Arnon continues to support her.

Elizabeth McGovern married English producer and director Simon Curtis in 1992. They live in London and have two daughters. She continued a modest acting career while focusing on her family.

Shauna Beal lives in Malibu, California, down the street from Arnon's beach house, and maintains a good relationship with her ex-boss and father of her daughter Maayan. Arnon sees Maayan often and the two have a warm father-daughter relationship.

Amanda Coetzer has tamed the beast. "At age sixty-five I finally feel like I've settled down," Milchan said. The two travel together and are raising their son Shimon as a loving family.

Benjamin Blumberg was deeply hurt by his less-than-cordial dismissal as head of LAKAM. He retreated to his humble apartment in Tel Aviv and changed his last name to Vered. In 1986 he, along with others, started a company called Optomic Technologies, which manufactures electronics and lasers for military use. In 1998, he left the company for health reasons. In a secret ceremony in the 1990s, he received the Israel Prize for national security, the highest award that Israel bestows on its heroes.

Rafi Eitan went on to a successful political career as the head of Israel's Gil (Pensioners) Party. He served in the Knesset and as special minister without portfolio, advising the prime minister on national security matters. Since the Pollard affair in 1985, Eitan has not been allowed to travel to the United States, where he could be arrested if he did. He spends his leisure time sculpting, and one of his works can be found in Milchan's living room in Malibu.

LAKAM was officially disbanded as a result of the Pollard affair in 1985. However, it continues to operate worldwide, except in the United States, under a new name.

Richard and Emilie Smyth continue to live with their cats in a trailer park next to the railroad tracks in Lompoc, California. They make a modest living by holding commodity trading seminars at a nearby hotel. When we met with him, it was difficult to convince Smyth that we were not FBI agents, plotting a new trap for him – understandable paranoia, given his life experiences.

Milchan's longtime assistant and keeper of the secrets, Dvora Ben Yitzhak, continued to work for Milchan Bros. until her retirement in 2000, after thirty-five years in the service of Milchan and LAKAM. Today she volunteers for a charity organization called PUSH, which provides special education help to underprivileged children.

Roman Polanski was under house arrest in Gstaad, Switzerland, awaiting extradition to Los Angeles for the 1977 case involving sex with then thirteen-year-old Samantha Geimer. Although Geimer has requested that the matter be dropped, the district attorney in Los Angeles continues to pursue the matter thirty-three years later. On July 12, 2010, Swiss authorities announced that they would not extradite Polanski to the US, in part due to a fault in the American request for extradition. Polanski is now free, although charges against him still stand in California.

Terry Gilliam continues on his path as a controversial director. J.K. Rowling, author of the Harry Potter series, was a fan of Gilliam's work. Consequently, he was Rowling's first choice to direct *Harry Potter and the Philosopher's Stone* in 2000. However, remembering *Brazil*, *The Adventures of Baron Munchausen*, and Gilliam's difficult temperament in general,

Warner Bros. refused to consider the director. Instead they selected Chris Columbus for the job. By 2006, Terry Gilliam renounced his American citizenship and cannot spend more than thirty days of any year in the United States.

Oliver Stone also continues to be controversial, spending time with South American dictator Hugo Chavez and going from one drug-related arrest to the next.

* * *

Israel gained its modern nuclear deterrence capabilities because of the covert efforts of many people, but Milchan was one of the most essential. Most of its nuclear program was developed before the introduction of international antiproliferation treaties such as the NPT. The fathers of Israel's bomb were the products of, and direct witnesses to, the most horrific period in human history and were determined to never let it happen again. Over the years, the United States has tacitly accepted Israel's status as the only nuclear power in the Middle East.

That monopoly is currently challenged by a fundamentalist Islamic regime in Iran, a regime that denies the Holocaust and maintains deep ties to proxy terror organizations such as Hezbollah and Hamas, who represent an existential threat to Israel. To counter the growing threat, the renamed LAKAM and the Mossad have kicked into high gear. Every known computer system sent to Iran over the past decade has been bugged with monitoring devices. Every possible high-tech system, such as aircraft electronics and spare parts, has been tampered with.

It is widely reported that Israel is directly responsible for the penetration of the Stuxnet worm into computers that control Iran's uranium enrichment program, and its spinning centrifuges. The Stuxnet is considered the most sophisticated cyber attack since the dawn of the digital age, setting Iran's nuclear program back at least a number of years. On January 15, 2011, the *New York Times* reported that the Stuxnet worm was tested at Israel's Dimona nuclear reactor, where Israel uses identical centrifuges. As reported for the first time in this book, the reason Iran and Israel's centrifuges are identical is because both countries obtained the design from the same source in the early 1970s: the German-based company Urenco.

The war that Milchan was recruited for in his youth has never ended, just taken on new dimensions.

* * *

Milchan was surprised when we approached him with the news that we had written a book about his life and were offering him a chance to respond. His first instinct was to probe the depth of our knowledge. He quickly understood that we had done our homework. Within a few days, we found ourselves in Milchan's armored black Cadillac SUV, with tinted windows and satellite television, on our way to a meeting with him at one of his homes. The vehicle stopped on a busy highway in front of a massive door with no hint of what lay behind it. We entered the door into a luscious tropical courtyard leading to another door where his English butler, John, graciously awaited us.

We then entered a plush world of expensive art adorning every available space, with the gentle sound of ocean waves lapping against the sandy beach in the background. We were ushered into a small library stacked wall-to-wall with art books about every major artist of the last five hundred years.

Milchan arrived, casually dressed and in a cheerful mood, but also in a little pain from a recent shoulder injury. "I overdid it in tennis; now I'm paying the price," he said with a smile. He suggested that we begin with a toast and asked John to bring a round of shots of his favorite tequila, slices of lime, and bottles of Stella Artois beer. He then took us on a tour, obsessively adjusting the sophisticated track lighting illuminating the million-dollar works of art throughout the house. At one point we entered his private, state-of-the-art movie theater, where he screens his latest productions, and later, the large gym downstairs where he tries to defeat the aging process.

The man is clearly likable and charming when he wants to be, a demeanor that we were carful not to mistake for weakness or naïveté. He seemed open, but very controlled when it came to the information that he revealed. Only when pressed with hard, inconvenient evidence did he tend to give way. That is Milchan.

When legendary media mogul Sumner Redstone told us that he considers Milchan to be "Mr. Israel," he had little idea how accurate his sentiments actually are. If one could imagine a single, indispensible person in the middle who knows where all of the bodies are buried when it comes to Israel's secret wars, it would be none other than this heavyweight Hollywood producer, who spends his life seamlessly moving between the worlds of fame and secrecy, fantasy and reality, war and peace.

Mathew McConaughey and Kevin Spacey starred in Arnon Milchan's production of *A Time To Kill*, based on a John Grisham novel.

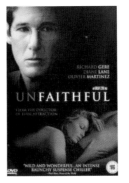

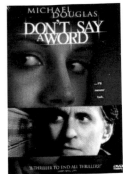

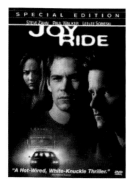

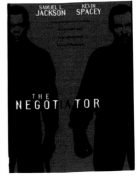

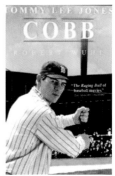

Appendix A

The Smoking Gun

Smoking-gun evidence exists of aggressive American spying on Israel in the form of a secret memo sent by US secretary of state Condoleezza Rice clearly instructing US personnel to spy on Israel. The secret cable was released by Wikileaks and published by the *Guardian* November 28, 2010.[1]

> Friday, 31 October 2008, 15:25
>
> S E C R E T STATE 116392
> NOFORN
> **EO 12958** DECL: 09/18/2033
>
> [...]
>
> G. Information Infrastructure and Telecommunications Systems (INFR-3).
>
> – Current specifications, vulnerabilities, capabilities, and planned upgrades to national telecommunications infrastructure, networks,

---

1. The memo was written by Rice as part of her instructions to collect information on "Palestinian issues." The section relating to spying on Israel was buried, perhaps purposefully, towards the end of the memo in section G, a bombshell that went largely unnoticed by the press until well over a month after the memo was leaked.

and technologies used by government and military authorities, intelligence and security services, and the public sector.

– Details about command, control, and communications systems and facilities. --National leadership use of and dependencies on a dedicated telecommunications infrastructure.

– Details about national and regional telecommunications policies, programs, regulations, and training.

– Information about current and planned upgrades to public sector communications systems and technologies used by government, military personnel, and the civil sector, including cellular phone networks, mobile satellite phones, very small aperture terminals (VSAT), trunked and mobile radios, pagers, prepaid calling cards, firewalls, encryption, international connectivity, use of electronic data interchange, and cable and fiber networks.

– Information about wireless infrastructure, cellular communications capabilities and makes and models of cellular phones and their operating systems, to include second generation and third generation systems.

– Details about the use of satellites for telecommunication purposes, including planned system upgrades.

– Details about internet and intranet use and infrastructure, including government oversight.

– Details about foreign and domestic telecommunications service providers and vendors.

– Plans and efforts to acquire US export-controlled telecommunications equipment and technology.

– Plans and efforts to export or transfer state-of-the art telecom-munications equipment and technology.

– Details about information repositories associated with radio fre-quency identification (RFID)-enabled systems used for passports, government badges, and transportation systems.

– Official and personal phone numbers, fax numbers, and e-mail addresses of principal civilian and military leaders.

RICE

Appendix B

Novels of "Jon Schiller"

While in exile, Richard Kelly Smyth began to try his hand at writing novels under his pseudonym Dr. Jon Schiller.

These self-published books are a treasure trove of information about his relationship with Milchan, mixing fiction with real events along with many hints about how and where their interactions occurred. His writings also indicate Smyth's obsession with the man whom he clearly on one hand admires, yet on the other holds primarily responsible for destroying his life.

One of the first books that he wrote in exile is called *Ibex*, in which he describes the events surrounding the Israeli-Iranian deal to develop a network of sophisticated electronic surveillance outposts to spy on Iran's neighbors in the 1970s. He uses fictitious names, easily recognizable to anyone with basic knowledge of the real story, attached to characters entirely based on real people. Smyth gives Milchan the name Amnon Milchbucher – almost as creative as Milco – and Rockwell International is called Associated Aviation Corporation. For his own character he uses the name Dr. Bradford Kelly.

Ibex goes into great detail about Kelly's activities in Israel. Smyth accurately describes the locations of specific offices deep inside Israel's Ministry of Defense in Tel Aviv, as well as offices and restaurants that Kelly and Milchbucher frequented, and specific individuals that they met with, such as former Mossad chief Meir Amit and Ministry of Defense chief of operations Yitzhak Ironi. Only someone with detailed knowledge of these specific locations and personalities – people who were not exactly household names and who went out of their way to maintain their anonymity – would have been able to describe them so accurately in a novel. Many of the details could only have come from direct knowledge of the locations and characters involved. It's not the kind of subject that can be researched, nor merely the product of someone's colorful imagination.

Clearly, in writing these books Smyth was venting and dropping heavy hints. The books are awkwardly written and heavy on cheap sex scenes, and were never picked up by a publisher despite Smyth's repeated efforts. Perhaps Smyth's true feelings toward Milchan can be deciphered from *Ibex*'s ending, when the character resembling Smyth kills the Amnon Milchbucher character in a massive explosion in his Paris apartment. Of course, not many people knew who Milchan was at the time, and fewer knew about his apartment in Paris.

The next book that Smyth wrote in exile, also under the name Dr. Jon Schiller, was called *Masada: Never Again*. In that book, Milchan's character is named Dani Sharon and Milchan Bros. is called Rehovot Trading. Benjamin Blumberg is called Benni Yamin.

Incredibly, in *Masada: Never Again*, Smyth accurately describes the exact location of the top-secret LAKAM offices in Tel Aviv. The story describes Milchan as an Israeli superagent with his hand in every Mossad and LAKAM operation since the early 1960s. The story is greatly embellished, presumably to make for a more exciting read. For example, Smyth describes how, to avoid suspicion from US satellites monitoring the Dimona reactor, Dani Sharon (Milchan) personally drives to the reactor to pick up a neutron bomb, placing it in the trunk of his convertible and driving it to a Negev air force base and into the belly of a waiting C-130 Hercules, which flies him immediately to Port Elizabeth, South Africa. Dani Sharon then places the bomb on a waiting sailboat with a small crew and sails it to Prince Edward Island in the South Atlantic, where he wires the bomb for detonation, fights off US and Soviet snoops attempting to intercept him, makes his way back to the sailboat, and detonates the nuke once he reaches a safe distance.

All of this is in reference to Israel's nuclear test on September 22, 1979, in the South Atlantic. His description is an absurd portrayal, but serves as an indication that Smyth was well aware of Milchan's activities beyond Milco, as well as the nature of Israel's secret relationship with South Africa. Other scenes have a much truer ring to them, such as a meeting that the Smyth character had with the Milchan character at the Orlando airport, where he transfers sensitive material to Dani Sharon relating to solid rocket fuel that he had obtained. We know that Smyth worked at the rocket manufacturer Martin Marietta in Orlando for a short period of time. We know that during that time Milco was in operation. We know that his description of an airport drop-off was a typical LAKAM method of operation.

In these books, Smyth is desperately trying to tell his story without actually telling it. He could not even bring himself to use his own name or the names of others whom he vividly describes. He creates fictional stories while planting elements of his own real experiences to buttress the credibility of the plot. In some instances, it appears that he's trying to mislead investigators about his activities and about the circumstances of his escape before trial.

A relentless obsession with his former friend Milchan comes through in all of his writings. These books were the author's acts of self-therapy, and it's not at all clear whether his former friend Milchan is even aware of their existence.

Appendix C

Arnon Milchan Filmography

Love and Other Drugs – 2010
  Executive Producer

Vampires Suck – 2010
  Executive Producer

Knight and Day – 2010
  Executive Producer

Marmaduke – 2010
Executive Producer

Mirrors 2 – 2010
  Executive Producer

Alvin and the Chipmunks
The Squeakquel – 2009
  Executive Producer

Fantastic Mr. Fox – 2009
  Executive Producer

Aliens in the Attic – 2009
  Executive Producer

Bride Wars – 2009
  Executive Producer

Marley and Me – 2008
  Executive Producer

Mirrors – 2008
  Executive Producer

Meet Dave – 2008
  Executive Producer

Shutter – 2008
  Executive Producer

Jumper – 2008
  Executive Producer

Meet the Spartans – 2008
  Executive Producer

Alvin and the Chipmunks – 2007
  Executive Producer

Epic Movie – 2007
  Executive Producer

Deck the Halls – 2006
  Producer

The Fountain – 2006
  Producer

My Super Ex-Girlfriend – 2006
  Producer

Just My Luck – 2006
  Producer

The Sentinel – 2006
  Producer

Date Movie – 2006
  Producer

Big Momma's House 2 – 2006
  Executive Producer

Bee Season – 2005
  Executive Producer

Stay – 2005
  Producer

Little Manhattan – 2005
  Producer

Mr. and Mrs. Smith – 2005
  Producer

Elektra – 2005
  Producer

First Daughter – 2004
  Executive Producer

Man on Fire – 2004
  Producer

The Girl Next Door – 2004
  Executive Producer

Runaway Jury – 2003
  Producer

Down with Love – 2003
  Executive Producer

Daredevil – 2003
  Producer

Unfaithful – 2002
  Executive Producer

Life or Something Like It – 2002
  Producer

High Crimes – 2002
  Producer

Joe Somebody – 2001
  Executive Producer

Black Knight – 2001
  Producer

Joy Ride – 2001
  Executive Producer

Don't Say a Word – 2001
  Producer

Freddy Got Fingered – 2001
  Executive Producer

Tigerland – 2000
  Producer

Big Momma's House – 2000
  Executive Producer

Up at the Villa – 2000
  Executive Producer

Noriega: God's Favorite – 2000
  Executive Producer

Fight Club – 1999
  Executive Producer

A Midsummer Night's
Dream – 1999
  Executive Producer

Entrapment – 1999
  Executive Producer

Goodbye Lover – 1999
  Executive Producer

Simply Irresistible – 1999
  Executive Producer

The Hunt for the Unicorn
Killer – 1999
  Producer

Dangerous Beauty – 1998
  Producer

City of Angels – 1998
  Executive Producer

The Negotiator – 1998
  Producer

The Devil's Advocate – 1997
  Producer

The Man Who Knew Too
Little – 1997
  Producer

Free Willy 3: The Rescue – 1997
  Coproducer

Breaking Up – 1997
  Executive Producer

Murder at 1600 – 1997
  Producer

L.A. Confidential – 1997
  Producer

A Time to Kill – 1996
  Producer

Bogus – 1996
  Producer

The Sunchaser – 1996
  Producer

Tin Cup – 1996
  Executive Producer

The Mirror Has Two
Faces – 1996
  Producer

Carpool – 1996
  Producer

Under Siege 2:
Dark Territory – 1995
  Producer

Copycat – 1995
  Producer

Free Willy 2:
The Adventure Home – 1995
  Executive Producer

Boys on the Side – 1995
  Producer

Empire Records – 1995
  Producer

Heat – 1995
  Producer

The New Age – 1994
  Producer

The Client – 1994
  Producer

Second Best – 1994
  Executive Producer

Cobb – 1994
  Executive Producer

Sommersby – 1993
  Producer

Striking Distance – 1993
  Producer

Free Willy – 1993
  Executive Producer

Made in America – 1993
  Producer

Heaven and Earth – 1993
  Producer

The Nutcracker – 1993
  Executive Producer

Six Degrees of
Separation – 1993
  Producer

Under Siege – 1992
  Producer

The Power of One – 1992
  Producer

The Mambo Kings – 1992
  Producer

Memoirs of an Invisible
Man – 1992
  Producer

That Night – 1992
  Producer

JFK – 1991
  Executive Producer

Switch – 1991
  Executive Producer

Guilty by Suspicion – 1991
  Producer

Q&A – 1990
  Coproducer

Pretty Woman – 1990
  Coproducer

Big Man on Campus – 1990
  Producer

Family Business – 1989
  Producer

The War of the Roses – 1989
  Coproducer

Who's Harry Crumb? – 1989
  Coproducer

Man on Fire – 1987
  Producer

Legend – 1986
  Producer

Stripper – 1986
  Producer

Brazil – 1985
  Producer

Once upon a Time in
America – 1984
  Producer

The King of Comedy – 1983
  Producer

Masada – 1980
  Producer

Dizengoff 99 – 1979
  Producer

The Medusa Touch – 1978
  Producer

Black Joy – 1977
  Producer

Index

C

K

L

V

U

W

Y

Z